BENSON and **HEDGES**®
SNOOKER YEAR

SIXTH EDITION EDITED BY TERRY SMITH
ASSOCIATE EDITOR TERRY GRIFFITHS

PELHAM BOOKS

Stephen Greene Press

PELHAM BOOKS

Published by the Penguin Group
27 Wrights Lane, London W8 5TZ, England
Viking Penguin Inc., 40 West 23rd Street, New York, New York 10010, USA
The Stephen Greene Press, 15 Muzzey Street, Lexington, Massachusetts 02173, USA
Penguin Books Australia Ltd, Ringwood, Victoria, Australia
Penguin Books Canada Ltd, 2801 John Street, Markham, Ontario, Canada L3R 1B4
Penguin Books (NZ) Ltd, 182–190 Wairau Road, Auckland 10, New Zealand

Penguin Books Ltd, Registered Offices: Harmondsworth, Middlesex, England

First published by Pelham Books simultaneously in hardback and paperback 1989

Typeset, printed and bound in Great Britain by
BPCC Hazell Books Ltd
Member of BPCC Ltd
Aylesbury, Bucks, England

A CIP catalogue record for this book is available from the British Library

ISBN 0 7207 1910 0

CONTENTS

ACKNOWLEDGEMENTS

When I sat down to begin compiling the Sixth Edition of the *Benson and Hedges Snooker Year*, it was difficult to believe another twelve months had passed. The 1988/89 season was certainly hectic but that's usually the case for any thriving industry.

Many people have once again helped me prepare the *Snooker Year* and I would like to thank Alexander Clyde (*Evening Standard*), Bruce Beckett (Press Assciation), Bob Holmes (*Evening Standard* and *Observer*), Chris Bradley, John Dee, Gaye Jones, Ian Morrison and Mark Taylor for their tremendous contributions.

Martyn Blake, secretary of the WPBSA, David Ford, chief executive of the B&SCC, and world-famous referees Len Ganley and John Street have all provided background information so vital to this edition.

And finally, associate editor Terry Griffiths, the world number 5, has taken a hard-hitting look at snooker as the sport moves into the 1990s.

It's a fact that covering snooker is, despite the pressures, still a lot of fun and everybody in the game must take credit for that.

No book is complete without pictures and additional photographs have been provided by Chris Bradley (on pages 127, 128, 129); John Hawken (on pages 32, 67 above); and Gaye Jones (on page 139).

Once again, Benson and Hedges and Pelham Books are to be praised for the continued development of a snooker publication which hopefully has grown in stature every year.

Incredibly, three ladies – my wife Eileen Smith, Pat Mead and Ruth Baldwin – have continued to put up with my occasional tantrum since I started editing the *Benson and Hedges Snooker Year* three years ago. Again, my thanks go to them for all their work in compiling the facts and figures, typing the many, many thousands of words, and editing the copy. The designer this year was Penny Mills and I am sure you will agree she has done a superb job.

HAS THE FUN GONE OUT OF SNOOKER?

by Terry Griffiths

Professional snooker is still in a very healthy state. There have never been more tournaments, more prize money and more interest in the game. Even so, we must beware of over-exposure and concentrate on guaranteeing that this success continues in the 1990s.

I definitely feel that there has been too much snooker on British television screens in the past couple of years and I would certainly think about reducing the number of events we have been showing. In fact ITV have decreased their commitment by not screening the International this season – something I think the WPBSA should have already started to look at.

We must leave the viewing public – who are so vital for our game – wanting more, which means giving them fewer events. But what we do show must be top-quality tournaments – events they will remember from year to year. The Embassy World Championship could be called anything, but it will always be 'The Embassy'. It's our premier event, and of course there are many other quality tournaments on the calendar like the Benson and Hedges Masters. The Masters will always be a major tournament. It is staged very well and features the top sixteen players in the world. This has become established over so many years and it's always on in the same month at the same venue. We must maintain the standard of high-quality snooker like this, which could mean reducing the number of hours on TV.

That leaves a problem, however, because it is obviously difficult for the WPBSA to start turning down sponsorship deals worth £300,000 a year when the majority of our members don't earn £20,000 a year. They have to act on behalf of the full membership and if they started refusing sponsorship there would be a hue and cry from all the players. But in the long term I do believe the increase in the number of events has been bad for the game.

I have heard criticism that snooker

WHO SAID THAT?

'That's nice – is there any money in it?'

▲

– *Tony Drago after hearing that his three-minute frame during the Fidelity Unit Trusts International was the quickest on record.*

---

events are becoming stereotyped. I watch all sports on TV, but let's take a look at golf in which tournaments are now looking like the same events all the time – the same players playing the same sort of tournament over eighteen holes. They have the World Matchplay once a year, which I do find different, and obviously the Open, which is always tremendous. But the effect of the same format for events is that I don't watch golf so much – and some people might be having just the same thoughts about snooker.

Another problem, I think, is that there is a lack of characters. No, I will rephrase that – snooker has a lot of great characters who have been turned into robots because of the way the sport has gone. In some cases, the fun has gone out of the game. You don't see as many people having a laugh and a joke when they are trailing in

Keep on laughing: Dennis Taylor (left) and Willie Thorne, two of snooker's great characters.

about slow play, especially when Cliff Thorburn played Eddie Charlton in the World Championship and the match didn't finish until 2.39am. I know the time because I was there! But if Thorburn plays Charlton it's always going to be a long match because they are on the slower side and both of them play an extremely high standard of safety play.

I thought the publicity for the Thorburn/Charlton match was unfair because my game with Silvino Francisco at the World Championship was longer and worse! I watched the Thorburn/Charlton game and I thought the standard was very high. I don't think it was a turn-off for the public, because you have to have different

a match like they did five or six years ago, but this is purely because of the pressure and money involved these days.

I used to go out after matches and mix with my fellow professionals, but that happens less and less frequently these days – just in case you have to play them the following week. The characters are there but they don't express themselves as much and that's bad from the public's point of view.

Another reason for this is that we hardly play any exhibition shows any more, mainly because we haven't got enough time, though some people say we are too expensive. Exhibitions used to be a load of fun because you met snooker fans, cracked a few jokes and did a few trick shots. If you do that a lot you carry it through to the tournaments, but in today's market the top players play very few exhibitions.

Unlike players such as Dennis Taylor, Cliff Thorburn and myself, many of the game's new players have been brought straight up in the tournament world. They are good players, nice people, practise very hard and dress immaculately, but they are all getting a bit stereotyped.

I have been reading a lot in the media

Chatting away: Eddie Charlton talks snooker with Martin Griffiths, Terry's father. Charlton came under fire for slow play during the World Championship.

sorts of games and it did get a lot of media coverage.

If everyone played like Stephen Hendry, the game would die immediately because there is nothing more monotonous than somebody knocking in breaks of 70 every go. It's great to see but it doesn't happen all the time for all players, and if you had a dozen Stephen Hendrys, the thoughtful side of snooker would fade away because the game would look too easy.

The greatest matches have been when a safety player has come up against an out-and-out potter because you have a contrast in styles. I honestly don't think the slow play does any real harm to the game.

So where do we go in the 1990s? We had this surge in the 1980s and if I must criticise then it would be that our administrative side hasn't moved forward as quickly as the game. I feel that as we reach the 1990s the WPBSA could have a much stronger base. But even so we are very sound financially, we have lots of tournaments and there have never been more amateur players taking up the game.

When I was on the committee and vice-chairman of the WPBSA in the early '80s I tried very hard to purchase property for our offices somewhere central like Birmingham which would have included an arena to play in. Now I am afraid we have to go to Blackpool – which is, of course, very central if you live in Blackpool! The conditions are not ideal, with sixteen tables, and the first time I went there it reminded me of a circus. It would be nice to have our own big arena somewhere in the Midlands where we could establish a base for the public to come along to.

Without being too critical of the WPBSA, it's very difficult for a group of men heavily involved in snooker to make decisions to cope with the growth of a sport like this which was so dramatic in such a short space of time.

This season we have started to move abroad in a big way, but I don't think it's

Before the final: Terry Griffiths (right) with John Parrott before the start of the ICI European Open in Deauville, France.

right to take thirty-two players for major ranking tournaments. It's got to be more streamlined, with just eight or sixteen taking part in the final stages. It's very optimistic to go to places like Hong Kong, Thailand and Dubai, but the board have made the decision and, apart from Dubai, I will be competing because it's very important to play in the ranking tournaments. Even so, the ICI European Open in Deauville last winter was like being in the middle of the desert. The French had hardly seen snooker, and even though I reached the final, the place took a lot out of me. I had lost my edge. Being away for that amount of time certainly damaged my game for the rest of the season.

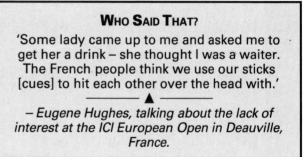

WHO SAID THAT?

'Some lady came up to me and asked me to get her a drink – she thought I was a waiter. The French people think we use our sticks [cues] to hit each other over the head with.'

▲

– Eugene Hughes, talking about the lack of interest at the ICI European Open in Deauville, France.

I hope that next season we start taking sixteen players to these countries and play off the early rounds on four tables with the semi-finals and finals on one table. The event should last about a week because the early matches, in terms of spectators, are often a waste of time.

Overseas tournaments will be a success but that will probably be in another ten years. I am forty-two now and I don't feel I will be travelling all over the world when I am past fifty, although I will still play in all the events in this country.

I am keener now than I have ever been and I have a greater understanding of the game. I hear a lot of talk about all the young players coming into the game, but I am now up to number 5 and this is the highest I have ever been. The only younger players who have really made the breakthrough have been people like Stephen Hendry, John Parrott, Neal Foulds and Jimmy White. There certainly has not been a glut of young superstars and, anyway, I think that if your health is good, age doesn't make much difference.

Who has been our greatest player? Steve Davis is streets ahead of anyone I have played – and I mean a long way ahead.

Starstruck: Steve Davis holds aloft the Embassy World Championship trophy for a record-equalling sixth time.

Davis is the most complete player in the world – he delivers the cue straight, straighter than anyone I have ever seen, and he does it day in and day out. His appetite for the game is incredible and he just never seems to flag, even though he has won everything in the game. I have watched most sports and I have never seen anyone perform at the same level as Davis for so long.

Yes, Davis is the greatest player the game has ever seen. I only hope that I can beat him a few times and collect some more titles myself.

WHO SAID THAT?

'I am not perfect, but I am a lot closer. I know every department of my technical game and I can fine tune it when there is a slight problem.'

▲

– Steve Davis after winning the Fidelity Unit Trusts International.

SPONSOR'S INTRODUCTION

Welcome to the Sixth Edition of the *Benson and Hedges Snooker Year*, which we hope you will continue to find an invaluable reference to an increasingly popular sport.

We are delighted that the popularity of *Benson and Hedges Snooker Year* continues apace. Much praise must go to our Editor, Terry Smith, not just for the astounding detail of his background to another year's action-packed snooker, but also for his ability to put it all between covers in such an entertaining way.

We welcome to this edition Terry Griffiths as our new Associate Editor and hope that readers will enjoy both his insight and wit.

To the longest-running snooker sponsorship, the Benson and Hedges Masters, we have this year added support for the sport at its grassroots level in the Benson and Hedges Snooker Challenge for Scottish amateurs. Its British-record entry of 3,750 players, including many talented newcomers, provides evidence, if ever we needed it, that the sport of snooker has a bright future too.

We are pleased to be a part of it.

Barry Jenner
Marketing Manager, Benson and Hedges

WHERE IT'S ALL HAPPENING IN THE 1989/90 SEASON

PROPOSED SNOOKER TOURNAMENT DATES

DATES	EVENT	VENUE
1989		
May 30–31	The International (Prelims)	Norbreck Castle Hotel, Blackpool
Jun 1–2	Rothmans Grand Prix (Prelims)	Norbreck Castle Hotel, Blackpool
Jun 3–5	Hong Kong Open (Prelims)	Norbreck Castle Hotel, Blackpool
Jun 6–8	555 Asian Open (Prelims)	Norbreck Castle Hotel, Blackpool
Jun 9–11	Dubai Classic (Prelims)	Norbreck Castle Hotel, Blackpool
Jul 30–Aug 6	Lion Brown New Zealand Masters	Wellington
Aug 7–13	Hong Kong Open	Hong Kong
Aug 17–27	555 Asian Open	Bangkok, Thailand
Aug 26–31	Non-ranking Professional Tournament (Non-qualifiers Hong Kong Open)	Clacton Snooker Centre
Sept 2–3	StormSeal UK Open (Prelims)	Norbreck Castle Hotel, Blackpool
Sept 4–5	Mercantile Credit Classic (Prelims)	Norbreck Castle Hotel, Blackpool
Sept 6–7	British Open (Prelims)	Norbreck Castle Hotel, Blackpool
Sept 13–17	Regal Masters	Scottish Exhibition Centre, Glasgow
Sept 18–21	The International (Last 64)	Trentham Gardens, Stoke-on-Trent
Sept 23–30	The International (Last 16)	Trentham Gardens, Stoke-on-Trent
Oct 9–12	Rothmans Grand Prix (Last 64)	Hexagon Theatre, Reading
Oct 14–21	Rothmans Grand Prix (Last 32, TV stages)	Hexagon Theatre, Reading
Oct 27–Nov 3	Dubai Classic	Al Nasr Stadium, Dubai
Nov 17–22	StormSeal UK Open (Last 64)	Guild Hall, Preston
Nov 25–Dec 3	StormSeal UK Open (Last 16, TV stages)	Guild Hall, Preston
Dec 8–17	Everest World Matchplay	International Hall, Brentwood

DATES	EVENT	VENUE
1990		
Jan 2–4	Mercantile Credit Classic (Last 64)	Norbreck Castle Hotel, Blackpool
Jan 6–13	Mercantile Credit Classic (Last 16, TV stages)	Norbreck Castle Hotel, Blackpool
Jan 12–17	Non-Ranking Professional Tournament (Non-qualifiers UK Open)	Venue to be announced
Jan 19–21	Overseas Ranking Tournament (Prelims)	Norbreck Castle Hotel, Blackpool
Jan 22–27	Embassy World Championship (Prelims)	Norbreck Castle Hotel, Blackpool
Feb 4–11	Benson and Hedges Masters	Wembley Conference Centre, London
Feb 12–17	Senator Windows Welsh Championship	Newport Centre
Feb 18–21	British Open (Last 64)	Assembly Rooms, Derby
Feb 23–Mar 3	British Open (Last 32, TV stages)	Assembly Rooms, Derby
Mar 6–12	Non-Ranking Professional Tournament	Venue to be announced
Mar 6–17	Overseas Ranking Tournament	Venue to be announced
Mar 21–24	Fersina Windows World Cup	Bournemouth International Centre
Mar 25–26	Embassy World Championship (5th round)	Guild Hall, Preston
Mar 27–Apr 1	Benson and Hedges Irish Masters	Goffs, County Kildare
Mar 27–28	Pro-Ticket Tournament	Guild Hall, Preston
Mar 29–30	Professional Challenges	Guild Hall, Preston
Apr 13–29	Embassy World Championship (Last 32, TV stages)	Crucible Theatre, Sheffield

PROPOSED BILLIARDS TOURNAMENT DATES

DATES	EVENT	VENUE
1989		
Sept 14–18	Radiant Classic Invitation	New Delhi
Dec 4–8	British Open	Venue to be announced
1990		
Mar 4–8	Strachan UK Championship	Marton Country Club, Middlesbrough
Date to be announced	World Championship	Venue to be announced

All dates and venues may be subject to change without prior notification.

PLAYERS' RANKINGS AND HOW THEY EARN THOSE VITAL POINTS

Snooker's ranking tournaments schedule is increasing in size every year and during the 1989/90 season the players will be playing in ten different ranking tournaments all over the world. The 1988/89 season saw the number of ranking tournaments grow to eight and now two more have been added. This season there will be six tournaments, as usual, based in the United Kingdom – the International, the Rothmans Grand Prix, the StormSeal UK Open, the Mercantile Credit Classic, the British Open and the Embassy World Championship. On the overseas front, four tournaments have been scheduled – the Hong Kong Open, the Asian Open, the Dubai Classic and one other event, yet to be announced.

Each player's ranking has been worked out on the points obtained in the preceding two seasons – the 1989/90 ranking is therefore based on performances in the 1987/88 and 1988/89 seasons. Obviously, with the tremendous increase in the number of tournaments the World Professional Billiards and Snooker Association (WPBSA) did discuss whether to base the rankings on the performances of just one season. But they decided that it was fairer to stay with the two-year system, which means that fourteen tournaments have been taken into account for the ranking positions for the current season.

In many other sports the players find their rankings adjusted after every tournament. Unfortunately, although this might be a fairer system, it is impossible to achieve in snooker because the qualifying rounds for most tournaments are carried out well in advance of the actual events.

Ranking points are awarded in all tournaments, apart from the World Championship, as follows:

Winner	6	points
Runner-up	5	points
Losing semi-finalist	4	points
Losing quarter-finalist	3	points
Fifth-round loser	2	points
Fourth-round loser	1	point
Third-round loser	1	merit point
Second-round loser	1	'A' point
First-round loser		Frames won

In the World Championship, which is the most prestigious tournament of the season, higher points are awarded. In previous years there have been only four qualifying preliminary rounds but last sea-

Dropping down: Jimmy White who slipped two places to number 4.

son an extra round was added to cope with the record entry. This meant that frames won in first-round matches did not count as had been the case in previous years. The points awarded in the World Championship are as follows:

Winner	10	points
Runner-up	8	points
Losing semi-finalist	6	points
Losing quarter-finalist	4	points
Second-round loser	2	points
First-round loser	1	ranking point unless member of top sixteen who receives 2 merit points
Fifth-round prelim-round loser	2	merit points
Fourth-round prelim-round loser	1	merit point
Third-round prelim-round loser	1	'A' point
Second-round prelim-round loser		Frames won in match

Putting on the style: Mark Johnston-Allen who started the season at number 52 after just one season as a professional.

Putting on a brave face: Canadian Kirk Stevens who slumped to number 50 in the world.

In the event of ties on ranking points, the player who has picked up most ranking points in the most recent season is allocated a higher placing. If there is still a tie, the player with the greatest number of merit points is given the higher placing. If scores are still equal, the number of merit points in the preceding season applies. In the unlikely event that players are still level, their positions are decided on 'A' points, followed by frames won. If, by a remote chance, the players still cannot be separated, their performances in the preceding World Championship will determine their ranking order; and, if this method fails, the other ranking tournaments are worked through in reverse order until the players' positions can be established.

THE OFFICIAL WPBSA WORLD RANKING LIST 1989/90

(1988/89 positions in brackets)

POSITION	NAME	R	M	A	F
1 (1)	S. Davis (Eng)	64	2	—	—
2 (7)	J. Parrott (Eng)	48	1	—	—
3 (4)	S. Hendry (Scot)	46	1	—	—
4 (2)	J. White (Eng)	43	1	—	—
5 (5)	T. Griffiths (Wales)	39	2	—	—
6 (9)	M. Hallett (Eng)	33	4	—	—
7 (6)	C. Thorburn (Can)	33	2	—	—
8 (10)	Dennis Taylor (NI)	29	1	—	—
9 (13)	W. Thorne (Eng)	28	1	—	—
10 (24)	D. Mountjoy (Wales)	25	4	—	—
11 (11)	J. Johnson (Eng)	24	3	—	—
12 (8)	A. Knowles (Eng)	24	4	—	—
13 (15)	J. Virgo (Eng)	22	1	—	—
14 (31)	A. Meo (Eng)	20	7	—	—
15 (22)	D. Reynolds (Eng)	19	6	—	—
16 (32)	S. James (Eng)	17	4	1	—
17 (41)	M. Clark (Eng)	16	6	—	8
18 (16)	C. Wilson (Wales)	16	3	—	—
19 (25)	S. Newbury (Wales)	15	7	—	—
20 (3)	N. Foulds (Eng)	15	6	—	—
21 (26)	B. West (Eng)	14	7	—	—
22 (19)	E. Charlton (Aust)	14	7	—	—
23 (12)	S. Francisco (SA)	14	6	—	—
24 (17)	A. Higgins (NI)	13	7	—	—
25 (14)	P. Francisco (SA)	13	8	—	—
26 (39)	D. Roe (Eng)	12	4	2	—
27 (21)	E. Hughes (Rep Ire)	11	7	—	—
28 (23)	D. O'Kane (NZ)	11	3	3	—
29 (29)	R. Chaperon (Can)	11	6	—	—
30 (20)	A. Drago (Malta)	11	8	—	—
31 (34)	W. Jones (Wales)	10	7	2	—
32 (18)	R. Williams (Eng)	10	11	—	—
33 (28)	David Taylor (Eng)	9	11	—	—
34 (30)	S. Longworth (Eng)	9	10	—	—
35 (102)	A. Robidoux (Can)	8	5	1	—
36 (43)	D. Fowler (Eng)	8	8	1	—
37 (38)	J. Wych (Can)	8	6	3	—
38 (27)	J. Spencer (Eng)	8	9	—	—
39 (45)	Gary Wilkinson (Eng)	8	5	2	9
40 (35)	J. O'Boye (Eng)	8	6	4	—
41 (51)	A. Chappel (Wales)	7	9	1	—
42 (33)	J. Campbell (Aust)	7	6	3	—
43 (50)	S. Duggan (Eng)	6	5	5	—
44 (54)	P. Browne (Rep Ire)	6	3	7	—
45 (48)	M. Macleod (Scot)	6	9	1	—
46 (56)	N. Gilbert (Eng)	6	8	2	5
47 (52)	M. Bennett (Wales)	5	6	5	—
48 (67)	C. Roscoe (Wales)	4	3	4	14
49 (55)	R. Edmonds (Eng)	4	5	6	—
50 (37)	K. Stevens (Can)	4	8	1	—
51 (46)	G. Cripsey (Eng)	4	8	4	—
52 (—)	M. Johnston-Allen (Eng)	3	2	4	3
53 (—)	D. Morgan (Wales)	3	—	4	—
54 (40)	R. Reardon (Wales)	3	9	2	—
55 (44)	W. King (Aust)	3	6	6	—
56 (36)	D. Martin (Eng)	3	12	2	—
57 (42)	T. Murphy (NI)	3	9	3	—
58 (64)	J. McLaughlin (NI)	2	7	6	5
59 (—)	I. Graham (Eng)	2	3	2	—
60 (73)	J. Chambers (Eng)	2	3	2	10
61 (60)	R. Bales (Eng)	2	—	6	7
62 (49)	A. Jones (Eng)	2	10	12	—
63 (57)	D. Gilbert (Eng)	2	7	4	—
64 (58)	M. Fisher (Eng)	2	2	7	—
65 (62)	L. Dodd (Eng)	1	12	9	5
66 (81)	John Rea (Scot)	1	8	2	12
67 (61)	J. Wright (Eng)	1	7	3	—
68 (63)	M. Gauvreau (Can)	1	3	7	—
69 (—)	C. Edwards (Eng)	1	2	10	5
70 (119)	R. Marshall (Eng)	1	1	3	18
71 (—)	A. Wilson (Eng)	1	1	5	11
72 (—)	N. Terry (Eng)	1	1	4	4
73 (90)	G. Scott (Eng)	1	1	4	14
74 (116)	A. Harris (Eng)	1	—	6	22
75 (53)	K. Owers (Eng)	1	8	6	—
76 (72)	M. Smith (Eng)	1	7	4	7
77 (66)	R. Foldvari (Aust)	1	6	6	8
78 (65)	G. Miles (Eng)	1	6	6	10
79 (70)	B. Rowswell (Eng)	1	5	7	6
80 (68)	P. Medati (Eng)	1	4	7	15
81 (59)	P. Houlihan (Eng)	1	3	10	—
82 (69)	P. Gibson (Eng)	1	3	3	4
83 (71)	V. Harris (Eng)	1	—	7	14
84 (74)	J. Donnelly (Scot)	1	—	4	30

POSITION	NAME	R	M	A	F
85 (84)	W. Oliver (Eng)	—	6	6	11
86 (82)	M. Morra (Can)	—	6	3	16
87 (75)	M. Bradley (Eng)	—	5	7	11
88 (86)	J. Bear (Can)	—	5	3	27
89 (83)	F. Davis (Eng)	—	5	5	13
90 (—)	M. Price (Eng)	—	3	3	4
91 (95)	Glen Wilkinson (Aust)	—	3	5	7
92 (89)	I. Williamson (Eng)	—	3	7	15
93 (77)	B. Harris (Eng)	—	3	6	11
94 (85)	E. Sinclair (Scot)	—	3	5	34
95 (92)	J. Dunning (Eng)	—	3	5	28
96 (93)	E. Lawlor (Eng)	—	3	5	16
97 (76)	M. Wildman (Eng)	—	3	6	13
98 (—)	S. Campbell (Eng)	—	2	3	16
99 (—)	M. Rowing (Eng)	—	2	2	5
100 (101)	T. Whitthread (Eng)	—	2	6	14
101 (80)	A. Kearney (Rep Ire)	—	2	6	18
102 (100)	M. Darrington (Eng)	—	2	4	27
103 (87)	J. van Rensburg (SA)	—	2	4	25
104 (118)	J. Smith (Eng)	—	1	8	19
105 (113)	F. Ellis (SA)	—	1	6	13
106 (114)	J. Fitzmaurice (Eng)	—	1	5	14
107 (117)	S. Meakin (Eng)	—	1	4	21
108 (111)	D. Hughes (Eng)	—	1	4	17
109 (115)	D. Sheehan (Rep Ire)	—	1	3	39
110 (108)	M. Watterson (Eng)	—	1	2	25
111 (124)	P. Thornley (Can)	—	1	1	7
112 (88)	M. Gibson (Scot)	—	1	9	14
113 (79)	R. Grace (SA)	—	1	7	19
114 (98)	P. Watchorn (Rep Ire)	—	1	6	21
115 (94)	J. Meadowcroft (Eng)	—	1	6	16
116 (91)	G. Rigitano (Can)	—	1	5	25
117 (99)	Jack Rea (NI)	—	1	2	23

POSITION	NAME	R	M	A	F
118 (78)	G. Foulds (Eng)	—	—	9	17
119 (110)	W. Kelly (Rep Ire) (NT)	—	—	6	14
120 (104)	G. Jenkins (Aust) (NT)	—	—	4	23
121 (96)	I. Black (Scot) (NT)	—	—	4	15
122 (97)	B. Mikkelsen (Can) (NT)	—	—	3	18
123 (103)	P. Fagan (Rep Ire) (NT)	—	—	3	21
124 (105)	P. Burke (Rep Ire) (NT)	—	—	2	22
125 (112)	D. Chalmers (Eng) (NT)	—	—	2	29
126 (107)	I. Anderson (Aust) (NT)	—	—	2	11
127 (106)	F. Jonik (Can) (NT)	—	—	2	8
128 (121)	D. Mienie (SA) (NT)	—	—	1	19
129 (109)	J. Rempe (USA) (NT)	—	—	1	16
130 (—)	J. Grech (Malta) (NT)	—	—	1	—
131 (123)	D. Heaton (Eng) (NT)	—	—	1	15
132 (120)	C. Everton (Wales) (NT)	—	—	1	10
133 (125)	D. Greaves (Eng) (NT)	—	—	—	12
134 (129)	B. Bennett (Eng) (NT)	—	—	—	9
135 (127)	M. Parkin (Eng) (NT)	—	—	—	6
136 (122)	J. Hargreaves (Eng) (NT)	—	—	—	4
137 (128)	B. Demarco (Scot) (NT)	—	—	—	2
138 (131)	E. McLaughlin (Scot) (NT)	—	—	—	1
139 (130)	J. Caggianello (Can) (NT)	—	—	—	—
140 (126)	M. Hines (SA) (NT)	—	—	—	—
141 (136)	L. Condo (Aust) (NT)	—	—	—	—
142 (137)	M. Francisco (SA) (NT)	—	—	—	—
143 (135)	J. Giannaros (Aust) (NT)	—	—	—	—
144 (132)	S. Mizerak (USA) (NT)	—	—	—	—
145 (134)	P. Morgan (Aust) (NT)	—	—	—	—
146 (138)	W. Saunderson (Can) (NT)	—	—	—	—
147 (133)	G. Watson (Can) (NT)	—	—	—	—
148 (—)	S. Frangie (Aust) (NT)	—	—	—	—
149 (—)	W. Potasnik (Aust) (NT)	—	—	—	—

Key to table
R – ranking ponts
M – Merit points
A – 'A' points
F – Frames won
NT – Non-tournament status

NATIONALITIES
Aust – Australia
Can – Canada
Eng – England
Malta – Malta
NI – Northern Ireland
NZ – New Zealand
Rep Ire – Republic of Ireland
Scot – Scotland
SA – South Africa
Wales – Wales
USA – United States of America

NEW FACES FOR 1989/90

Snooker's professional ranks have, as the television boom has shown, been dominated by players from the British Isles. But, as the game moves into the 1990s, there is a growing awareness that it must attract more players from overseas – particularly with four ranking tournaments planned outside the UK this season.

This season there has been a small but significant step with two of the new professionals coming from Canada and Thailand. They are Brady Gollan and James Wattana, the 1988 world amateur champion from Bangkok, who has been based in the UK in Bradford, learning his trade.

The method of selecting the new professionals is complicated. The bottom ten professionals in the rankings have to play off for their places against the world amateur champion, the English amateur champion and eight players who qualified through a series of three pro-ticket tournaments. (The top twenty-six in this series play off in Preston to reduce the field to eight.) The ten winners then automatically take their place or continue as full members of the WPBSA. If any professional loses his match, he can opt for non-tournament status, which means he can still play in the World Championship.

Last season three professionals decided to accept non-tournament status while the remaining seven took on the amateurs and all of them lost. Here we take a look at the ten new professionals who are competing on the circuit in the 1989/90 season.

Join the club: Chairman John Virgo (centre) welcomes snooker's ten new professionals for 1989/90 to the WPBSA headquarters. They are (left to right) Ian Brumby, James Wattana, Brian Morgan, Duncan Campbell, Steve Murphy, Nick Dyson, Brady Gollan, Nigel Bond, Barry Pinches and Andrew Cairns.

JAMES WATTANA

Date of birth: 17 January 1970   *Star sign:* Capricorn

World amateur champion James Wattana – full name Wattana Pu-Ob Orm – also topped the pro-ticket table and did not have to play off in Preston after Canadian Bernie Mikkelsen opted for non-tournament status. Wattana, from Bangkok, Thailand, was impressive on the amateur circuit last season, winning the Asian Championship and the Hong Kong Kent Challenge and reaching the finals of the first two pro-ticket events. Victory in Brean Sands followed the runner-up spot in Puckpool, but it was his 11–8 victory over English champion Barry Pinches in the World Amateur Championship final in Sydney that confirmed his status as the world's number 1 amateur.

A national hero in Thailand, Wattana first came to British notice in 1986 when, in winning the Camus Thailand Masters, he enjoyed victories over three world champions – Steve Davis, Dennis Taylor and Terry Griffiths – at the age of sixteen! Now based in Bradford, Wattana speaks almost fluent English and has made England his home. He even confesses to liking the British weather.

Star from the East: Thailand's James Wattana.

BARRY PINCHES

Date of birth: 1 July 1970   *Star sign:* Cancer

Like Wattana, Barry Pinches qualified automatically for the play-offs as English amateur champion and did not have to play in Preston when his opponent opted for non-tournament status.

Based originally in his home town of Norwich, Pinches played snooker under the government-sponsored Youth Training Scheme, together with some thirty-seven other aspiring amateurs nationwide.

After considerable success on the amateur circuit, Pinches sprung to the fore with a dogged 13–6 victory over Craig Edwards in the 1988 BCE English Amateur final in Bradford, but was unable to complete an English double when he lost 13–11 to Nigel Bond in the 1989 final. He finished runner-up to James Wattana in the World Amateur Championship in Sydney.

DUNCAN CAMPBELL

Date of birth: 24 September 1966   *Star sign:* Libra

Duncan Campbell, who was number 2 overall on the pro-ticket circuit, was not called on to play in the Preston play-offs and was drafted straight into the professional ranks. He has been playing snooker since the age of fourteen and a half and holds the record for a break by an amateur in Scotland – a 142.

Sponsored by Ian Doyle before the Scottish businessman took charge of Stephen Hendry, Campbell reached the last eight and then the final of the first two pro-ticket events in 1988. In the third event he lost in the last 128, but would have still finished in the top six overall had he not bothered to enter. He was runner-up in the 1986 Scottish Amateur Championship.

STEVE MURPHY

Date of birth: 23 September 1969   *Star sign:* Libra

Watched by close friend and mentor Eugene Hughes, Dubliner Steve Murphy capped a timely return to form with a 9–4 victory over South African Derek Mienie in the play-offs in Preston. Hughes had opened his house to his young fellow countryman for a time when Murphy found himself with nowhere to stay when he first came over to England. Based at the same Ilford Snooker Club as the Republic of Ireland number 1, Murphy repaid that kindness by taking the English amateur circuit by storm.

Last season, in the space of two months, stylish potter Murphy won the Daily Mirror UK Under-19 title, led the Republic of Ireland to its first victory in the Pontin's Junior Home Internationals and picked up the Player of the Series prize in the senior competition on the Isle of Man. He also finished fourth in the pro-ticket table after victory in the first event in Puckpool.

Back in Ireland, however, he twice missed out on a trip to the World Amateur Championship in Sydney, finishing runner-up in both the national championship and the ranking table.

Irish hopeful: Steve Murphy.

ANDREW CAIRNS

Date of birth: 12 July 1968   *Star sign:* Cancer

Andrew Cairns, formerly an employee at a Blackpool promenade cafe, is under the wing of local referee and coach Dale Rawcliffe. He defeated Ian Anderson 9–4 to gain professional status, having finished in seventh place overall at the pro-ticket events. In that pro-ticket series his record was: semi-final (Isle of Wight); last thirty-two (Brean Sands); last sixty-four (Prestatyn).

Cairns was in the Lancashire team which lost to Essex in the final of the 1988 Inter County Championship. In the 1988 English Amateur Championship, he was beaten in the last thirty-two 4-2 by Danny Murphy, though he compiled breaks of 68 and 105 in the two frames he won.

NICK DYSON

Date of birth: 19 December 1969   *Star sign:* Sagittarius

Nick Dyson, who left school at the age of sixteen, having passed several CSE examinations including government and politics, was formerly based at his father's snooker centre in Macclesfield where he was a YTS graduate along with Barry Pinches. He could have made a career out of football, having signed schoolboy forms with Manchester City, but instead chose snooker rather than the left wing at Maine Road and last season finished tenth on the pro-ticket circuit.

Winner of the Riley National Championship, Stockport-based Dyson has three brothers, Justin, now twenty-three (but at the age of sixteen the Cheshire junior champion), Jonathan and Ben. Father Norman has now sold all his interests in local snooker clubs in order to devote more time to his son's professional career. Dyson defeated Dave Chalmers 9–2 (including a break of 99 in frame 11) to gain professional status.

BRIAN MORGAN

Date of birth: 16 July 1968   *Star sign:* Cancer

Brian Morgan, world junior champion in 1988, is following in illustrious footsteps. He is playing under the wing of Essex professional Vic Harris – the man who discovered Steve Davis. With Harris' coaching and the support of his backers at Benfleet Snooker Centre, Morgan demonstrated his ability by winning the World Junior Championship in 1988. Not selected by the Billiards and Snooker Control Council, the usually shy Morgan promptly borrowed his air fare, flew to Thailand and won the title.

After finishing eleventh in the pro-ticket table, Morgan gained his professional status with a 9–0 whitewash of the Republic of Ireland's Pascal Burke in the play-offs.

BRADY GOLLAN

Date of birth: 28 March 1965   *Star sign:* Aries

Canadian Brady Gollan, from Kelowna, British Columbia, defeated Patsy Fagan 9–2 in the play-offs to confirm his place among this season's 128 full tournament professionals. The 1988 Canadian amateur champion set a championship record break of 135 on his way to a quarter-final place in the World Amateur Championship in Sydney last year. He also reached the last eight in 1986.

Gollan is a former employee at a factory which made fibre-glass boats. He is based at the Crystal Palace Snooker Lounge in Calgary, and plays out of Stockport when in England.

Canadian cracker: Calgary's Brady Gollan.

NIGEL BOND

Date of birth: 15 November 1965   *Star sign:* Scorpio

A former England international, Nigel Bond enjoyed considerable success in amateur tournaments and pro-ams before turning professional. He earned his pro ticket when racing to a 9–0 victory in just 162 minutes against Ian Black of Scotland. Bond finished twentieth overall on the pro-ticket circuit and in 1989 won the prestigious Websters Pro-Am at the Piccadilly Snooker Club in Manchester.

Formerly employed by Derbyshire Dale District Council, Bond worked for two years in the treasurer's department. His amateur career ended in glory when he won the English Championship, defeating the holder, Barry Pinches, 13–11 in the final.

IAN BRUMBY

Date of birth: 17 September 1964   *Star sign:* Virgo

A Liverpool football supporter, Ian Brumby was seventeen before he started playing snooker on a full-size table. This former North West champion was the lowest of the pro-ticket qualifiers at Preston in twenty-first place, but he gained professional status by beating Bill Kelly 9–3.

Brumby formerly worked with his father – the boss – at a Speake butcher's factory but left in 1986 to play on the circuit full-time. He is looked after by veteran Sid Lane, a retired businessman who has been his guide and mentor since 1984. He practises at Hunts Cross Snooker Club and like John Parrott, a former practice partner, and George Scott is a full-blooded Scouser.

WHO SAID THIS?

'Hearn is not just a thorn in the side of the WPBSA – he is a thorn in the side of snooker. He is a disruptive influence who has insulted the board's integrity.'

– *John Virgo, talking about Barry Hearn after the Matchroom chairman had been banned from the WPBSA board and press rooms.*

'I find this extremely childish – are they keeping the champagne for themselves and their friends?'

– *Barry Hearn, talking about the WPBSA ban.*

'I only watched two frames of snooker during my suspension. I turned the TV on, saw Steve Davis score two centuries and turned it off thinking, "What's new?".'

– *Cliff Thorburn.*

'That's not a bad amount – if you are a gerbil and like eating sawdust.'

– *Kirk Stevens after being told he had earned just over £7,000 in the first half of the season.*

'I think I have become a better player since becoming chairman of the WPBSA. It has given me a fuller life.'

– *John Virgo.*

'My broken foot has not been put in plaster because the doctor at this hospital believes in the "natural" healing process. My eyes and head are a bit sore and I am tired.'

– *Alex Higgins, talking from his hospital bed, after falling out of a window in Manchester and breaking his left foot. He also needed twelve stitches in a head wound.*

'This deal could be worth up to £40 million for us in guaranteeing sponsorship and promoting overseas television sales.'

– *Del Simmons, the WPBSA's contracts negotiator, after signing an £11 million six-year deal with the BBC.*

'I shut myself away in a private room for six hours for six days. It was just me and a snooker table.'

– *Stephen Hendry, talking about the way he played himself out of his bad start to the season.*

'I don't like the qualifying rounds when you are watched by three men and a dog. It is much better when the tournament proper gets under way.'

– *John Parrott.*

	Lion Brown NZ Masters	LEP Hong Kong Masters	Foster's Professional	Fidelity Unit Trusts International	Dubai Duty Free Masters	LEP Matchroom Championship	Rothmans Grand Prix	BCE Canadian Masters	Tennents UK Open	Everest World Matchplay	Norwich Union European Grand Prix
1 S. Davis	–	3,571	–	45,000 4,500(HB)	12,000	50,000 5,000(HB)	105,000*	24,000	24,000	100,000	50,000
2 J. Parrott	–	3,571	5,825	984.37	–	–	3,148.43	6,000	12,000	40,000	–
3 S. Hendry	11,250	–	8,500 2,000(HB)	3,375	.	–	3,148.43	12,000	48,000	20,000	–
4 J. White	–	28,571 2,714(HB)	–	27,000	5,000	12,500	9,750	40,000	3,875	20,000	25,000
5 D. Mountjoy	–	–	–	2,179.68	–	–	4,875	3,000	80,000 8,000(HB)	–	–
6 T. Griffiths	–	3,571	–	984.37	5,000	6,250	9,750	6,000	24,000	10,000	12,500
7 A. Meo	–	3,571	–	6,750	8,000	6,250	3,148.43	875	1,750	–	7,500
8 N. Foulds	–	10,714	–	2,179.68	25,000	12,500	4,875	875	3,875	–	7,500
9 Dennis Taylor	–	7,143	–	6,750	5,000	25,000	19,500	6,000 4,000(HB)	6,000	10,000	12,500
10 M. Hallett	6,750	–	12,500	2,179.68	–	–	4,875	12,000	1,750	10,000	–
11 C. Thorburn	–	–	–	–	5,000	6,250	–	6,000	12,000	5,000	7,500
12 W. Thorne	–	7,143	–	3,375	8,000 2,000(HB)	6,250	1,421.87	1,937.50	6,000	5,000	7,500
13 A. Higgins	–	–	–	984.37	–	–	39,000	875	3,875	–	–
14 D. Reynolds	2,600	–	–	13,500	–	–	3,148.43	1937.50	6,000	–	–
15 J. Johnson	4,400 750(HB)	–	–	6,750	–	–	3,148.43	1,937.50	6,000	10,000	–
16 W. Jones	–	–	–	984.37	–	–	3,148.43	–	1,750	–	–
17 A. Knowles	3,700	–	–	2,179.68	–	–	4,875	875	6,000	5,000	–
18 J. Virgo	–	–	–	2,179.68	–	–	1,421.87	3,000	12,000	–	–
19 A. Robidoux	–	–	–	2,179.68	–	–	19,500	875	1,750	–	–
20 S. Francisco	–	–	–	2,179.68	–	–	1,421.87	875	3,875	–	–
21 P. Francisco	–	–	–	984.37	–	–	1,421.87	875	3,875	5,000	–
22 C. Wilson	–	–	–	984.37	–	–	4,875	3,000	3,875	–	–
23 M. Clark	–	–	–	984.37	–	–	1,421.87	1,937.50	3,875	–	–
24 D. O'Kane	2,600	–	–	2,179.68	–	–	3,148.43	875	3,875	–	–
25 B. West	–	–	–	6,750	–	–	3,148.43	875	12,000	–	–
26 S. James	–	–	–	13,500	–	–	3,148.43	3,000	3,875	–	–
27 A. Drago	–	–	–	2,179.68	–	–	3,148.43	875	1,750	–	–
28 E. Hughes	–	–	5,825	2,179.68	–	–	4,875	875	1,750	–	–
29 D. Roe	–	–	–	984.37	–	–	1,421.87	875	6,000	–	–
30 E. Charlton	–	–	–	984.37	–	–	3,148.43	1,937.50	1,750	–	–
31 Gary Wilkinson	–	–	–	–	–	–	3,148.43	875	3,875	–	–
32 P. Browne	–	–	–	–	–	–	–	875	–	–	–
33 R. Williams	–	–	–	3,375	–	–	9,750	875	3,875	–	–
34 David Taylor	–	–	–	3,375	–	–	1,421.87	3,000	1,750	–	–
35 R. Chaperon	–	–	–	3,375	–	–	3,148.43	875	1,750	–	–
36 S. Newbury	–	–	–	3,375	–	–	3,148.43	1,937.50	1,750	–	–
37 N. Gilbert	–	–	–	984.37	–	–	9,750	875	3,875	–	–
38 S. Longworth	–	–	–	2,179.68	–	–	1,421.87	3,000	1,750	–	–
39 S. Duggan	–	–	–	2,179.68	–	–	3,148.43	1,937.50	3,875	–	–
40 D. Fowler	–	–	–	984.37	–	–	1,421.87	1,937.50	6,000	–	–
41 J. Wych	–	–	–	3,375	–	–	–	875	1,750	–	–
42 J. McLaughlin	–	–	–	984.37	–	–	4,875	–	1,750	–	–
43 M. Macleod	–	–	–	2,179.68	–	–	1,421.87	1,937.50	–	–	–
44 D. Morgan	2,600	–	–	–	–	–	–	1,937.50	–	–	–
45 J. Spencer	–	–	–	3,375	–	–	3,148.43	1,937.50	1,750	–	–
46 M. Johnston-Allen	–	–	–	984.37	–	–	1,421.87	–	–	–	–
47 A. Chappel	–	–	–	984.37	–	–	1,421.87	875	1,750	–	–
48 K. Stevens	–	–	–	–	–	–	1,421.87	875	3,875	–	–
49 J. Campbell	–	–	–	2,179.68	–	–	1,421.87	–	1,750	–	–
50 M. Bennett	–	–	–	984.37	–	–	–	1,937.50	6,000	–	–
51 J. O'Boye	–	–	–	984.37	–	–	1,421.87 1,625(HB)	875	3,875	–	–
52 L. Dodd	–	–	–	2,179.68	–	–	1,421.87	875	1,750	–	–
53 W. King	2,600	–	–	984.37	–	–	–	3,000	1,750	–	–
54 R. Reardon	–	–	–	984.37	–	–	–	1,937.50	1,750	–	–
55 T. Murphy	–	–	–	984.37	–	–	–	875	1,750	–	–
56 John Rea	–	–	–	2,179.68	–	–	–	–	1,750	–	–
57 C. Roscoe	–	–	–	–	–	–	–	1,937.50	3,875	–	–
58 R. Edmonds	–	–	–	984.37	–	–	4,875	–	1,750	–	–
59 A. Jones	–	–	–	984.37	–	–	1,421.87	–	1,750	–	–
60 B. Rowswell	–	–	–	–	–	–	–	–	1,750	–	–

SNOOKER'S MONEY CAKE

Mercantile Credit Classic	ICI European Open	Benson and Hedges Masters	National Champion-ships	Anglian Windows British Open	Fersina Windows World Cup	Benson and Hedges Irish Masters	Professional Players Tournaments **	Matchroom League	Continental Airlines London Masters	Embassy World Champion-ship	TOTAL
1,203.12	–	20,000	–	10,500	14,400	11,316.01	–	70,000	6,000	105,000	661,490.13
8,250	40,000 2,000(HB)	36,000	10,000 1,300(HB)	21,000	–	11,316.01	–	30,000	10,000	63,000	314,394.81
8,250	3,000	62,000	–	5,250	2,700	16,764.46 2,933.78(HB)	–	25,000	25,000 3,000(HB)	31,500 10,500(HB)	310,171.67
1,203.12	12,000	13,000	–	3,390.62	14,400	6,705.78	–	17,000	6,000	15,750	263,859.52
55,000	3,000	–	10,500 1,200(HB)	5,250	4,500	–	–	–	–	4,429.68	181,934.36
4,125	24,000	13,000	6,000	1,531.25	4,500	6,705.78	–	9,000	2,500	15,750	165,167.40
2,664.06	875	–	575	70,000	–	–	–	15,000	–	31,500	158,458.49
2,664.06	875	20,000	5,000	5,250	14,400	6,705.78	–	13,000	2,500	4,429.68	142,343.20
2,664.06	1,937.50	6,750	–	1,531.25	2,700	4,191.11	–	–	2,500	7,875	132,041.92
1,203.12	12,000	6,750	15,500	21,000	–	6,705.78	–	–	–	15,750	128,963.58
16,500	6,000 2,000(HB)	13,000	1,904.76	5,250 1,750(HB)	4,500	4,191.11	–	20,000 5,000(HB)	–	4,429.68	126,275.55
16,500	3,000	6,750	2,500	5,250	–	–	–	11,000	–	7,875	101,502.37
2,664.06	1,937.50	–	5,000	3,390.62	2,700	27,242.25	4,550	5,000	–	3,445.31	100,664.11
2,664.06	–	–	1,250	42,000	–	–	–	–	–	15,750	96,474.99
4,125	3,000	6,750	2,500	10,500	–	–	–	–	–	4,429.68	64,330.61
33,000 5,500(HB)	875	–	750	1,531.25	–	–	250	–	–	7,875	55,664.05
4,125	875	13,000	1,250	3,390.62	–	4,191.11	250	–	–	4,429.68	54,141.09
4,125	3,000	6,750	575	3,390.62	–	–	–	–	–	7,875	44,317.17
–	3,000 1,000(HB)	–	6,428.57	3,390.62	–	–	625	–	–	3,445.31	42,194.18
4,125	875	6,750	–	1,531.25	9,000 1,800(HB)	–	–	–	–	7,875	40,307.80
1,203.12	875	6,750	–	10,500	–	–	4,100	–	–	4,429.68	40,014.04
2,664.06	1,937.50	6,750	750	5,250	4,500	–	–	–	–	4,429.68	39,015.61
8,250	6,000	–	575	10,500	–	–	750	–	–	3,445.31	37,739.05
2,664.06	875	–	–	3,390.62	9,000 1,800(HB)	–	250	–	–	4,429.68	35,087.47
1,203.12	875	–	575	5,250	–	–	250	–	–	3,445.31	34,371.86
2,664.06	875	–	575	1,531.25	–	–	–	–	–	4,429.68	33,598.42
2,664.06	875	–	–	3,390.62	9,000 1,800(HB)	–	250	–	2,500	3,445.31	31,878.10
2,664.06	1,937.50	–	900	3,390.62	2,700	–	–	–	–	4,429.68	31,526.54
1,203.12	1,937.50	–	1,250	3,390.62	–	–	3,000	–	–	7,875	29,937.48
1,203.12	6,000	–	714.29	1,531.25	2,700	–	250	–	–	7,875	28,093.96
1,203.12	1,937.50	–	5,000	1,531.25	–	–	5,300	–	–	4,429.68	27,299.98
8,250	1,937.50	–	900	1,531.25	–	–	5,975	–	–	4,429.68	26,598.43
1,203.12	1,937.50	–	575	1,531.25	–	–	–	–	–	3,445.31	26,567.18
4,125	875	–	575	1,531.25	–	–	5,000	–	–	3,445.31	25,098.43
2,664.06	875	–	595.24	1,531.25	4,500	–	–	–	–	4,429.68	23,743.66
4,125	875	–	2,500	1,531.25	–	–	–	–	–	4,429.68	23,671.86
1,203.12 1,375(HB)	–	–	–	1,531.25	–	–	200	–	–	3,445.31	23,239.05
1,203.12	1,937.50	–	2,500	3,390.62	–	–	600	–	–	3,445.31	21,428.10
1,203.12	875	–	–	–	–	–	–	–	–	7,875	21,093.73
1,203.12	3,000	–	1,250	1,531.25	–	–	350	–	–	1,804.68	19,482.79
–	6,000	–	3,571.43	1,531.25	–	–	–	–	–	1,804.68	18,907.36
1,203.12	875	–	2,500	–	–	4,191.11	450	–	–	1,804.68	18,633.28
1,203.12	1,937.50	–	1,250	3,390.62	2,700	–	225	–	–	1,804.68	18,049.97
–	–	–	750	3,390.62	–	–	1,500	–	–	4,429.68 2,625(HB)	17,232.80
1,203.12	–	–	575	1,531.25	–	–	–	–	–	3,445.31	16,965.61
–	1,937.50	–	–	5,250 7,000(HB)	–	–	350	–	–	–	16,943.74
4,125	1,937.50	–	150	3,390.62	–	–	1,975	–	–	–	16,609.36
1,203.12	875	–	1,071.43	–	4,500	–	–	–	–	1,804.68	15,626.10
–	3,000	–	1,904.76	1,531.25	–	–	650	–	–	–	15,137.56
–	1,937.50	–	2,500	1,531.25	–	–	–	–	–	–	14,890.62
–	875	–	–	–	–	–	–	–	–	4,429.68	14,085.92
1,203.12	875	–	–	1,531.25	–	–	800	–	–	3,445.31	14,081.23
1,203.12	875	–	–	–	2,700	–	600	–	–	–	13,712.49
2,664.06	875	–	750	1,531.25	–	–	–	–	–	1,804.68	12,296.86
1,203.12	875	–	450 300(HB)	–	2,700	–	725	–	–	1,804.68	11,667.17
–	–	–	2,000	1,531.25	–	–	250	–	–	3,445.31	11,156.24
1,203.12	–	–	150	3,390.62	–	–	350	–	–	–	10,906.24
–	875	–	–	–	–	–	–	–	–	1,804.68	10,289.05
–	875	–	–	1,531.25	–	–	–	–	–	3,445.31	10,007.80
–	–	–	2,500	–	–	–	1,825	–	–	3,445.31	9,520.31

	Lion Brown NZ Masters	LEP Hong Kong Masters	Foster's Professional	Fidelity Unit Trusts International	Dubai Duty Free Masters	LEP Matchroom Championship	Rothmans Grand Prix	BCE Canadian Masters	Tennents UK Open	Everest World Matchplay	Norwich Union European Grand Prix
61 I. Graham	–	–	–	–	–	–	–	3,000	–	–	–
62 D. Gilbert	–	–	–	–	–	–	1,421.87	–	1,750	–	–
63 D. Martin	–	–	–	984.37	–	–	1,421.87	875	1,750	–	–
64 K. Owers	–	–	–	984.37	–	–	–	875	1,750	–	–
65 G. Cripsey	–	–	–	984.37	–	–	–	–	–	–	–
66 M. Smith	–	–	–	–	–	–	1,421.87	875 1,000(HB)	1,750	–	–
67 C. Edwards	–	–	–	–	–	–	–	–	–	–	–
68 J. Wright	–	–	–	984.37	–	–	–	–	–	–	–
69 A. Kearney	–	–	–	–	–	–	–	–	1,750	–	–
70 R. Marshall	–	–	–	–	–	–	–	–	–	–	–
71 M. Price	–	–	–	984.37	–	–	–	875	–	–	–
72 P. Medati	–	–	–	–	–	–	1,421.87	875	1,750	–	–
73 R. Foldvari	–	–	–	–	–	–	1,421.87	–	–	–	–
74 J. Chambers	–	–	–	984.37	–	–	1,421.87	–	–	–	–
75 M. Morra	–	–	–	–	–	–	1,421.87	–	–	–	–
76 M. Gauvreau	–	–	–	–	–	–	–	1,937.50	–	–	–
77 J. Donnelly	–	–	–	–	–	–	–	–	–	–	–
78 A. Harris	–	–	–	–	–	–	–	–	–	–	–
79 N. Terry	–	–	–	–	–	–	1,421.87	–	–	–	–
80 Glen Wilkinson	–	–	–	–	–	–	–	–	–	–	–
81 S. Meakin	–	–	–	984.37	–	–	–	–	–	–	–
82 M. Rowing	–	–	–	–	–	–	–	–	1,750	–	–
83 P. Houlihan	–	–	–	–	–	–	1,421.87	–	–	–	–
84 R. Grace	–	–	–	–	–	–	–	–	–	–	–
85 G. Miles	–	–	–	984.37	–	–	–	–	–	–	–
86 R. Bales	–	–	–	–	–	–	–	–	–	–	–
87 M. Fisher	–	–	–	984.37	–	–	1,421.87	–	–	–	–
88 M. Bradley	–	–	–	–	–	–	1,421.87	–	–	–	–
89 T. Wilson	–	–	–	984.37	–	–	–	–	–	–	–
90 S. Campbell	–	–	–	–	–	–	–	875	–	–	–
91 I. Williamson	–	–	–	–	–	–	1,421.87	–	–	–	–
92 E. Sinclair	–	–	–	–	–	–	–	–	–	–	–
93 P. Thornley	–	–	–	–	–	–	–	–	–	–	–
94 B. Mikkelsen	–	–	–	–	–	–	–	–	–	–	–
95 F. Ellis	–	–	–	–	–	–	1,421.87	–	–	–	–
96 B. Oliver	–	–	–	–	–	–	–	875	–	–	–
97 J. Bear	–	–	–	–	–	–	–	–	–	–	–
98 G. Scott	–	–	–	–	–	–	–	1,937.50	–	–	–
99 M. Watterson	–	–	–	–	–	–	1,421.87	–	–	–	–
100 B. Harris	–	–	–	–	–	–	–	–	1,750	–	–
101 T. Whitthread	–	–	–	–	–	–	–	–	–	–	–
102 M. Darrington	–	–	–	–	–	–	–	–	–	–	–
103 M. Gibson	–	–	–	–	–	–	–	–	–	–	–
104 J. Smith	–	–	–	–	–	–	–	–	–	–	–
105 M. Hines	–	–	–	–	–	–	–	–	–	–	–
106 D. Sheehan	–	–	–	–	–	–	–	–	–	–	–
107 P. Watchorn	–	–	–	–	–	–	–	–	–	–	–
108 D. Hughes	–	–	–	–	–	–	–	–	–	–	–
109 J. Fitzmaurice	–	–	–	–	–	–	–	875	–	–	–
110 J. Caggianello	–	–	–	–	–	–	–	–	–	–	–
F. Jonik	–	–	–	–	–	–	–	–	–	–	–
112 J. Dunning	–	–	–	–	–	–	–	875	–	–	–
113 E. Lawlor	–	–	–	–	–	–	–	–	–	–	–
114 J. van Rensburg	–	–	–	–	–	–	–	–	–	–	–
D. Mienie	–	–	–	–	–	–	–	–	–	–	–
116 W. Werbeniuk	–	–	–	–	–	–	–	–	–	–	–
117 W. Potasnik	–	–	–	–	–	–	–	–	–	–	–
118 G. Watson	–	–	–	–	–	–	–	–	–	–	–
119 Jack Rea	–	–	–	–	–	–	–	–	–	–	–
120 E. McLaughlin	–	–	–	–	–	–	–	–	–	–	–
121 I. Anderson	–	–	–	–	–	–	–	–	–	–	–
G. Jenkins	–	–	–	–	–	–	–	–	–	–	–
123 B. Kelly	–	–	–	–	–	–	–	–	–	–	–
124 I. Black	–	–	–	–	–	–	–	–	–	–	–
125 V. Harris	–	–	–	–	–	–	–	–	–	–	–
126 B. Demarco	–	–	–	–	–	–	–	–	–	–	–
127 P. Burke	–	–	–	–	–	–	–	–	–	–	–
128 G. Rigitano	–	–	–	–	–	–	–	–	–	–	–
129 G. Greaves	–	–	–	–	–	–	–	–	–	–	–
130 J. Giannaros	–	–	–	–	–	–	–	–	–	–	–
131 D. Heaton	–	–	–	–	–	–	–	–	–	–	–
132 L. Condo	–	–	–	–	–	–	–	–	–	–	–
P. Morgan	–	–	–	–	–	–	–	–	–	–	–
134 P. Gibson	–	–	–	–	–	–	–	–	–	–	–
J. Grech	–	–	–	–	–	–	–	–	–	–	–
136 B. Bennett	–	–	–	–	–	–	–	–	–	–	–
C. Everton	–	–	–	–	–	–	–	–	–	–	–
S. Frangie	–	–	–	–	–	–	–	–	–	–	–

* Includes £40,000 bonus for completing a Grand Prix and Rothmans Matchroom League double.
** This column represents the combined prize money from 3 events in Glasgow, Brixham and Leeds.

Mercantile Credit Classic	ICI European Open	Benson and Hedges Masters	National Champion-ships	Anglian Windows British Open	Fersina Windows World Cup	Benson and Hedges Irish Masters	Professional Players Tournaments **	Matchroom League	Continental Airlines London Masters	Embassy World Champion-ship	TOTAL
–	–	–	1,250	1,531.25	–	–	100	–	–	3,445.31	9,326.56
–	875	–	575	–	–	–	725	–	–	3,445.31	8,792.18
1,203.12	–	–	575	–	–	–	–	–	–	1,804.68	8,614.04
–	875	–	–	1,531.25	–	–	1,225	–	–	1,804.68	8,170.30
2,664.06	875	–	1,250	1,531.25	–	–	525	–	–	–	7,829.68
–	–	–	–	–	–	–	800	–	–	1,804.68	7,651.55
–	1,937.50	–	1,250	1,531.25	–	–	600	–	–	1,804.68	7,123.43
2,664.06	–	–	–	1,531.25	–	–	1,275	–	–	–	6,454.68
–	–	–	450	–	2,700	–	575	–	–	–	5,475
1,203.12	–	–	575	3,390.62	–	–	300	–	–	–	5,468.74
–	–	–	1,250	–	–	–	425	–	–	1,804.68	5,339.05
–	–	–	575	–	–	–	575	–	–	–	5,196.87
–	–	–	1,047.62 142.86(HB)	1,531.25	–	–	675	–	–	–	4,818.60
–	1,937.50	–	–	–	–	–	300	–	–	–	4,643.74
–	875	–	1,071.43 476.19(HB)	–	–	–	475	–	–	–	4,319.49
–	–	–	595.24	1,531.25	–	–	175	–	–	–	4,238.99
–	–	–	750	–	2,700	–	775	–	–	–	4,255
2,664.06	–	–	575	–	–	–	975	–	–	–	4,214.06
2,664.06	–	–	–	–	–	–	–	–	–	–	4,085.93
1,203.12	–	–	190.48	–	–	–	625	–	–	1,804.68	3,823.28
–	–	–	–	–	–	–	2,800	–	–	–	3,784.37
–	–	–	–	–	–	–	175	–	–	1,804.68	3,729.68
–	–	–	575	1,531.25	–	–	–	–	–	–	3,528.12
–	–	–	3,038 127(HB)	–	–	–	325	–	–	–	3,490
1,203.12	–	–	575	–	–	–	675	–	–	–	3,437.49
–	–	–	–	3,390.62	–	–	–	–	–	–	3,390.62
–	–	–	–	–	–	–	925	–	–	–	3,331.24
1,203.12	–	–	–	–	–	–	625	–	–	–	3,249.99
–	1,937.50	–	–	–	–	–	300	–	–	–	3,221.87
1,203.12	–	–	–	–	–	–	625	–	–	–	2,703.12
–	–	–	575	–	–	–	625	–	–	–	2,621.87
–	875	–	312.50	–	–	–	1,300	–	–	–	2,487.50
–	–	–	595.24	–	–	–	–	–	–	1,804.68	2,399.92
–	–	–	1,904.76	–	–	–	450	–	–	–	2,354.76
–	–	–	760	–	–	–	125	–	–	–	2,306.87
–	875	–	–	–	–	–	450	–	–	–	2,220
–	–	–	595.24	1,531.25	–	–	–	–	–	–	2,126.49
–	–	–	–	–	–	–	–	–	–	–	1,937.50
–	–	–	–	–	–	–	375	–	–	–	1,796.87
–	–	–	–	–	–	–	–	–	–	–	1,750
–	–	–	–	1,531.25	–	–	125	–	–	–	1,656.25
1,203.12	–	–	–	–	–	–	300	–	–	–	1,503.12
–	–	–	750	–	–	–	750	–	–	–	1,500
1,203.12	–	–	–	–	–	–	200	–	–	–	1,403.12
–	–	–	1,266	–	–	–	125	–	–	–	1,391
1,203.12	–	–	–	–	–	–	150	–	–	–	1,353.12
–	–	–	450	–	–	–	800	–	–	–	1,250
1,203.12	–	–	–	–	–	–	–	–	–	–	1,203.12
–	–	–	–	–	–	–	225	–	–	–	1,100
–	–	–	1,071.43	–	–	–	–	–	–	–	1,071.43
–	–	–	1,071.43	–	–	–	–	–	–	–	1,071.43
–	–	–	–	–	–	–	175	–	–	–	1,050
–	875	–	–	–	–	–	–	–	–	–	875
–	–	–	760	–	–	–	–	–	–	–	760
–	–	–	760	–	–	–	–	–	–	–	760
–	–	–	–	–	–	–	750	–	–	–	750
–	–	–	476.19	–	–	–	125	–	–	–	601.19
–	–	–	595.24	–	–	–	–	–	–	–	595.24
–	–	–	450	–	–	–	125	–	–	–	575
–	–	–	312.50	–	–	–	200	–	–	–	512.50
–	–	–	476.19	–	–	–	–	–	–	–	476.19
–	–	–	476.19	–	–	–	–	–	–	–	476.19
–	–	–	–	–	–	–	475	–	–	–	475
–	–	–	312.50	–	–	–	125	–	–	–	437.50
–	–	–	–	–	–	–	425	–	–	–	425
–	–	–	312.50	–	–	–	100	–	–	–	412.50
–	–	–	150	–	–	–	250	–	–	–	400
–	–	–	–	–	–	–	375	–	–	–	375
–	–	–	–	–	–	–	350	–	–	–	350
–	–	–	190.48	–	–	–	125	–	–	–	315.48
–	–	–	–	–	–	–	225	–	–	–	225
–	–	–	190.48	–	–	–	–	–	–	–	190.48
–	–	–	190.48	–	–	–	–	–	–	–	190.48
–	–	–	–	–	–	–	175	–	–	–	175
–	–	–	–	–	–	–	175	–	–	–	175
–	–	–	–	–	–	–	100	–	–	–	100
–	–	–	–	–	–	–	100	–	–	–	100
–	–	–	–	–	–	–	100	–	–	–	100

THE TOP THIRTY-TWO – THEIR CAREERS SO FAR (AND A SECRET WISH)

STEVE DAVIS

World ranking: number 1
Date of birth: 22 August 1957
Star sign: Leo

My secret wish: To be able to sing like Otis Redding

Steve Davis once again dominated world snooker – even though he went four months without winning a title. Between the start of the season and Christmas, Davis won five titles – the Fidelity Unit Trusts International, the Rothmans Grand Prix, the LEP Matchroom Championship, the Everest World Matchplay and the Norwich Union European Grand Prix.

But then there was a barren spell as he failed to retain the Mercantile Credit Classic title, withdrew from the ICI European Open and was beaten in the two Benson and Hedges Masters events and the Anglian Windows British Open. However, as always, Davis answered the doubters by collecting a record sixth Embassy World Championship and, just for good measure, won the Matchroom League for the third successive year.

He also helped England win the Fersina Windows World Cup to bring his total earnings for the 1988/89 season to a record £661,490. Davis' total yearly income now amounts to nearly £1.5 million and he continues to be one of the highest-paid sportsmen in Britain.

Record breaker: Steve Davis with a collection of 5,000 records at his Essex home.

BEST PERFORMANCES

Embassy World Championship:
Winner 1981 (beat Doug Mountjoy 18–12)
Winner 1983 (beat Cliff Thorburn 18–6)
Winner 1984 (beat Jimmy White 18–16)
Winner 1987 (beat Joe Johnson 18–14)
Winner 1988 (beat Terry Griffiths 18–11)
Winner 1989 (beat John Parrott 18–3)

Other Ranking Tournaments

Fidelity Unit Trusts International:
Winner 1983 (beat Clifff Thorburn 9–4)
Winner 1984 (beat Tony Knowles 9–2)
Winner 1987 (beat Cliff Thorburn 12–5)
Winner 1988 (beat Jimmy White 12–6)

Other Ranking Tournaments (continued)

Rothmans Grand Prix:	Winner 1985 (beat Dennis Taylor 10–9)
	Winner 1988 (beat Alex Higgins 10–6)
BCE Canadian Masters:	Runner-up 1988 (lost to Jimmy White 9–4)
Tennents UK Open:	Winner 1984 (beat Alex Higgins 16–8)
	Winner 1985 (beat Willie Thorne 16–14)
	Winner 1986 (beat Neal Foulds 16–7)
	Winner 1987 (beat Jimmy White 16–14)
Mercantile Credit Classic:	Winner 1984 (beat Tony Meo 9–8)
	Winner 1987 (beat Jimmy White 13–12)
	Winner 1988 (beat John Parrott 13–11)
ICI European Open;	Did not enter
Anglian Windows British Open:	Winner 1986 (beat Willie Thorne 12–7)

Current Non-ranking Tournaments

Benson and Hedges Masters:	Winner 1982 (beat Terry Griffiths 9–5)
	Winner 1988 (beat Mike Hallett 9–0)
Benson and Hedges Irish Masters:	Winner 1983 (beat Ray Reardon 9–2)
	Winner 1984 (beat Terry Griffiths 9–1)
	Winner 1987 (beat Willie Thorne 9–1)
	Winner 1988 (beat Neal Foulds 9–4)
Everest World Matchplay:	Winner 1988 (beat John Parrott 9–5)

Other Wins

Pontin's Open: 1978, 1979
Coral UK: 1980, 1981
Lada Classic: 1981 (played December 1980)
English Professional: 1981, 1985
Yamaha International Masters: 1981, 1982, 1984
Jameson International: 1981
Pot Black: 1982, 1983
Pontin's Professional: 1982
Tolly Cobbold Classic: 1982, 1983, 1984
Winfield Masters: 1982
Langs Supreme Scottish Masters: 1982, 1983, 1984

Hofmeister World Doubles: 1982, 1983, 1985, 1986
Camus Hong Kong Masters: 1984
Riley Hong Kong Masters: 1987
Camus Singapore Masters: 1985
BCE Canadian Masters: 1986
Brazilian Masters: 1986
Camus China Masters: 1986
Matchroom League: 1987, 1988, 1989
LEP Matchroom Trophy: 1988
Fersina Windows World Cup: 1981, 1983, 1988, 1989
Norwich Union European Grand Prix: 1988

WORLD RANKING POSITIONS

1980/81	13		1984/85	1		1987/88	1
1981/82	2		1985/86	1		1988/89	1
1982/83	4		1986/87	1		1989/90	1
1983/84	1						

JOHN PARROTT

World ranking: number 2
Date of birth: 11 May 1964
Star sign: Taurus

My secret wish: To own a winning horse in the Champion Hurdle at Cheltenham

John Parrott finally 'arrived' in the 1988/89 season. After many years of trying to win his first major trophy, he travelled to Deauville and won the inaugural ICI European Open with a 9–8 final defeat of Terry Griffiths.

Crossword king: John Parrott fills in time at the ICE European Open in France.

Parrott, who finished second on the money list behind Steve Davis with £314,394, also made the finals of the Everest World Matchplay, the Benson and Hedges Masters, the Continental Airlines London Masters and the Embassy World Championship. Unfortunately for him, he was totally outplayed by defending champion Davis in the Embassy final and received an 18–3 beating.

Even so, it was still the greatest season of Parrott's professional career. In June 1989 he married his long-time girlfriend, Karen.

BEST PERFORMANCES

Embassy World Championship:	Runner-up 1989 (lost to Steve Davis 18–3)

Other Ranking Tournaments

Fidelity Unit Trusts International:	Quarter-finalist 1985 (lost to Dennis Taylor 5–1)
Rothmans Grand Prix:	Semi-finalist 1987 (lost to Stephen Hendry 9–7)
BCE Canadian Masters:	Quarter-finalist 1988 (lost to Mike Hallett 5–3)
Tennents UK Open:	Semi-finalist 1986 (lost to Neal Foulds 9–3)
Mercantile Credit Classic:	Runner-up 1988 (lost to Steve Davis 13–11)
ICI European Open:	Winner 1989 (beat Terry Griffiths 9–8)
Anglian Windows British Open	Semi-finalist 1988 (lost to Mike Hallett 9–8)
	Semi-finalist 1989 (lost to Dean Reynolds 9–8)

Current Non-ranking Tournaments

Benson and Hedges Masters:	Runner-up 1989 (lost to Stephen Hendry 9–6)
Benson and Hedges Irish Masters:	Semi-finalist 1989 (lost to Alex Higgins 6–4)
Everest World Matchplay:	Runner-up 1988 (lost to Steve Davis 9–5)

Other Wins

Junior Pot Black: 1982, 1983	Pontin's Professional: 1988
Pontin's Open: 1982, 1986	Kent China Cup: 1988

WORLD RANKING POSITIONS

1984/85	20	1986/87	17	1988/89	7
1985/86	18	1987/88	13	1989/90	2

STEPHEN HENDRY

World ranking: number 3
Date of birth: 13 January 1969
Star sign: Capricorn

My secret wish: To be rock singer Jon Bon Jovi for a day

Stephen Hendry, who has been setting records since he turned professional, earned another place in the record books when, at twenty, he became the youngest winner of the Benson and Hedges Masters at Wembley. It was an outstanding performance from the youthful Scot, who eventually went on to move one place up the rankings to number 3.

But, deep down, Hendry will be disappointed with his season as he failed to win a ranking tournament. He was beaten by Doug Mountjoy in the final of the Tennents UK Open and then suffered a 16–9 reverse against Steve Davis in the semifinal of the Embassy World Championship. That world defeat was even more cruel because Hendry, in the third session, had produced one of the most inspired performances of the entire event. He had also suffered another final defeat – this time 9–8 – by Alex Higgins in the Benson and Hedges Irish Masters.

Hendry still earned more than £300,000 during the season and his income from all sources topped the £700,000 mark.

Heading for the top: Stephen Hendry who moved up one place to number 3.

BEST PERFORMANCES

Embassy World Championship:	Semi-finalist 1989 (lost to Steve Davis 16–9)

Other Ranking Tournaments

Fidelity Unit Trusts International:	Semi-finalist 1987 (lost to Cliff Thorburn 9–1)
Rothmans Grand Prix:	Winner 1987 (beat Dennis Taylor 10–7)
BCE Canadian Masters:	Semi-finalist 1988 (lost to Steve Davis 9–5)
Tennents UK Open:	Runner-up 1988 (lost to Doug Mountjoy 16–12)
Mercantile Credit Classic:	Semi-finalist 1987 (lost to Steve Davis 9–3)
ICI European Open:	Round 5 1989 (lost to Mike Hallett 5–3)
Anglian Windows British Open:	Winner 1988 (beat Mike Hallett 13–2)

Current Non-ranking Tournaments

Benson and Hedges Masters:	Winner 1989 (beat John Parrott 9–6)
Benson and Hedges Irish Masters:	Runner-up 1989 (lost to Alex Higgins 9–8)
Everest World Matchplay:	Semi-finalist 1988 (lost to John Parrott 9–6)

Other Wins

British Isles Under-16: 1983
Scottish Amateur: 1984, 1985
Scottish Professional: 1986, 1987, 1988

Winfield Masters: 1987
Foster's World Doubles: 1987
Lion Brown New Zealand Masters: 1988

WORLD RANKING POSITIONS

1986/87	51	1988/89	4
1987/88	23	1989/90	3

JIMMY WHITE

World ranking: number 4
Date of birth: 2 May 1962
Star sign: Taurus

My secret wish: To play
professional football for Chelsea

Jimmy White won the BCE Canadian Masters title with a 9–4 thrashing of Steve Davis but the Whirlwind was far from pleased with his overall results in the 1988/89 season. He dropped two places down the rankings and knows that his form must improve if he is to get back and challenge Davis again for the number 1 spot.

He did reach the final of the Fidelity Unit Trusts International where he was beaten 12–6 by Davis and the semi-final of the ICI European Open where he lost 5–4 to Terry Griffiths. Many players would have settled for reaching the quarter-final of the Embassy World Championship, but White knows that he should have played better as he lost 13–7 to John Parrott.

White has recently moved house from Wimbledon to the Surrey countryside with his wife, Maureen, and their three daughters.

What style: Jimmy White waits to drive at the Royal Hong Kong Golf Club the day after he won the LEP International Masters.

BEST PERFORMANCES

Embassy World Championship:	Runner-up 1984 (lost to Steve Davis 18–16)

Other Ranking Tournaments

Fidelity Unit Trusts International:	Runner-up 1985 (lost to Cliff Thorburn 12–10) Runner-up 1988 (lost to Steve Davis 12–6)
Rothmans Grand Prix:	Winner 1986 (beat Rex Williams 10–6)
BCE Canadian Masters:	Winner 1988 (beat Steve Davis 9–4)
Tennents UK Open:	Runner-up 1987 (lost to Steve Davis 16–14)
Mercantile Credit Classic;	Winner 1986 (beat Cliff Thorburn 13–12)
ICI European Open:	Semi-finalist 1989 (lost to Terry Griffiths 5–4)
Anglian Windows British Open:	Winner 1987 (beat Neal Foulds 13–9)

Current Non-ranking Tournaments

Benson and Hedges Masters:	Winner 1984 (beat Terry Griffiths 9–5)
Benson and Hedges Irish Masters:	Winner 1985 (beat Alex Higgins 9–5) Winner 1986 (beat Willie Thorne 9–5)
Everest World Matchplay:	Semi-finalist 1988 (lost to Steve Davis 9–5)

Other Wins

British Isles Under-16: 1977	Hofmeister World Doubles: 1984
Pontin's Autumn Open: 1978	Carlsberg Challenge: 1984, 1985
English Amateur: 1979	Pot Black: 1986
World Amateur: 1980	Camus Malaysian Masters: 1986
Indian Amateur: 1980	Fersina Windows World Cup: 1988, 1989
Langs Supreme Scottish Masters: 1981	LEP International Masters: 1988
Northern Ireland Classic: 1981	

WORLD RANKING POSITIONS

1981/82	21	1984/85	7	1987/88	2
1982/83	10	1985/86	7	1988/89	2
1983/84	11	1986/87	5	1989/90	4

TERRY GRIFFITHS

World ranking: number 5
Date of birth: 16 October 1947
Star sign: Libra

My secret wish: To walk out in front of a sell-out crowd at Cardiff Arms Park and play rugby for Wales

Terry Griffiths, once again, proved that he is one of the most consistent players the game has ever seen. There were no titles in the 1988/89 season but he reached the final of the ICI European Open, in which he lost to John Parrott 9–8, and the quarter-final of the Embassy World Championship.

Wherever he is playing, Terry, a committed home-lover, cannot wait to get back to his family and friends in Wales but understands fully the demands placed on players in recent years. Unfortunately, he lost his Welsh Championship title to his good friend Doug Mountjoy and was relegated from the Matchroom League.

Solid as ever: Welshman Terry Griffiths at number 5 after reaching the final of the ICI European Open.

BEST PERFORMANCES

Embassy World Championship:	Winner 1979 (beat Dennis Taylor 24–16)

Other Ranking Tournaments

Fidelity Unit Trusts International:	Semi-finalist 1983 (lost to Cliff Thorburn 9–8)
Rothmans Grand Prix:	Quarter-finalist 1982 (lost to Jimmy White 5–2)
	Quarter-finalist 1985 (lost to Cliff Thorburn 5–1)
BCE Canadian Masters:	Quarter-finalist 1988 (lost to Steve Davis 5–3)
Tennents UK Open:	Semi-finalist 1988 (lost to Doug Mountjoy 9–4)
Mercantile Credit Classic:	Quarter-finalist 1984 (lost to Steve Davis 5–4)
	Quarter-finalist 1985 (lost to Cliff Thorburn 5-4)
	Quarter-finalist 1987 (lost to Jimmy White 5–3)
	Quarter-finalist 1988 (lost to Steve Newbury 5–4)
ICI European Open:	Runner-up 1989 (lost to John Parrott 9–8)
Anglian Windows British Open:	Quarter-finalist 1986 (lost to Willie Thorne 5–4)

Current Non-ranking Tournaments

Benson and Hedges Masters:	Winner 1980 (beat Alex Higgins 9–5)
Benson and Hedges Irish Masters:	Winner 1980 (beat Doug Mountjoy 9–8)
	Winner 1981 (beat Ray Reardon 9–7)
	Winner 1982 (beat Steve Davis 9–5)
Everest World Matchplay:	Quarter-finalist 1988 (lost to Jimmy White 9–5)

Other Wins

Welsh Amateur: 1975
English Amateur: 1977, 1978
State Express World Cup: 1979, 1980
Pontin's Professional: 1981, 1985, 1986
Coral UK: 1982
Lada Classic: 1982

Pontin's Open: 1983
Pot Black: 1984
Welsh Professional: 1985, 1986, 1988
Camus Hong Kong Masters: 1985
BCE Belgian Classic: 1986

WORLD RANKING POSITIONS

1979/80	8	1983/84	9	1987/88	6
1980/81	5	1984/85	8	1988/89	5
1981/82	3	1985/86	8	1989/90	5
1982/83	14	1986/87	10		

MIKE HALLETT

World ranking: number 6
Date of birth: 6 July 1959
Star sign: Cancer

My secret wish: To be a fighter pilot taking a plane through the sound barrier

Mike Hallett continued his march up the rankings with a move of three places to number 6. After a poor start to the season, Hallett reached the semi-finals of the BCE Canadian Masters and the ICI European Open. He also became a winner for the first time in his professional career and there was no bigger smile than his when he beat John Parrott 9–7 to take the English professional title in Bristol. 'I have waited a long time for this win,' he said.

But his biggest disappointment came in the Embassy World Championship when he was crushed 13–3 by Steve Davis in the quarter-final – just one year after losing 13–1 to the same player in the second round. Hallett is determined that defeats like that will only make him a more experienced player, however, and he is looking to move into snooker's top four this season.

A winner at last: English champion Mike Hallett.

BEST PERFORMANCES

Embassy World Championship:	Quarter-finalist 1987 (lost to Neal Foulds 13–9)
	Quarter-finalist 1989 (lost to Steve Davis 13–3)

Other Ranking Tournaments

Fidelity Unit Trusts International:	Semi-finalist 1987 (lost to Steve Davis 9–3)
Rothmans Grand Prix:	Round 3 (last 16) 1983 (lost to Tony Meo 5–3)
	Round 3 (last 16) 1984 (lost to Kirk Stevens 5–3)
	Round 5 1986 (lost to Jimmy White 5–3)
	Round 5 1988 (lost to Dennis Taylor 5–2)
BCE Canadian Masters:	Semi-finalist 1988 (lost to Jimmy White 9–2)
Tennents UK Open:	Quarter-finalist 1987 (lost to Joe Johnson 9–7)
Mercantile Credit Classic:	Round 1 (last 16) 1984 (lost to Tony Knowles 5–3)
ICI European Open:	Semi-finalist 1989 (lost to John Parrott 5–4)
Anglian Windows British Open:	Runner-up 1988 (lost to Stephen Hendry 13–2)

Current Non-ranking Tournaments

Benson and Hedges Masters:	Runner-up 1988 (lost to Steve Davis 9–0)
Benson and Hedges Irish Masters:	Quarter-finalist 1989 (lost to Steve Davis 5–4)
Everest World Matchplay:	Quarter-finalist 1988 (lost to Steve Davis 9–2)

	Other Wins	
British Isles Under-16: 1975		Foster's Professional: 1988
Foster's World Doubles: 1987		English Professional: 1989

WORLD RANKING POSITIONS

1980/81	–	1984/85	25	1987/88	16
1981/82	29	1985/86	28	1988/89	9
1982/83	31	1986/87	27	1989/90	6
1983/84	32				

CLIFF THORBURN

World ranking; number 7
Date of birth: 16 January 1948
Star sign: Capricorn

My secret wish: To be on the eighteenth green in the US Masters Golf Tournament with a seven-stroke lead knowing I could six-putt and still win the title

Cliff Thorburn missed the first two ranking tournaments of the 1988/89 season through suspension, but even so the consistency that has always been Thorburn's trademark kept him in snooker's top ten at number 7. There is no more durable a competitor on the circuit, and he proved that in the Embassy World Championship when he made Eddie Charlton wait until 2.39am before losing his first-round match 10–9. It was the second latest finish in the history of snooker – Thorburn and Terry Griffiths hold the record at 3.51am in 1983. Thorburn lost his Canadian title to newcomer Alain Robidoux.

Consistent: Cliff Thorburn who kept his place in the top ten despite being banned from two tournaments at the start of the season.

BEST PERFORMANCES

Embassy World Championship:	Winner 1980 (beat Alex Higgins 18–16)

Other Ranking Tournaments

Fidelity Unit Trusts International:	Winner 1985 (beat Jimmy White 12–10)
Rothmans Grand Prix:	Runner-up 1984 (lost to Dennis Taylor 10–2)
BCE Canadian Masters:	Quarter-finalist 1988 (lost to Stephen Hendry 5–4)
Tennents UK Open:	Semi-finalist 1984 (lost to Alex Higgins 9–7)

Other Ranking Tournaments (continued)

Mercantile Credit Classic:	Runner-up 1985 (lost to Willie Thorne 13–8) Runner-up 1986 (lost to Jimmy White 13–12)
ICI European Open:	Quarter-finalist 1989 (lost to Jimmy White 5–3)
Anglian Windows British Open:	Semi-finalist 1987 (lost to Jimmy White 9–5) Semi-finalist 1988 (lost to Stephen Hendry 9–5)

Current Non-ranking Tournaments

Benson and Hedges Masters:	Winner 1983 (beat Ray Reardon 9–7) Winner 1985 (beat Doug Mountjoy 9–6) Winner 1986 (beat Jimmy White 9–5)
Benson and Hedges Irish Masters:	Semi-finalist 1981 (lost to Terry Griffiths 6–5) Semi-finalist 1986 (lost to Willie Thorn 6–4)
Everest World Matchplay:	Round 1 1988 (lost to Joe Johnson 9–4)

Other Wins

Canadian Open: 1974, 1978, 1979, 1980
Pot Black: 1981
State Express World Team Classic: 1982

Winfield Masters: 1983
Canadian Professional: 1984, 1985, 1986, 1987
Langs Supreme Scottish Masters: 1985, 1986

WORLD RANKING POSITIONS

1976/77	3	1981/82	1	1986/87	2
1977/78	6	1982/83	3	1987/88	4
1978/79	5	1983/84	3	1988/89	6
1979/80	5	1984/85	3	1989/90	7
1980/81	2	1985/86	2		

DENNIS TAYLOR

World ranking: number 8
Date of birth: 19 January 1949
Star sign: Capricorn

My secret wish: To be all square with Ian Woosnam and Jack Nicklaus at the last hole in a golf tournament and score a birdie to win

Dennis Taylor, world champion in 1985, enjoyed, by his standards, an 'average' season. In 1987/88 he had won a glut of titles, but there was to be no repeat last season in which his best performance was in the Rothmans Grand Prix when he reached the semi-final only to be crushed 9–1 by eventual winner Steve Davis.

In the Embassy World Championship Taylor came safely through his first-round match against Eugene Hughes; however, after a really tough encounter, he lost 13–10 to John Parrott in the second round.

Taylor is still one of the best-known faces in snooker and has a time-consuming love of golf.

Moving up: Dennis Taylor who jumped from number 10 to number 8.

BEST PERFORMANCES

| Embassy World Championship: | Winner 1985 (beat Steve Davis 18–17) |

Other Ranking Tournaments

Fidelity Unit Trusts International:	Semi-finalist 1985 (lost to Cliff Thorburn 9–5)
Rothmans Grand Prix:	Winner 1984 (beat Cliff Thorburn 10–2)
BCE Canadian Masters:	Quarter-finalist 1988 (lost to Jimmy White 5–3)
Tennents UK Open:	Semi-finalist 1985 (lost to Willie Thorne 9–7)
Mercantile Credit Classic:	Quarter-finalist 1988 (lost to John Parrott 5–1)
ICI European Open:	Round 4 1989 (lost to Doug Mountjoy 5–3)
Anglian Windows British Open:	Quarter-finalist 1985 (lost to Kirk Stevens 5–2)
	Quarter-finalist 1987 (lost to Tony Knowles 5–4)

Current Non-ranking Tournaments

Benson and Hedges Masters:	Winner 1987 (beat Alex Higgins 9–8)
Benson and Hedges Irish Masters:	Semi-finalist 1984 (lost to Terry Griffiths 5–4)
	Semi-finalist 1987 (lost to Willie Thorne 6–2)
Everest World Matchplay:	Quarter-finalist 1988 (lost to Stephen Hendry 9–7)

Other Wins

Irish Professional: 1982, 1985, 1986, 1987
Costa del Sol Classic: 1984
Guinness World Cup: 1985
BCE Canadian Masters: 1985
Camus Thailand Masters: 1985
Kit-Kat Break for World Champions: 1985
Winfield Masters: 1986

Car Care Plan World Cup: 1986
Tuborg World Cup: 1987
Carling Challenge: 1987
Labatt Canadian Masters: 1987
Matchroom Trophy: 1987
British Caledonian Tokyo Masters: 1987

WORLD RANKING POSITIONS

1976/77	9	1981/82	5	1986/87	3
1977/78	4	1982/83	13	1987/88	8
1978/79	8	1983/84	13	1988/89	10
1979/80	2	1984/85	11	1989/90	8
1980/81	6	1985/86	4		

WILLIE THORNE

World ranking: number 9
Date of birth: 4 March 1954
Star sign: Pisces

My secret wish: To be a professional footballer like my best friend, Gary Lineker

Willie Thorne's best performance in a ranking tournament last season came in the Mercantile Credit Classic when he reached the semi-final before losing 9–4 to Wayne Jones. That sort of form helped Thorne move four places up the rankings to number 9. His biggest disappointment came in the World Championship when he made a series of bad mistakes and was hammered 13–4 by Stephen Hendry in the second round.

Thorne, known as snooker's Mr Maximum, finally achieved one hundred 147s in his career, though only one has come in a tournament – against Tommy Murphy in the 1987 Tennents UK Open.

BEST PERFORMANCES

Embassy World Championship:	Quarter-finalist 1982 (lost to Alex Higgins 13–10)
	Quarter-finalist 1986 (lost to Cliff Thorburn 13–6)

Other Ranking Tournaments

Fidelity Unit Trusts International:	Quarter-finalist 1983 (lost to Eddie Charlton 5–0)
	Quarter-finalist 1984 (lost to Eugene Hughes 5–2)
Rothmans Grand Prix:	Semi-finalist 1983 (lost to Tony Knowles 9–7)
BCE Canadian Masters:	Round 4 1988 (lost to Doug Mountjoy 5–4)
Tennents UK Open:	Runner-up 1985 (lost to Steve Davis 16–14)
Mercantile Credit Classic:	Winner 1985 (beat Cliff Thorburn 13–8)
ICI European Open:	Round 5 1989 (lost to Jimmy White 5–3)
Anglian Windows British Open:	Runner-up 1986 (lost to Steve Davis 12–7)

Current Non-ranking Tournaments

Benson and Hedges Masters:	Quarter-finalist 1986 (lost to Steve Davis 5–4)
	Quarter-finalist 1987 (lost to Cliff Thorburn 5–3)
Benson and Hedges Irish Masters:	Runner-up 1986 (lost to Jimmy White 9–5)
	Runner-up 1987 (lost to Steve Davis 9–1)
Everest World Matchplay:	Round 1 1988 (lost to Mike Hallett 9–8)

Other Wins

British Isles Under-16: 1970	Camus Hong Kong Masters: 1986
British Isles Under-19: 1973	Matchroom Trophy: 1986
Pontin's Open: 1980	Kent China Cup: 1987
Pontin's Professional: 1984	

WORLD RANKING POSITIONS

1976/77	–		1981/82	22	1986/87	7
1977/78	20		1982/83	16	1987/88	11
1978/79	15		1983/84	18	1988/89	13
1979/80	17		1984/85	12	1989/90	9
1980/81	19		1985/86	11		

DOUG MOUNTJOY

World ranking: number 10
Date of birth: 8 June 1942
Star sign: Gemini

My secret wish: To be a rock and
roll singer like Elvis Presley

Doug Mountjoy finished the season with three titles under his belt – an incredible performance for a man who started the campaign at number 24. With the help of top coach Frank Callan, Welshman Mountjoy completely remodelled his game and suddenly became a winner. He took the Tennents UK Open with a 16–12 defeat of Stephen Hendry and seven weeks later collected the Mercantile Credit Classic with a 13–11 victory over his close friend Wayne Jones. That made Mountjoy only the second man – apart from Steve Davis – to win successive ranking events, and he followed that by beating Terry Griffiths to capture the Welsh Professional title.

Towards the end of the season, Mountjoy's form briefly deserted him and he was disappointed with going out in the first round of the Embassy World Championship. But there was an added bonus waiting for him when he was promoted to this season's Matchroom League.

BEST PERFORMANCES

Embassy World Championship:	Runner-up 1981 (lost to Steve Davis 18–12)

Other Ranking Tournaments

Fidelity Unit Trusts International:	Quarter-finalist 1983 (lost to Cliff Thorburn 5–2)
Rothmans Grand Prix:	Quarter-finalist 1984 (lost to Cliff Thorburn 5–3)
BCE Canadian Masters:	Round 5 1988 (lost to Terry Griffiths 5–4)
Tennents UK Open:	Winner 1988 (beat Stephen Hendry 16–12)
Mercantile Credit Classic:	Winner 1989 (beat Wayne Jones 13–11)
ICI European Open:	Round 5 1989 (lost to Cliff Thorburn 5–0)
Anglian Windows British Open:	Round 5 1987 (lost to Cliff Thorburn 5–4)
	Round 5 1989 (lost to John Parrott 5–2)

Current Non-ranking Tournaments

Benson and Hedges Masters:	Winner 1977 (beat Ray Reardon 7–6)
Benson and Hedges Irish Masters:	Winner 1979 (beat Ray Reardon 6–5)

Other Wins

Welsh Amateur: 1968, 1976	Pontin's Professional: 1979, 1983
World Amateur: 1976	State Express World Cup: 1979, 1980
Pontin's Open: 1974, 1976	Champion of Champions: 1980
Pot Black: 1978, 1985	Welsh Professional: 1980, 1982, 1984, 1987, 1989
Coral UK: 1978	Camus Hong Kong Masters: 1983

WORLD RANKING POSITIONS

1977/78	14		1982/83	7		1986/87	14
1978/79	14		1983/84	12		1987/88	14
1979/80	13		1984/85	15		1988/89	24
1980/81	14		1985/86	15		1989/90	10
1981/82	6						

JOE JOHNSON

World ranking: number 11
Date of birth: 29 July 1952
Star sign: Leo

My secret wish: To have a number 1 chart hit

Joe Johnson, the 1986 world champion, knows his end-of-term report for the 1988/89 season might have read: 'Satisfactory but could have done better.' Johnson maintained his position at number 11 but managed to reach just two quarter-finals in ranking tournaments – the Fidelity Unit Trusts International and the Anglian Windows British Open. On both occasions he lost to Dean Reynolds. Johnson's usually sound World Championship form also deserted him as he was beaten 10–5 by Tony Meo in the first round.

BEST PERFORMANCES

Embassy World Championship: Winner 1986 (beat Steve Davis 18–12)

Other Ranking Tournaments

Fidelity Unit Trusts International:	Quarter-finalist 1985 (lost to Neal Foulds 5–2)
	Quarter-finalist 1988 (lost to Dean Reynolds 5–1)
Rothmans Grand Prix:	Runner-up 1983 (lost to Tony Knowles 9–8)
BCE Canadian Masters:	Round 4 1988 (lost to Steve James 5–4)
Tennents UK Open:	Semi-finalist 1987 (lost to Jimmy White 9–4)
Mercantile Credit Classic:	Semi-finalist 1985 (lost to Cliff Thorburn 9–2)
ICI European Open:	Round 5 1989 (lost to Martin Clark 5–4)
Anglian Windows British Open:	Quarter-finalist 1989 (lost to Dean Reynolds 5–4)

Current Non-ranking Tournaments

Benson and Hedges Masters:	Semi-finalist 1988 (lost to Steve Davis 6–3)
Benson and Hedges Irish Masters:	Quarter-finalist 1987 (lost to Terry Griffiths 5–0)
	Quarter-finalist 1988 (lost to Steve Davis 5–0)
Everest World Matchplay:	Quarter-finalist 1988 (lost to John Parrott 9–7)

Other Wins

British Isles Under-19: 1971   Langs Supreme Scottish Masters: 1987

WORLD RANKING POSITIONS

1980/81	–	1984/85	19	1987/88	5
1981/82	–	1985/86	16	1988/89	11
1982/83	–	1986/87	8	1989/90	11
1983/84	23				

TONY KNOWLES

World ranking: number 12
Date of birth: 13 June 1955
Star sign: Gemini

My secret wish: To play tennis well enough to reach a final at Wimbledon

Tony Knowles was certain he was going to win his first title for many years last season but it was not to be and he slipped out of snooker's top ten. Knowles failed to reach the quarter-final of any ranking tournaments and was particularly displeased with

his first-round exit to David Roe in the Embassy World Championship.

Knowles still enjoys a hectic life away from the circuit – water-skiing in the Lake District and making regular visits to his holiday home in Tenerife.

Dropping down: Tony Knowles who has slipped out of the top ten to number 12.

BEST PERFORMANCES

Embassy World Championship:	Semi-finalist 1983 (lost to Cliff Thorburn 16–15) Semi-finalist 1985 (lost to Dennis Taylor 16–5) Semi-finalist 1986 (lost to Joe Johnson 16–8)

Other Ranking Tournaments

Fidelity Unit Trusts International:	Winner 1982 (beat David Taylor 9–6)
Rothmans Grand Prix:	Winner 1983 (beat Joe Johnson 9–8)
BCE Canadian Masters:	Round 3 1988 (lost to Colin Roscoe 5–2)
Tennents UK Open:	Quarter-finalist 1984 (lost to Kirk Stevens 9–7) Quarter-finalist 1985 (lost to Jimmy White 9–4)
Mercantile Credit Classic:	Semi-finalist 1988 (lost to John Parrott 9–4)
ICI European Open:	Round 3 1989 (lost to Danny Fowler 5–2)
Anglian Windows British Open:	Semi-finalist 1987 (lost to Neal Foulds 9–2)

Current Non-ranking Tournaments

Benson and Hedges Masters:	Semi-finalist 1984 (lost to Terry Griffiths 6–4) Semi-finalist 1986 (lost to Cliff Thorburn 6–4)
Benson and Hedges Irish Masters:	Semi-finalist 1985 (lost to Jimmy White 6–4)
Everest World Matchplay:	Round 1 1988 (lost to Dennis Taylor 9–7)

Other Wins

British Isles Under-19: 1972, 1974   State Express World Team Classic: 1983
Pontin's Autumn Open: 1979   Winfield Masters: 1984

WORLD RANKING POSITIONS

1981/82	20	1984/85	2	1987/88	7
1982/83	15	1985/86	3	1988/89	8
1983/84	4	1986/87	4	1989/90	12

JOHN VIRGO

World ranking: number 13
Date of birth: 4 March 1946
Star sign: Pisces

My secret wish: To be a bus conductor. As a kid I always wanted to ring the bell!

John Virgo is a busy man. He is chairman of the WPBSA, a member of the BBC commentary squad and a highly successful snooker cabaret performer. And, despite his hectic schedule, he's also managed to improve his position in the rankings, moving up two places to number 13.

Virgo's best performance in a ranking tournament came in the Tennents UK Open where he narrowly lost 9–8 to Doug Mountjoy, the eventual winner, in the quarter-final. Virgo won the respect of many people when he owned up to a foul that nobody else saw in the second round of the Embassy World Championship against Jimmy White – an honest move that undoubtedly cost him the match as he ultimately lost 13–12.

BEST PERFORMANCES

Embassy World Championship:	Semi-finalist 1979 (lost to Dennis Taylor 19–12)

Other Ranking Tournaments

Fidelity Unit Trusts International:	Semi-finalist 1982 (lost to David Taylor 9–5)
Rothmans Grand Prix:	Semi-finalist 1982 (lost to Jimmy White 10–4)
BCE Canadian Masters:	Round 5 1988 (lost to John Parrott 5–4)
Tennents UK Open:	Quarter-finalist 1988 (lost to Doug Mountjoy 9–8)
Mercantile Credit Classic:	Quarter-finalist 1985 (lost to Willie Thorne 5–1)
ICI European Open:	Round 5 1989 (lost to Eddie Charlton 5–4)
Anglian Windows British Open:	Semi-finalist 1986 (lost to Willie Thorne 9–4)

Current Non-ranking Tournaments

Benson and Hedges Masters:	Round 1 1980 (lost to Cliff Thorburn 5–3)
	Round 1 1983 (lost to Doug Mountjoy 5–1)
	Round 1 1984 (lost to Ray Reardon 5–3)
	Round 1 1989 (lost to Jimmy White 5–2)

Other Wins

British Isles Under-16: 1962
British Isles Under-19: 1965
Coral UK: 1979

Pontin's Professional: 1980
Bombay International: 1980
Professional Snooker League: 1984

WORLD RANKING POSITIONS

1977/78	18		1982/83	19		1986/87	19
1978/79	19		1983/84	14		1987/88	19
1979/80	10		1984/85	18		1988/89	15
1980/81	12		1985/86	19		1989/90	13
1981/82	13						

TONY MEO

World ranking: number 14
Date of birth: 4 October 1959
Star sign: Libra

My secret wish: To be a boxer – as long as they don't hit me back!

Tony Meo enjoyed a 1988/89 season that ranked as one of the most spectacular recoveries of all time. This former top ten player started the season at number 31 and looked destined for a further downward slide. But towards the end he suddenly emerged from the snooker shadows to win the Anglian Windows British Open with a 13–6 defeat of Dean Reynolds. More was to follow as he capitalised on his revival to reach the semi-final of the Embassy World Championship before losing 16–7 to John Parrott. Now back in snooker's top sixteen, Meo will this season be hoping to move forward yet again into snooker's higher reaches.

First time: Tony Meo who won his first ranking tournament – the Anglian Windows British Open.

BEST PERFORMANCES

Embassy World Championship:	Semi-finalist 1989 (lost to John Parrott 16–7)

Other Ranking Tournaments

Fidelity Unit Trusts International:	Quarter-finalist 1988 (lost to Steve James 5–1)
Rothmans Grand Prix:	Semi-finalist 1983 (lost to Joe Johnson 9–6)
BCE Canadian Masters:	Round 3 1988 (lost to Marcel Gauvreau 5-0)
Tennents UK Open:	Round 2 (last 16) 1984 (lost to Steve Davis 9–7)
	Round 5 1985 (lost to Steve Davis 9–5)
Mercantile Credit Classic:	Runner-up 1984 (lost to Steve Davis 9–8)
ICI European Open:	Round 3 1989 (lost to David Roe 5–1)
Anglian Windows British Open:	Winner 1989 (beat Dean Reynolds 13–6)

Current Non-ranking Tournaments

Benson and Hedges Masters:	Semi-finalist 1982 (lost to Steve Davis 6–4)
	Semi-finalist 1987 (lost to Alex Higgins 6–2)
Benson and Hedges Irish Masters:	Quarter-finalist 1982 (lost to Terry Griffiths 5–3)
	Quarter-finalist 1983 (lost to Ray Reardon 5–4)
	Quarter-finalist 1984 (lost to Steve Davis 5–4)
	Quarter-finalist 1986 (lost to Jimmy White 5–2)
	Quarter-finalist 1987 (lost to Steve Davis 5–2)

Other Wins

British Isles Under-19: 1978
Winfield Masters: 1981, 1985
Hofmeister World Doubles: 1982, 1983, 1985, 1986

State Express World Team Classic: 1983
English Professional: 1986, 1987

WORLD RANKING POSITIONS

1980/81	–	1984/85	10	1987/88	20
1981/82	18	1985/86	10	1988/89	31
1982/83	24	1986/87	11	1989/90	14
1983/84	15				

DEAN REYNOLDS

World ranking: number 15
Date of birth: 11 January 1963
Star sign: Capricorn

My secret wish: To play professional football in the First Division

Dean Reynolds was another player who produced an outstanding snooker recovery after sliding out of the top sixteen. Now this determined left-hander from Grimsby is back at the top after earning a place in the final of the Anglian Windows British Open and then getting through to the last eight of the Embassy World Championship. In both those tournaments he was beaten by Tony Meo. At the start of the season Reynolds also earned a semi-final place in the Fidelity Unit Trusts International.

Back in the top sixteen: Dean Reynolds is there again after good performances in the Fidelity Unit Trusts International, the Anglian Windows British Open and the Embassy World Championship.

BEST PERFORMANCES

Embassy World Championship:	Quarter-finalist 1989 (lost to Tony Meo 13-9)

Other Ranking Tournaments

Fidelity Unit Trusts International:	Semi-finalist 1988 (lost to Jimmy White 9–5)
Rothmans Grand Prix:	Quarter-finalist 1982 (lost to Eddie Charlton 5–2)
	Quarter-finalist 1984 (lost to Steve Davis 5–0)
BCE Canadian Masters:	Round 4 1988 (lost to Cliff Wilson 5–4)
Tennents UK Open:	Round 5 1986 (lost to Steve Davis 9–5)
	Round 5 1988 (lost to Terry Griffiths 9–6)
Mercantile Credit Classic:	Semi-finalist 1987 (lost to Jimmy White 9–8)
ICI European Open:	Did not enter
Anglian Windows British Open:	Runner-up 1989 (lost to Tony Meo 13–6)

Current Non-ranking Tournaments

Benson and Hedges Masters: Round 1 1983 (lost to Ray Reardon 5–1)
                              Round 1 1988 (lost to Steve Davis 5–2)

Other Wins

British Isles Under-19: 1981   English Professional: 1988
Junior Pot Black: 1981

WORLD RANKING POSITIONS

1982/83	22	1985/86	24	1988/89	22
1983/84	19	1986/87	29	1989/90	15
1984/85	22	1987/88	15		

STEVE JAMES

World ranking: number 16
Date of birth: 2 May 1961
Star sign: Taurus

My secret wish: To be the world motor-cycle champion

Steve James enjoyed his usual spectacular season off the table! James, who seems to bounce happily from one catastrophe to another, started the season by falling into a boating lake. Then at Reading a practice room roof fell on his head and later, in the most bizarre incident of all, he disarmed a knife-wielding drunken Australian on a flight home from Bangkok.

On the table James made the top sixteen for the first time but will be disappointed with his season's work overall. He started by reaching the semi-final of the Fidelity Unit Trusts International but then struggled and finally lost to John Parrott in the first round of the Embassy World Championship.

Mr Mishap: Speed king Steve James who came into the top sixteen for the first time at number 16.

BEST PERFORMANCES

Embassy World Championship:	Quarter-finalist 1988 (lost to Cliff Thorburn 13–11)

Other Ranking Tournaments

Fidelity Unit Trusts International:	Semi-finalist 1988 (lost to Steve Davis 9–1)
Rothmans Grand Prix:	Round 4 1988 (lost to Mike Hallett 5–2)
BCE Canadian Masters:	Round 5 1988 (lost to Steve Davis 5–0)
Tennents UK Open:	Round 4 1988 (lost to Cliff Thorburn 9–6)
Mercantile Credit Classic:	Round 4 1989 (lost to Paddy Browne 5–4)
ICI European Open:	Round 3 1989 (lost to Mark Johnston-Allen 5–1)
Anglian Windows British Open:	Round 4 1987 (lost to Rex Williams 5–2)
	Round 4 1988 (lost to Jimmy White 5–1)

Other Wins

No significant wins

WORLD RANKING POSITIONS

1987/88	67	1988/89	32	1989/90	16

MARTIN CLARK

World ranking: number 17
Date of birth: 27 October 1968
Star sign: Scorpio

My secret wish: To play centre forward for Wolverhampton Wanderers, but unfortunately I'm not tall enough!

Martin Clark has made a tremendous impact after just two seasons as a professional. He first entered the rankings at number 41 and then narrowly missed out on a top sixteen place, starting this season at number 17. The reason for that was his failure in the World Championship when he was surprisingly beaten 10–4 by Canadian Bob Chaperon in the final qualifying round.

Despite that setback, Clark, certainly a player of top eight material, can look back on a highly successful season in which he reached three successive quarter-finals.

On the brink: Martin Clark, who narrowly missed out on a place in the top sixteen, takes it easy with a 'friend'.

BEST PERFORMANCES

Embassy World Championship:	Qualifying round 5 1989 (lost to Bob Chaperon 10–4)

Other Ranking Tournaments

Fidelity Unit Trusts International:	Round 5 1987 (lost to Joe O'Boye 5–2)
Rothmans Grand Prix:	Round 4 1987 (lost to Mick Fisher 5–4)
BCE Canadian Masters:	Round 4 1988 (lost to Dennis Taylor 5–4)
Tennents UK Open:	Round 4 1988 (lost to Danny Fowler 9–6)
Mercantile Credit Classic:	Quarter-finalist 1989 (lost to Willie Thorne 5–4)
ICI European Open:	Quarter-finalist 1989 (lost to Tery Griffiths 5–1)
Anglian Windows British Open:	Quarter-finalist 1989 (lost to Mike Hallett 5–3)

Other Wins

British Isles Under-19: 1984

WORLD RANKING POSITIONS

1988/89	41	1989/90	17

CLIFF WILSON

World ranking: number 18
Date of birth: 10 May 1944
Star sign: Taurus

My secret wish: I only ever had one wish – to make loads and loads of money. It's never come true!

Cliff Wilson lasted just one season in the world's top sixteen as he dropped down two places to number 18. But that won't worry Welshman Wilson as he keeps plugging away at a snooker career that he treats with a smile – win or lose.

Wilson did not reach the last eight of any ranking tournament and fared badly in the first round of the Embassy World Championship as he was hammered 10–1 by Steve Duggan. In fact, he has never progressed past the first round in snooker's premier event.

The joker: Cliff Wilson who was awarded Gold Card Life Membership of the Official Monster Raving Loony Party. Wilson joined other Gold Card members like Eddie 'The Eagle' Edwards, Ronald Reagan, Ian Botham and Michael Jackson's chimpanzee, Bubbles.

BEST PERFORMANCES

Embassy World Championship:
Round 1 1980 (lost to Doug Mountjoy 10–6)
Round 1 1981 (lost to David Taylor 10–6)
Round 1 1982 (lost to Eddie Charlton 10–5)
Round 1 1983 (lost to Doug Mountjoy 10–2)
Round 1 1986 (lost to Eddie Charlton 10–6)
Round 1 1988 (lost to Joe Johnson 10–7)
Round 1 1989 (lost to Steve Duggan 10–1)

Other Ranking Tournaments

Fidelity Unit Trusts International:
Quarter-finalist 1982 (lost to Tony Knowles 5–4)
Quarter-finalist 1986 (lost to Cliff Thorburn 5–1)

Rothmans Grand Prix:
Quarter-finalist 1985 (lost to Dennis Taylor 5–2)

BCE Canadian Masters:
Round 5 1988 (lost to Stephen Hendry 5–1)

Tennents UK Open:
Round 2 (last 16) 1984 (lost to Cliff Thorburn 9–3)

Mercantile Credit Classic:
Quarter-finalist 1987 (lost to Dean Reynolds 5–1)

ICI European Open:
Round 4 1989 (lost to Alain Robidoux 5–0)

Anglian Windows British Open:
Round 5 1987 (lost to John Virgo 5–2)
Round 5 1989 (lost to Dean Reynolds 5–0)

Current Non-ranking Tournaments

Benson and Hedges Masters:
Round 1 1989 (lost to Steve Davis 5–2)

Other Wins

British Isles Under-19: 1952, 1953
Welsh Amateur: 1956, 1977, 1979

World Amateur: 1978

WORLD RANKING POSITIONS

1980/81	–	1984/85	23	1987/88	17
1981/82	23	1985/86	22	1988/89	16
1982/83	26	1986/87	23	1989/90	18
1983/84	20				

STEVE NEWBURY

World ranking: number 19
Date of birth: 21 April 1956
Star sign: Taurus

My secet wish: To be a long-distance lorry driver or a police-car driver

Steve Newbury moved into the top twenty for the first time at number 19, which means he has jumped twenty-six places in the last two years. He reached the last sixteen in the Fidelity Unit Trusts Inter-

Hit man: Steve Newbury moves into the top twenty at number 19.

national and the Mercantile Credit Classic but was unlucky on his World Championship debut when he met defending champion Steve Davis in the first round. Newbury showed plenty of spirit, but eventually went down 10–5.

BEST PERFORMANCES

Embassy World Championship:	Round 1 1989 (lost to Steve Davis 10–5)

Other Ranking Tournaments

Fidelity Unit Trusts International:	Round 2 (last 16) 1984 (lost to Tony Knowles 5–4)
	Round 5 1988 (lost to Joe Johnson 5–2)
Rothmans Grand Prix:	Quarter-finalist 1987 (lost to Dennis Taylor 5–2)
BCE Canadian Masters:	Round 4 1988 (lost to John Virgo 5–2)
Tennents UK Open:	Round 3 1985 (lost to Kirk Stevens 9–7)
	Round 3 1987 (lost to John Parrott 9–5)
	Round 3 1988 (lost to Colin Roscoe 9–7)
Mercantile Credit Classic:	Semi-finalist 1988 (lost to Steve Davis 9–2)
ICI European Open:	Round 3 1989 (lost to Alain Robidoux 5–0)
Anglian Windows British Open:	Round 3 (last 16) 1985 (lost to Dennis Taylor 5–3)

Other Wins

Welsh Amateur: 1980

WORLD RANKING POSITIONS

1985/86	34		1987/88	45	1989/90	19
1986/87	40		1988/89	25		

NEAL FOULDS

World ranking: number 20
Date of birth: 13 July 1963
Star sign: Cancer

My secret wish: To open the batting, and bowl leg breaks for Middlesex at Lord's

---

Neal Foulds was glad to see the back of the 1988/89 season as a 10–9 defeat by Wayne Jones in the first round of the Embassy World Championship confirmed that he had lost his position in the world's top sixteen. The season had started brightly when Foulds beat Steve Davis to win the Dubai Duty Free Masters, but then followed a disappointing run of results as he struggled to recapture the form that took him to the number 3 position in the world ranking list.

He was a member of England's Fersina Windows World Cup-winning team for the second successive year, but his ranking of number 20 means that he will be out of the side this season. Away from snooker Foulds owns a string of greyhounds and likes nothing better than relaxing with a night at the dogs.

BEST PERFORMANCES

Embassy World Championship:	Semi-finalist 1987 (lost to Joe Johnson 16–9)

Other Ranking Tournaments

Fidelity Unit Trusts International:	Winner 1986 (beat Cliff Thorburn 12–9)
Rothmans Grand Prix:	Semi-finalist 1984 (lost to Dennis Taylor 9–3)
	Semi-finalist 1986 (lost to Rex Williams 9–8)
BCE Canadian Masters:	Round 3 1988 (lost to Warren King 5–3)
Tennents UK Open:	Runner-up 1986 (lost to Steve Davis 16–7)
Mercantile Credit Classic:	Quarter-finalist 1986 (lost to Doug Mountjoy 5–3)
ICI Euopean Open:	Round 3 1989 (lost to Martin Clark 5–3)
Anglian Windows British Open:	Runner-up 1987 (lost to Jimmy White 13–9)

Current Non-ranking Tournaments

Benson and Hedges Masters:	Semi-finalist 1989 (lost to John Parrott 6–5)
Benson and Hedges Irish Masters:	Runner-up 1988 (lost to Steve Davis 9–4)

Other Wins

British Isles Under-19: 1982	Fersina Windows World Cup: 1988, 1989
Pontin's Open: 1984	Dubai Duty Free Masters: 1988
Pontin's Professional: 1987	

WORLD RANKING POSITIONS

1984/85	30		1986/87	13		1988/89	3
1985/86	23		1987/88	3		1989/90	20

BARRY WEST

World ranking: number 21
Date of birth: 24 October 1958
Star sign: Scorpio

Barry West, the publicity-shy Yorkshireman, ended another consistent season, this time moving five places up the rankings to number 21. In the first ranking tournament of the season he reached the quarter-final of the Fidelity Unit Trusts International before going down 5–2 to Jimmy White and also came through to the last eight in the Tennents UK Open before losing to Terry Griffiths 9–5. This season West will be looking to move into the top sixteen for the first time.

BEST PERFORMANCES

Embassy World Championship:	Round 1 1987 (lost to Ray Reardon 10–5)
	Round 1 1988 (lost to Doug Mountjoy 10–6)

Other Ranking Tournaments

Fidelity Unit Trusts International:	Quarter-finalist 1988 (lost to Jimmy White 5–2)
Rothmans Grand Prix:	Round 4 1988 (lost to Terry Griffiths 5–1)
BCE Canadian Masters:	Round 3 1988 (lost to Steve Duggan 5–3)
Tennents UK Open:	Quarter-finalist 1985 (lost to Steve Davis 9–1)
	Quarter-finalist 1988 (lost to Terry Griffiths 9–5)
Mercantile Credit Classic:	Round 5 1987 (lost to Dean Reynolds 5–3)
	Round 5 1988 (lost to Terry Griffiths 5–2)
ICI European Open:	Round 3 1989 (lost to Murdo Macleod 5–4)
Anglian Windows British Open:	Round 5 1989 (lost to Peter Francisco 5–1)

Other Wins

No significant wins

WORLD RANKING POSITIONS

1986/87	30	1988/89	26
1987/88	29	1989/90	21

EDDIE CHARLTON

World ranking: number 22
Date of birth: 31 October 1929
Star sign: Scorpio

My secret wish: To be a politician

Eddie Charlton, at sixty, is one of the oldest professionals on the circuit but is still one of the toughest players to beat. The durable Australian slipped just three places on the rankings to number 22 after enjoying another incident-packed season.

In the ICI European Open in France he was involved in a verbal row with John Virgo but went on to reach the quarter-final before losing 5–1 to John Parrott. In the World Championship Charlton reached the last sixteen after surviving the first round with a 10–9 defeat of Canadian Cliff Thorburn – the match ending at 2.39 am to make it the second latest finish in the World Championship. Charlton, despite his age, is still one of the fittest players on the circuit.

BEST PERFORMANCES

Embassy World Championship:	Runner-up 1973 (lost to Ray Reardon 38–32)
	Runner-up 1975 (lost to Ray Reardon 31–30)

Other Ranking Tournaments

Fidelity Unit Trusts International:	Semi-finalist 1983 (lost to Steve Davis 9–2)
Rothmans Grand Prix:	Semi-finalist 1982 (lost to Ray Reardon 10–7)
BCE Canadian Masters:	Round 4 1988 (lost to Ian Graham 5–2)
Tennents UK Open:	Round 2 (last 16) 1984 (lost to Willie Thorne 9–7)
Mercantile Credit Classic:	Quarter-finalist 1984 (lost to Mark Wildman 5–4)
ICI European Open:	Quarter-finalist 1989 (lost to John Parrott 5–1)
Anglian Windows British Open:	Round 5 1986 (lost to John Virgo 5–4)

Current Non-ranking Tournaments

Benson and Hedges Masters:	Semi-finalist 1975 (lost to John Spencer 5–2)
	Semi-finalist 1976 (lost to Ray Reardon 5–4)
	Semi-finalist 1983 (lost to Cliff Thorburn 6–5)
Benson and Hedges Irish Masters:	Quarter-finalist 1983 (lost to Steve Davis 5–1)
	Quarter-finalist 1985 (lost to Tony Knowles 5–3)

Other Wins

Pot Black: 1972, 1973, 1980
World Matchplay: 1976
Limosin International: 1979

Kronenbrau 1308 Classic: 1979
Australian Professional: 1964–67, 1969–84

WORLD RANKING POSITIONS

1976/77	3		1981/82	8		1986/87	25
1977/78	3		1982/83	5		1987/88	26
1978/79	3		1983/84	6		1988/89	19
1979/80	3		1984/85	6		1989/90	22
1980/81	3		1985/86	12			

SILVINO FRANCISCO

World ranking: number 23
Date of birth; 3 May 1946
Star sign: Taurus

My secret wish: To be a professional cricketer and play at Lord's

South African Silvino Francisco did not enjoy the best of seasons. He reached the last sixteen of only two ranking events – the Mercantile Credit Classic and the Embassy World Championship. That lack of success saw him drop eleven places down the rankings to number 23.

Francisco was also involved in off-the-table problems which hardly helped his form. There were allegations of betting irregularities in his 5–1 first-round defeat by Terry Griffiths in the Benson and Hedges Masters – claims that Francisco dismissed as 'rubbish'. There were also libel proceedings against John Virgo and Rex Williams for remarks made on television during the 1985 Dulux British Open. The matter was eventually settled out of court; Francisco received costs and a small sum by way of compensation.

He was a member of the Rest of the World team which lost 9–8 to England in the Fersina Windows World Cup final.

Cheerful: Silvino Francisco still stays happy despite dropping out of the top sixteen to number 23.

BEST PERFORMANCES

Embassy World Championship:	Quarter-finalist 1982 (lost to Ray Reardon 13–8)

Other Ranking Tournaments

Fidelity Unit Trusts International:	Semi-finalist 1984 (lost to Tony Knowles 9–6)
Rothmans Grand Prix:	Semi-finalist 1986 (lost to Jimmy White 9–6)
BCE Canadian Masters:	Round 3 1988 (lost to Murdo Mcleod 5–4)
Tennents UK Open:	Round 5 1985 (lost to Terry Griffiths 9–5)
	Round 5 1987 (lost to Terry Griffiths 9–3)
Mercantile Credit Classic:	Quarter-finalist 1987 (lost to Stephen Hendry 5–0)
ICI European Open:	Round 3 1989 (lost to Jim Wych 5–1)
Anglian Windows British Open:	Winner 1985 (beat Kirk Stevens 12–9)

Current Non-ranking Tournaments

Benson and Hedges Masters:	Quarter-finalist 1987 (lost to Dennis Taylor 5–3)

Other Wins

South African Amateur: 1968, 1969, 1974, 1977   South African Professional: 1985, 1986

WORLD RANKING POSITIONS

1979/80	–	1983/84	21	1987/88	10
1980/81	–	1984/85	17	1988/89	12
1981/82	–	1985/86	13	1989/90	23
1982/83	17	1986/87	12		

ALEX HIGGINS

World ranking: number 24
Date of birth: 18 March 1949
Star sign: Pisces

My secret wish: To have the talent and skill to play football like George Best in front of a 50,000 crowd at Old Trafford, the home of Manchester United

Alex Higgins, even though he started the season down at number 17, worked his way through another season with his name seldom out of the headlines – on and off the table! He was involved in an after-match dispute at a Professional Players Tournament in Glasgow for which he was given a suspended fine of £1,500, but then showed his career was far from over as he magnificently reached the final of the Rothmans Grand Prix only to lose to Steve Davis.

Then came an incident in Manchester that was spectacular even by Higgins' standard. He fell out of the second-floor window of a flat, split his head open and broke his left foot in many places. Higgins, lucky to be alive and walking only with the aid of crutches, defied doctor's orders to cross the Channel just a few days later to play in the ICI European Open in France. He spent the next few weeks hopping round the table while he carried on playing. He was still limping when, against all the odds, he won the Irish Championship and then became the first Irishman to win the Benson and Hedges Irish Masters with a breathtaking 9–8 defeat of Stephen Hendry.

The following day he had to fly back to take part in a World Championship qualifying match against professional newcomer Darren Morgan. Unfortunately, Higgins lost 10–8 and failed to appear in the final stages at the Crucible Theatre for the first time in his career. This season he has slipped to number 24 in the rankings.

BEST PERFORMANCES

Embassy World Championship:	Winner 1972 (beat John Spencer 37–32)
	Winner 1982 (beat Ray Reardon 18–15)

Other Ranking Tournaments

Fidelity Unit Trusts International:	Quarter-finalist 1984 (lost to Steve Davis 5–1)
Rothmans Grand Prix:	Runner-up 1988 (lost to Steve Davis 10–6)
BCE Canadian Masters:	Round 3 1988 (lost to Martin Clark 5–3)
Tennents UK Open:	Runner-up 1984 (lost to Steve Davis 16–8)
Mercantile Credit Classic:	Quarter-finalist 1986 (lost to Rex Williams 5–2)
ICI European Open:	Round 4 1989 (lost to Willie Thorne 5–1)
Anglian Windows British Open:	Semi-finalist 1985 (lost to Silvino Francisco 9–6)
	Semi-finalist 1986 (lost to Steve Davis 9–3)

Current Non-ranking Tournaments

Benson and Hedges Masters:	Winner 1978 (beat Cliff Thorburn 7–5)
	Winner 1981 (beat Terry Griffiths 9–6)
Benson and Hedges Irish Masters:	Winner 1989 (beat Stephen Hendry 9–8)

Other Wins

Northern Ireland Amateur: 1968
All-Ireland: 1968
Canadian Open: 1975, 1977
Pontin's Open: 1977
Tolly Cobbold Classic: 1979, 1980
Padmore/Super Crystalate International: 1980
British Gold Cup: 1980

Coral UK: 1983
Irish Professional: 1983, 1989
Hofmeister World Doubles: 1984
Guinness World Cup: 1985
Car Care Plan World Cup: 1986
Tuborg World Cup: 1987

WORLD RANKING POSITIONS

1976/77	2	1981/82	11	1986/87	6
1977/78	5	1982/83	2	1987/88	9
1978/79	7	1983/84	5	1988/89	17
1979/80	11	1984/85	9	1989/90	24
1980/81	4	1985/86	9		

PETER FRANCISCO

World ranking: number 25
Date of birth: 14 February 1962
Star sign: Aquarius

My secret wish: To have a free and peaceful world

Peter Francisco's stay in the top sixteen lasted just one season and he started the 1989/90 campaign in twenty-fifth place, having been plagued in 1988/89 by injury and illness. He displaced bones in his neck while carrying out work on a pond he was installing at his Essex home, and just before Christmas he contracted viral meningitis. Predictably his form suffered, and until the Anglian Windows British Open he had won only one match in a ranking tournament. In the Open, Francisco produced his best form of the season to reach the last eight before losing 5–3 to Tony Meo, the eventual winner. He was a first-round casualty in the World Championship.

Disappointing season: South African Peter Francisco who was dogged by injury and illness.

BEST PERFORMANCES

Embassy World Championship:	Round 1 1988 (lost to Willie Thorne 10–6)
	Round 1 1989 (lost to Dean Reynolds 10–7)

Other Ranking Tournaments

Fidelity Unit Trusts International:	Semi-finalist 1986 (lost to Cliff Thorburn 9–7)
Rothmans Grand Prix:	Semi-finalist 1987 (lost to Dennis Taylor 9–4)
BCE Canadian Masters:	Round 3 1988 (lost to Ian Graham 5–3)
Tennents UK Open:	Round 4 1985 (lost to Rex Williams 9–7)
	Round 4 1986 (lost to Jimmy White 9–5)
	Round 4 1987 (lost to Steve Davis 9–6)
	Round 4 1988 (lost to David Roe 9–7)
Mercantile Credit Classic:	Round 5 1986 (lost to Steve Davis 5–0)
	Round 5 1987 (lost to Silvino Francisco 5–1)
	Round 5 1988 (lost to Dennis Taylor 5–3)
ICI European Open:	Round 3 1989 (lost to John Campbell 5–0)
Anglian Windows British Open:	Quarter-finalist 1989 (lost to Tony Meo 5–3)

Current Non-ranking Tournaments

Benson and Hedges Masters:	Round 1 1989 (lost to Neal Foulds 5–2)
Everest World Matchplay:	Round 1 1988 (lost to Terry Griffiths 9–7)

DAVID ROE

World ranking: number 26
Date of birth: 11 September 1965
Star sign: Virgo

My secret wish: To be lead singer in a group like Simply Red

David Roe is surely one day heading for a place in snooker's top sixteen after establishing himself in the top thirty-two for the first time at number 26. Roe has an exciting style that proved too much for Tony Knowles in the first round of the Embassy World Championship. But then inexperience reared its ugly head in the next round when he lost 13–12 to Mike Hallett after leading 12–10.

One to watch: Derby's David Roe.

BEST PERFORMANCES

Embassy World Championship: Round 2 1989 (lost to Mike Hallett 13–12)

Other Ranking Tournaments

Fidelity Unit Trusts International:	Round 4 1987 (lost to Steve James 5–3)
Rothmans Grand Prix:	Round 4 1987 (lost to Tony Knowles 5–2)
BCE Canadian Masters:	Round 3 1988 (lost to Jimmy White 5–3)
Tennents UK Open:	Round 5 1987 (lost to Jimmy White 9–5) Round 5 1988 (lost to Cliff Thorburn 9–8)
Mercantile Credit Classic:	Round 3 1989 (lost to John Parrott 5–2)
ICI European Open:	Round 4 1989 (lost to Joe Johnson 5–2)
Anglian Windows British Open:	Round 5 1988 (lost to Joe O'Boye 5–1)

Other Wins

No significant wins

WORLD RANKING POSITIONS

| 1987/88 | 83 | 1988/89 | 39 | 1989/90 | 26 |

EUGENE HUGHES

World ranking: number 27
Date of birth: 4 November 1955
Star sign: Scorpio

My secret wish: To be a
professional footballer with
Manchester United

Eugene Hughes did not enjoy the most successful of seasons, but his best display came in the Rothmans Grand Prix where he reached the last sixteen. He stayed in the top thirty-two at number 27 but will this season be looking for much improved form. At the World Championship he was way below par as he was hammered 10–3 by Dennis Taylor. Hughes remains one of the most jovial professional players.

BEST PERFORMANCES

Embassy World Championship:	Round 2 1986 (lost to Cliff Thorburn 13–6)

Other Ranking Tournaments

Fidelity Unit Trusts International:	Semi-finalist 1984 (lost to Steve Davis 9–3)
	Semi-finalist 1986 (lost to Neal Foulds 9–8)
Rothmans Grand Prix:	Quarter-finalist 1983 (lost to Willie Thorne 5–1)
BCE Canadian Masters:	Round 3 1988 (lost to Mark Bennett 5–2)
Tennents UK Open:	Round 5 1986 (lost to Wayne Jones 9–5)
Mercantile Credit Classic:	Round 2 (last 16) 1985 (lost to Ray Reardon 5–1)
	Round 5 1986 (lost to Joe Johnson 5–1)
ICI European Open:	Round 4 1989 (lost to Martin Clark 5–1)
Anglian Windows British Open:	Quarter-finalist 1985 (lost to Alex Higgins 5–2)

Current Non-ranking Tournaments

Benson and Hedges Irish Masters:	Quarter-finalist 1985 (lost to Steve Davis 5–4)
	Quarter-finalist 1986 (lost to Cliff Thorburn 5–1)

Other Wins

British Isles Under-19: 1975
Republic of Ireland Amateur: 1978, 1979
All-Ireland: 1979

Guinness World Cup: 1985
Car Care Plan World Cup: 1986
Tuborg World Cup: 1987

WORLD RANKING POSITIONS

1982/83	–	1985/86	21	1988/89	21
1983/84	35	1986/87	20	1989/90	27
1984/85	27	1987/88	24		

DENE O'KANE

World ranking: number 28
Date of birth: 24 February 1963
Star sign: Pisces

My secret wish: To be an actor

Dene O'Kane, a former New Zealand amateur champion, didn't even want to return to the British circuit after spending Christmas 1988 at home with his family.

But he came back and in just three months clocked up a £1,000 phone bill keeping in touch with the other side of the world. O'Kane's most memorable and unfortunate moment of last season came in the final of the Fersina Windows World Cup when he lost a last-frame decider to England's Steve Davis knowing that winning would have given his Rest of the World team a shock victory.

BEST PERFORMANCES

Embassy World Championship:	Quarter-finalist 1987 (lost to Jimmy White 13–6)

Other Ranking Tournaments

Fidelity Unit Trusts International:	Round 1 (last 32) 1984 (lost to Willie Thorne 5–3) Round 4 1986 (lost to Ken Owers 5–0) Round 4 1988 (lost to Jim Wych 5–4)
Rothmans Grand Prix:	Round 4 1988 (lost to Alex Higgins 5–0)
BCE Canadian Masters:	Round 3 1988 (lost to Darren Morgan 5–2)
Tennents UK Open:	Round 5 1987 (lost to Willie Thorne 9–7)
Mercantile Credit Classic:	Round 4 1986 (lost to Doug Mountjoy 5–3) Round 4 1989 (lost to Willie Thorne 5–3)
ICI European Open:	Round 3 1989 (lost to Tony Chappel 5–0)
Anglian Windows British Open:	Quarter-finalist 1985 (lost to Steve Davis 5–1) Quarter-finalist 1988 (lost to John Parrott 5–2)

Other Wins

New Zealand Amateur: 1980	

WORLD RANKING POSITIONS

1985/86	32	1987/88	35	1989/90	28
1986/87	39	1988/89	24		

BOB CHAPERON

World ranking: number 29
Date of birth: 18 May 1958
Star sign: Taurus

My secret wish: To be lead guitarist in a world-famous rock and roll band

---

Bob Chaperon began the 1988/89 season confident of a push towards the top sixteen. But this determined Canadian from Sudbury, Ontario, didn't enjoy the best of fortune and was grateful to consolidate his place in the top thirty-two by staying at number 29. He reached the last thirty-two of the Mercantile Credit Classic and then thrashed the talented Martin Clark 10–4 to reach the first round proper of the World Championship. Unfortunately, he was beaten 10–6 by Terry Griffiths.

BEST PERFORMANCES

Embassy World Championship:	Round 1 1988 (lost to Mike Hallett 10–2) Round 1 1989 (lost to Terry Griffiths 10–6)

Other Ranking Tournaments

Fidelity Unit Trusts International:	Round 5 1986 (lost to Eugene Hughes 5–0)
	Round 5 1988 (lost to Tony Meo 5–4)
Rothmans Grand Prix:	Quarter-finalist 1987 (lost to John Parrott 5–2)
BCE Canadian Masters:	Round 3 1988 (lost to Ray Reardon 5–4)
Tennents UK Open:	Round 3 1986 (lost to David Taylor 9–8)
	Round 3 1987 (lost to David Taylor 9–6)
	Round 3 1988 (lost to Gary Wilkinson 9–0)
Mercantile Credit Classic:	Round 4 1989 (lost to John Virgo 5–1)
ICI European Open:	Round 3 1989 (lost to Craig Edwards 5–3)
Anglian Windows British Open:	Round 3 (last 16) 1985 (lost to Silvino Francisco 5–2)

Other Wins

Canadian Amateur: 1981

WORLD RANKING POSITIONS

1984/85	–	1986/87	53	1988/89	29
1985/86	44	1987/88	41	1989/90	29

TONY DRAGO

World ranking: number 30
Date of birth: 22 September 1965
Star sign: Virgo

My secret wish: To learn to play golf so I can join in with my snooker colleagues

Tony Drago set a world record during the Fidelity Unit Trusts International when he won a frame against Worksop's Danny Fowler in just three minutes. But after that his form slumped alarmingly and this likeable Maltese slid from number 20 on the rankings to number 30.

The highlight of the second half of his season was his inspired play during the Fersina Windows World Cup when he won eleven of his thirteen frames and helped the Rest of the World squad to reach the final where they gallantly lost 9–8 to England.

Winner: Tony Drago after collecting his Overseas Player of the Year award for the 1987/88 season. But he didn't live up to that promise and dropped ten places to number 30.

BEST PERFORMANCES

Embassy World Championship:	Quarter-finalist 1988 (lost to Steve Davis 13–4)

Other Ranking Tournaments

Fidelity Unit Trusts International:	Round 4 1986 (lost to Bob Chaperon 5–1)
Rothmans Grand Prix:	Round 5 1985 (lost to Cliff Wilson 5–2)
	Round 5 1987 (lost to Willie Thorne 5–2)
BCE Canadian Masters:	Round 3 1988 (lost to Danny Fowler 5–1)
Tennents UK Open:	Quarter-finalist 1986 (lost to Steve Davis 9–8)
Mercantile Credit Classic:	Round 4 1989 (lost to Terry Griffiths 5–0)
ICI European Open:	Round 3 1989 (lost to Mark Bennett 5–1)
Anglian Windows British Open:	Round 4 1989 (lost to Joe Johnson 5–3)

Other Wins

Malta Amateur: 1984

WORLD RANKING POSITIONS

1986/87	37	1988/89	20
1987/88	32	1989/90	30

WAYNE JONES

World ranking: number 31
Date of birth: 24 December 1959
Star sign: Capricorn

My secret wish: To be a professional boxer

Wayne Jones will never forget the 1988/89 season. He reached his first ranking tournament final – the Mercantile Credit Classic; his wife Jill gave birth to their first daughter, Clare; and he finished the season by taking his place in the top thirty-two at number 31. In the Mercantile event Jones beat world number 2 Jimmy White on his way to the final against his good friend Doug Mountjoy. Jones led Mountjoy 11–9 but finally lost four frames in a row to go down 13–11.

In the World Championship he scored a 10–9 victory over Neal Foulds in the first round but was then thrashed 13–3 by Dean Reynolds.

In the top thirty-two: Welshman Wayne Jones at number 31.

BEST PERFORMANCES

Embassy World Championship:	Round 2 1989 (lost to Dean Reynolds 13–3)

Other Ranking Tournaments

Fidelity Unit Trusts International:	Round 1 (last 32) 1984 (lost to David Taylor 5–4) Round 4 1987 (lost to Nigel Gilbert 5–4)
Rothmans Grand Prix:	Round 4 1985 (lost to Peter Francisco 5–3) Round 4 1986 (lost to Silvino Francisco 5–4) Round 4 1988 (lost to Jimmy White 5–1)
BCE Canadian Masters:	Round 2 1988 (lost to Colin Roscoe 5–4)
Tennents UK Open:	Quarter-finalist 1986 (lost to Alex Higgins 9–5)
Mercantile Credit Classic:	Runner-up 1989 (lost to Doug Mountjoy 13–11)
ICI European Open:	Withdrew from round 3
Anglian Windows British Open:	Round 2 (last 32) 1985 (lost to Bob Chaperon 5–2)

Other Wins

British Isles Under-16: 1976	Welsh Amateur: 1983

WORLD RANKING POSITIONS

1985/86	49	1987/88	34	1989/90	31
1986/87	56	1988/89	34		

REX WILLIAMS

World ranking: number 32
Date of birth: 20 July 1933
Star sign: Cancer

My secret wish: To catch a record trout or salmon

Rex Williams, one of the game's longest-serving professionals, dropped fourteen places in the rankings to number 32. It was hardly a memorable season for the former chairman of the WPBSA and his best performance came in reaching the last sixteen of the Fidelity Unit Trusts International where he lost 5–4 to Barry West. Away from the table Williams is a keen fisherman and is still a very successful businessman.

BEST PERFORMANCES

Embassy World Championship:	Semi-finalist 1969 (lost to John Spencer 37–12) Semi-finalist 1972 (lost to Alex Higgins 31–30) Semi-finalist 1974 (lost to Graham Miles 15–7)

Other Ranking Tournaments

Fidelity Unit Trusts International:	Round 5 1986 (lost to Steve Davis 5–4) Round 5 1988 (lost to Barry West 5–4)
Rothmans Grand Prix:	Runner-up 1986 (lost to Jimmy White 10–6)
BCE Canadian Masters:	Round 3 1988 (lost to George Scott 5–2)

Tennents UK Open:	Round 2 (last 16) 1984 (lost to Alex Higgins 9–7)
	Round 5 1985 (lost to Kirk Stevens 9–7)
Mercantile Credit Classic:	Semi-finalist 1986 (lost to Jimmy White 9–7)
ICI European Open:	Round 4 1989 (lost to Jimmy White 5–2)
Anglian Windows British Open:	Quarter-finalist 1988 (lost to Cliff Thorburn 5–2)

Current Non-ranking Tournaments

Benson and Hedges Masters:	Semi-finalist 1975 (lost to Ray Reardon 5–4)
Benson and Hedges Irish Masters:	Round 1 1988 (lost to Terry Griffiths 5–1)

Other Wins

British Isles Under-16: 1948, 1949   English Amateur: 1951
British Isles Under-19: 1951

WORLD RANKING POSITIONS

1976/77	6	1981/82	28	1986/87	16
1977/78	11	1982/83	–	1987/88	12
1978/79	17	1983/84	30	1988/89	18
1979/80	21	1984/85	31	1989/90	32
1980/81	–	1985/86	27		

WHO SAID THAT?

'It was good to see more snooker coverage from the BBC for the Fersina Windows World Cup when the amount of time allocated to sport generally is decreasing.'

– *WPBSA tournament director Paul Hatherell.*

'I was playing like a goose. I was even thinking of packing in snooker and going home to Sydney and taking out a bookmaker's licence.'

– *Warren King, looking back on his 1987/88 season.*

'It was embarrassing leaning over the snooker table being so fat. I used to break into a sweat calling "Heads or tails?" before the start of a match.'

– *Les Dodd, the Male Weightwatcher of the Year.*

'Anything's better than pouring someone's cold Sunday dinner over your own head.'

– *Worksop's Danny Fowler, a former dustman, now ranked number 36 in the world.*

'He's a big girl's blouse. The only other job he seems to want is God's and I don't think even he will get that. His players are just a flock of sheep.'

– *Cliff Wilson, talking about Barry Hearn.*

'I don't hate Steve Davis. I don't hate anybody.'

– *Alex Higgins.*

'I am fed up with wearing a red suit and a white beard and playing Santa Claus. I am playing so well that I don't think anybody in the whole world can beat me – I am not going to be a push-over this season.'

– *Jim Wych, the Canadian Professional Championship runner-up, looking ahead to the 1988/89 season.*

LOOKING BACK AT A YEAR ON THE CIRCUIT

FOSTER'S PROFESSIONAL

Mike Hallett was not going to let the fact that only four players contested the Foster's Professional tournament at the RTE Studios in Dublin stop him celebrating his first win as a professional.

'I just hope it's the first of many,' he said as he held up the trophy after an 8–5 final defeat of stablemate Stephen Hendry.

The Foster's is a 'made-for-television' event that does not rank as a major tournament. But it was a major breakthrough for Hallett as he put behind him the heartache of losing heavily in finals the previous season.

Hallett started with a 5–3 defeat of John Parrott while Hendry thrashed an out-of-touch Eugene Hughes 5–1. The final looked easy for Hendry as he opened a 4–1 lead, but then Hallett, after taking the last frame of the first session, raced to victory by winning six of the first seven frames at night.

Foster's Professional Results

SEMI-FINALS		FINAL	
S. Hendry (Scot)	5		
v		Hendry	5
E. Hughes (Rep Ire)	1		
		v	
J. Parrott (Eng)	3		
v		Hallett	8
M. Hallett (Eng)	5		
Losers:	£5,825	Loser:	£8,500
		Winner:	£12,500
High break: 99 – S. Hendry £2,000			

Previous Years' Results

YEAR	WINNER	RUNNER-UP	SCORE
1984	(Carlsberg) J. White (Eng)	A. Knowles (Eng)	9–7
1985	(Carlsberg) J. White (Eng)	A. Higgins (NI)	8–3
1986	(Carlsberg) Dennis Taylor (NI)	J. White (Eng)	8–3
1987	(Carling) Dennis Taylor (NI)	J. Johnson (Eng)	8–5

FIDELITY UNIT TRUSTS INTERNATIONAL

Steve Davis retained his title in the Fidelity Unit Trusts International, rocked back on his chair and declared: 'I have never played better.'

A few moments earlier he had put the finishing touches to a 12–6 victory over stablemate Jimmy White to collect the £45,000 first prize in the rural splendour of Trentham Gardens in Stoke-on-Trent. Davis was right. He had never played better – especially on the first day, when he opened a 10–4 lead.

White, desperately trying to play in a new cue tip after the original one had come off the previous night, was merely a spectator. Davis, supremely in control, left his opponent pointless in eight of the first fourteen frames.

But that was not all. After taking a 6–1 first-session lead, Davis then compiled breaks of 108, 101 and 104 in frames 9, 10 and 11 – the first time any professional had recorded three successive centuries under tournament conditions. White took the first two frames on day 2 but that only delayed the inevitable as Davis regained his composure for his 12–6 win.

'It's funny – I had never even scored three centuries in a row in practice before. When I got to the 70 mark in frame 11, I was shaking like a leaf as I realised what I was about to achieve,' said Davis, who also picked up £4,500 for the high-break prize of 135. 'In the first session I never missed a ball of any importance. I was that good, it was frightening.'

The problems with White's cue tip occurred at the end of the last frame in his 9–5 semi-final defeat of a revitalised Dean Reynolds. The new tip unfortunately hardened up and White said: 'Steve deserved to win, but I was not able to play my shots properly with the new tip.'

In the other semi-final Davis dismissed the challenge of world number 32 Steve James by a 9–1 margin, but James could

World beater: Tony Drago with the scoresheet that proved he had set a new world record by winning one frame in just three minutes. He went into the history books during a match with Danny Fowler at the Fidelity Unit Trusts International.

look back on his first major semi-final with pride and accept that no one could have lived with Davis in this form. James had scored a shock 5–2 win over Scotland's Stephen Hendry in the fifth round – on the day when he ended up in the Trentham Park lake after falling out of a paddle boat.

Snooker history was made in the third round when Tony Drago won the sixth frame of his 5–3 success over Danny Fowler in just three minutes.

Davis was on the brink of defeat in the fourth round when he came up against new Canadian champion Alain Robidoux who showed no fear as he opened leads of 3–1 and 4–3 before a relieved Davis came through 5–4 to win on the blue. Davis is usually reserved in his comments on other players but not so when discussing new boy Robidoux. He said: 'He is a great player. He should be in the top sixteen. We come from the same planet.'

Fidelity Unit Trusts International Results

FOURTH ROUND		FIFTH ROUND		QUARTER-FINALS		SEMI-FINALS		FINAL	
S. Davis (Eng)	5								
A. Robidoux (Can)	4	S. Davis	5						
John Rea (Scot)	4	v		S. Davis	5				
David Taylor (Eng)	5	David Taylor	1						
Dennis Taylor (NI)	5			v		S. Davis	9		
J. Campbell (Aust)	4	Dennis Taylor	5						
J. Wych (Can)	5	v		Dennis Taylor	2				
D. O'Kane (NZ)	4	Wych	2						
M. Hallett (Eng)	3					v		S. Davis	12
A. Meo (Eng)	5	Meo	5						
S. Francisco (SA)	2	v		Meo	1				
R. Chaperon (Can)	5	Chaperon	4						
M. Macleod (Scot)	2			v		James	1		
S. James (Eng)	5	James	5						
S. Hendry (Scot)	5	v		James	5				
S. Longworth (Eng)	3	Hendry	2					v	
N. Foulds (Eng)	3								
D. Reynolds (Eng)	5	Reynolds	5						
J. Virgo (Eng)	1	v		Reynolds	5				
J. Spencer (Eng)	5	Spencer	1						
J. Johnson (Eng)	5			v		Reynolds	5		
D. Mountjoy (Wales)	4	Johnson	5						
A. Knowles (Eng)	4	v		Johnson	1				
S. Newbury (Wales)	5	Newbury	2						
L. Dodd (Eng)	3					v		White	6
B. West (Eng)	5	West	5						
S. Duggan (Eng)	4	v		West	2				
R. Williams (Eng)	5	Williams	4						
W. Thorne (Eng)	5			v		White	9		
A. Drago (Malta)	2	Thorne	4						
J. White (Eng)	5	v		White	5				
E. Hughes (Rep Ire)	1	White	5						

Losers: £2,179.68	Losers: £3,375	Losers: £6,750	Losers: £13,500	Loser: £27,000
				Winner: £45,000

High break: 135 – S. Davis £4,500

Previous Years' Results

YEAR	WINNER	RUNNER-UP	SCORE
1981	(Jameson)		
	S. Davis (Eng)	Dennis Taylor (NI)	9–0
1982	(Jameson)		
	A. Knowles (Eng)	David Taylor (Eng)	9–6
1983	(Jameson)		
	S. Davis (Eng)	C. Thorburn (Can)	9–4
1984	(Jameson)		
	S. Davis (Eng)	A. Knowles (Eng)	9–2
1985	(Goya)		
	C. Thorburn (Can)	J. White (Eng)	12–10
1986	(BCE)		
	N. Foulds (Eng)	C. Thorburn (Can)	12–9
1987	(Fidelity)		
	S. Davis (Eng)	C. Thorburn (Can)	12–5

LEP MATCHROOM CHAMPIONSHIP

Steve Davis had won every major title on offer – except his own LEP Matchroom Championship. He filled that gap in his trophy cabinet when he beat defending champion Dennis Taylor 10–7 in the final at the Cliffs Pavilion, Southend.

At first it had looked as though Davis was going to miss out for the third year running when a determined Taylor went into a 5–4 lead at the end of the first session. However, Davis struck form at night as he reeled off breaks of 53, 83, 91 and 77 to collect the £50,000 first prize. There was also a £5,000 'extra' for the high break of 132 which Davis set during his 6–2 first-round triumph over Willie Thorne, who regretted a miss on the black that would have given him a break of 135.

LEP Matchroom Championship

FIRST ROUND		SEMI-FINALS		FINAL	
Dennis Taylor (NI)	6				
v		Taylor	6		
A. Meo (Eng)	4				
		v		Taylor	7
N. Foulds (Eng)	6				
v		N. Foulds	3		
T. Griffiths (Wales)	4			v	
J. White (Eng)	6				
v		White	4		
C. Thorburn (Can)	4				
		v		S. Davis	10
S. Davis (Eng)	6				
v		S. Davis	6		
W. Thorne (Eng)	2				
Losers: £6,250		Losers: £12,500		Loser: £25,000	
				Winner: £50,000	

High break: 132 – S. Davies £5,000

Previous Years' Results

YEAR	WINNER	RUNNER-UP	SCORE
1986	W. Thorne (Eng)	S. Davis (Eng)	10–9
1987	Dennis Taylor (NI)	W. Thorne (Eng)	10–3

ROTHMANS GRAND PRIX

Alex Higgins, down to number 17 on the world rankings, had been written off as a snooker has-been – a player whose best days were behind him. Higgins, world champion in 1972 and 1982, proved those critics wrong with a magnificent performance in the Rothmans Grand Prix at the Hexagon Theatre in Reading.

Irishman Higgins, against all the odds, came through to reach the final only to lose 10–6 to defending champion Steve Davis. But even in defeat he was cheered to the rafters by a sell-out crowd who had come to witness the Hurricane return to the snooker big time. Higgins picked up £39,000 – his biggest pay cheque since he turned professional in 1971.

Davis, because of a dispute between the sponsors and the Matchroom organisation, had not attended after-match press interviews. Even so, he did say: 'It takes a great champion to come back and needs a tremendous show of character. Alex has proved he's a great champion.'

Davis earned £65,000 and a £40,000 bonus for completing a Grand Prix and Matchroom League double. But that brief

Well played: Alex Higgins congratulates champion Steve Davis after the Rothmans Grand Prix final.

comment was his only remark during the entire tournament.

Higgins was a hit at the post-tournament gathering back at the Ramada Hotel. He said: 'I have come out of the wilderness into a crowded room. I just hope I can go one step further next year. I may not be the Hurricane of old but I still reckon I can get back to the top.'

The final had always pointed to a Davis win, especially as the world champion had won twenty-one of his previous twenty-five meetings with Higgins.

The semi-finals produced two totally different matches. Davis thrashed Dennis Taylor 9–1, while Higgins scraped home 9–7 in an outstanding match against new Canadian professional Alain Robidoux.

Robidoux had been like a breath of fresh air on the circuit as he battered Tony Meo 5–0, came back fom 4–0 down to stun Doug Mountjoy 5–4 and then overcame Nigel Gilbert by the same score. Gilbert,

Up in the air: Canadian Alain Robidoux gladly tears up his air ticket back home after reaching the semi-final of the Rothmans Grand Prix.

Rothmans Grand Prix Results

FOURTH ROUND		FIFTH ROUND		QUARTER-FINALS		SEMI-FINALS		FINAL	
S. Hendry (Scot)	1								
v		Mountjoy	4						
D. Mountjoy (Wales)	5								
				Robidoux	5				
A. Robidoux (Can)	5								
v		Robidoux	5						
A. Meo (Eng)	0								
						Robidoux	7		
N. Gilbert (Eng)	5								
v		N. Gilbert	5						
E. Charlton (Aust)	0								
				N. Gilbert	4				
A. Knowles (Eng)	5								
v		Knowles	4						
D. Reynolds (Eng)	3								
								Higgins	6
J. Parrott (Eng)	3								
v		Edmonds	3						
R. Edmonds (Eng)	5								
				Williams	4				
Gary Wilkinson (Eng)	2								
v		Williams	5						
R. Williams (Eng)	5								
						Higgins	9		
A. Higgins (NI)	5								
v		Higgins	5						
D. O'Kane (NZ)	0								
				Higgins	5				
N. Foulds (Eng)	5								
v		Foulds	3						
S. Duggan (Eng)	4								
									v
J. White (Eng)	5								
v		White	5						
W. Jones (Wales)	1								
				White	2				
J. McLaughlin (NI)	5								
v		J. McLaughlin	2						
J. Spencer (Eng)	3								
						Dennis Taylor	1		
Dennis Taylor (NI)	5								
v		Dennis Taylor	5						
R. Chaperon (Can)	4								
				Dennis Taylor	5				
M. Hallett (Eng)	5								
v		Hallett	2						
S. James (Eng)	2								
								S. Davis	10
T. Griffiths (Wales)	5								
v		Griffiths	5						
B. West (Eng)	1								
				Griffiths	3				
J. Johnson (Eng)	2								
v		E. Hughes	2						
E. Hughes (Rep Ire)	5								
						S. Davis	9		
C. Wilson (Wales)	5								
v		C. Wilson	1						
A. Drago (Malta)	4								
				S. Davis	5				
S. Davis (Eng)	5								
v		S. Davis	5						
S. Newbury (Wales)	1								

Losers: £3,148.43   Losers: £4,875   Losers: £9,750   Losers: £19,500   Loser: £39,000
Winner: £65,000

High break: 139 – D. Reynolds £6,500

who wears a white glove on his bridging hand, had also impressed by beating Eddie Charlton and Tony Knowles.

But Robidoux's dream looked in tatters as he trailed Higgins 8–1. Then Higgins relaxed and Robidoux suddenly came back to win six frames in a row to reduce the deficit to 7–8. The shock brought Higgins to his senses and he came through the sixteenth frame to reach the final.

Higgins laughed off a £100,000 tax demand from the Inland Revenue as he said: 'I promised I would be back – it's like the return of the Pink Panther. I am very popular and I know the television ratings will go up now I have reached the final.'

Previous Years' Results

YEAR	WINNER	RUNNER-UP	SCORE
1982	(Professional Players Tournament) R. Reardon (Wales)	J. White (Eng)	10–5
1983	(PPT) A. Knowles (Eng)	J. Johnson (Eng)	9–8
1984	Dennis Taylor (NI)	C. Thorburn (Can)	10–2
1985	S. Davis (Eng)	Dennis Taylor (NI)	10–9
1986	J. White (Eng)	R. Williams (Eng)	10–6
1987	S. Hendry (Scot)	Dennis Taylor (NI)	10–7

BCE CANADIAN MASTERS

Jimmy White delighted more than 1,000 Canadian fans as he collected his first ranking tournament trophy for eighteen months with a stunning 9–4 victory over Steve Davis in the final of the BCE Canadian Masters in Toronto.

Davis was not at his best, and by the end of the first session White had raced into a 5–2 lead. In the evening session White continued to pile in the breaks and eventually Davis caved in – his first defeat in a final since 1986. In that year Davis had lost his world title to Joe Johnson, but afterwards had won thirteen finals in succession.

White's last success over Davis had been in the same year, and since then they had played six matches, all of which the 'Wimbledon Whirlwind' had lost. 'I needed this win, I needed it badly,' said White, who ended a remarkable run of twenty-two match wins in a row by Davis.

Davis had almost predicted his defeat when he said: 'I am prepared to lose eventually and then it won't come as a shock.' Afterwards he added: 'The elastic

The master: Jimmy White with the BCE Canadian Masters trophy after a brilliant final win over Steve Davis in Toronto.

BCE Canadian Masters Results

FOURTH ROUND		FIFTH ROUND		QUARTER-FINALS		SEMI-FINALS		FINAL	
S. Davis (Eng)	5								
v		S. Davis	5						
G. Scott (Eng)	1			S. Davis	5				
J. Johnson (Eng)	4								
v		James	0						
S. James (Eng)	5			v		S. Davis	9		
W. Thorne (Eng)	4								
v		Mountjoy	4						
D. Mountjoy (Wales)	5			Griffiths	3				
T. Griffiths (Wales)	5								
v		Griffiths	5						
R. Reardon (Wales)	2							S. Davis	4
C. Thorburn (Can)	5								
v		Thorburn	5						
J. Spencer (Eng)	2			Thorburn	4				
I. Graham (Eng)	5								
v		Graham	4						
E. Charlton (Aust)	2			v		Hendry	5		
C. Wilson (Wales)	5								
v		Wilson	1						
D. Reynolds (Eng)	4			Hendry	5				
S. Hendry (Scot)	5								
v		Hendry	5					v	
D. Fowler (Eng)	2								
W. King (Aust)	5								
v		King	2						
S. Duggan (Eng)	4			Hallett	5				
M. Hallett (Eng)	5								
v		Hallett	5						
M. Gauvreau (Can)	3			v		Hallett	2		
J. Virgo (Eng)	5								
v		Virgo	4						
S. Newbury (Wales)	2			Parrott	3				
J. Parrott (Eng)	5								
v		Parrott	5						
D. Morgan (Wales)	3							White	9
C. Roscoe (Wales)	1								
v		David Taylor	2						
David Taylor (Eng)	5			Dennis Taylor	3				
Dennis Taylor (NI)	5								
v		Dennis Taylor	5						
M. Clark (Eng)	4			v		White	9		
M. Macleod (Scot)	3								
v		Longworth	0						
S. Longworth (Eng)	5			White	5				
J. White (Eng)	5								
v		White	5						
M. Bennett (Wales)	3								

Losers: £1,937.50   Losers: £3,000   Losers: £6,000   Losers: £12,000   Loser: £24,000
Winner: £40,000

High break: 132 – Dennis Taylor £4,000

band just snapped because Jimmy was playing at a higher level than me in every department throughout the game. Now I will just go away and put Humpty Dumpty back together again because a defeat like this brings you back to earth.'

White had given notice of his impressive form in the semi-final when he destroyed Mike Hallett 9–2 in a match which lasted just two hours, seventeen minutes.

In the other semi-final Davis clashed once again with Stephen Hendry. Hendry had been the victim of allegations concerning his personal life in a national newspaper – but he pushed that to the back of mind as he recovered from being 2–4 down to fire in breaks of 75 and 91 to lead 5–4. Then, however, he failed on the last red and Davis levelled at 5–5.

The world number 1 went 6–5 ahead before Hendry opened a 73–8 lead in the twelfth frame. Hendry promptly snookered himself, but even so Davis looked to have no chance as he needed three snookers. As Davis edged closer, Hendry left the final red just behind the blue, got down too quickly, missed the red and gave away a free ball to allow Davis to step in with a brilliant clearance of 42 to win the frame 74–73. From then on Davis was always going to win and he did just that, 9–5.

This was the first time a ranking tournament had been staged outside Britain – thirty-two players jetted across the Atlantic to take part. The opening stages were held in the Chimo Hotel, while the final rounds took place at the Minkler Auditorium in Toronto.

TENNENTS UK OPEN

Doug Mountjoy, seemingly with his best days behind him, started the season at number 24 in the world rankings. There seemed only one route available for the popular Welshman – downwards. But six months earlier Mountjoy had decided that 'enough was enough' and had been to see top snooker coach Frank Callan. Solid, unrelenting practice had been the order of the day, and all that work was going to blossom in the most remarkable way.

When the forty-six-year-old player went into the Tennents UK Open at the Guild Hall in Preston, nobody believed that he would eventually provide one of the fairy-tale stories of the season. But the tears were flowing on the final day as Doug and wife Yvonne celebrated his incredible 16–12 final victory over Stephen Hendry. In the background stood Callan, and Mountjoy said: 'This doesn't belong to me – I owe it all to Frank.'

Hendry, with two ranking tournament titles to his name the previous season, had gone into the final as the odds-on favour-

It's mine: Doug Mountjoy ends a ten-year wait for a major title with his victory in the Tennents UK Open.

ite. The bookmakers gave Mountjoy virtually no chance after Hendry's quite brilliant 9–3 battering of defending champion Steve Davis in the semi-final. Even so, Mountjoy had given notice of his outstanding form by beating his Welsh friend, Terry Griffiths, 9–4 to take his final place.

The final started with Mountjoy going 6–2 ahead, only for Hendry to level at 7–7 overnight.

Tennents UK Open Results

THIRD ROUND		FOURTH ROUND		FIFTH ROUND		QUARTER-FINALS		SEMI-FINALS		FINAL	
S. Davis (Eng)	9	S. Davis	9	S. Davis	9	S. Davis	9	S. Davis	3	Hendry	12
v W. King (Aust)	7	v		v							
R. Chaperon (Can)	0	Gary Wilkinson	3								
v Gary Wilkinson (Eng)	9										
M. Hallett (Eng)	6	Clark	6	Fowler	6						
v M. Clark (Eng)	9	v									
S. Longworth (Eng)	8	Fowler	9								
v D. Fowler (Eng)	9										
Dennis Taylor (NI)	9	Dennis Taylor	9	Dennis Taylor	4	Parrott	4				
v J. McLaughlin (NI)	5	v		v							
E. Hughes (Rep Ire)	8	O'Boye	4								
v J. O'Boye (Eng)	9										
J. Parrott (Eng)	9	Parrott	9	Parrott	9						
v D. Martin (Eng)	6	v									
J. Spencer (Eng)	7	N. Gilbert	8								
v N. Gilbert (Eng)	9										
C. Thorburn (Can)	9	Thorburn	9	Thorburn	9	Thorburn	2	Hendry	9		
v A. Robidoux (Can)	4	v		v							
S. James (Eng)	9	James	6								
v A. Kearney (Rep Ire)	1										
P. Francisco (SA)	9	P. Francisco	7	Roe	8						
v John Rea (Scot)	2	v									
A. Meo (Eng)	6	Roe	9								
v D. Roe (Eng)	9										
W. Thorne (Eng)	9	Thorne	9	Thorne	4	Hendry	9				
v D. Gilbert (Eng)	3	v		v							
E. Charlton (Aust)	7	Stevens	3								
v K. Stevens (Can)	9										
S. Hendry (Scot)	9	Hendry	9	Hendry	9						
v T. Murphy (NI)	4	v									
S. Newbury (Wales)	7	Roscoe	3								
v C. Roscoe (Wales)	9										

Round 1

Player	Score
N. Foulds (Eng)	9
M. Rowing (Eng)	4
D. Mountjoy (Wales)	9
W. Jones (Wales)	7
J. Johnson (Eng)	9
M. Smith (Eng)	2
R. Williams (Eng)	9
R. Harris (Eng)	4
J. Virgo (Eng)	9
B. Rowswell (Eng)	3
D. O'Kane (NZ)	9
R. Reardon (Wales)	8
A. Knowles (Eng)	9
J. Wych (Can)	4
A. Higgins (NI)	9
L. Dodd (Eng)	7
T. Griffiths (Wales)	9
K. Owers (Eng)	2
A. Drago (Malta)	7
S. Duggan (Eng)	9
C. Wilson (Wales)	9
R. Edmonds (Eng)	1
D. Reynolds (Eng)	9
A. Chappel (Wales)	4
S. Francisco (SA)	9
P. Medati (Eng)	8
B. West (Eng)	9
A. Jones (Eng)	5
J. White (Eng)	9
J. Campbell (Aust)	5
David Taylor (Eng)	4
M. Bennett (Wales)	9

Round 2

Player	Score
N. Foulds	4
Mountjoy	9
Johnson	9
Williams	7
Virgo	9
O'Kane	8
Knowles	9
Higgins	6
Griffiths	9
Duggan	2
C. Wilson	3
Reynolds	9
S. Francisco	4
West	9
White	6
M. Bennett	9

Round 3

Player	Score
Mountjoy	9
Johnson	5
Virgo	9
Knowles	3
Griffiths	9
Reynolds	6
West	9
M. Bennett	4

Quarter-finals

Player	Score
Mountjoy	9
Virgo	8
Griffiths	9
West	5

Semi-finals

Player	Score
Mountjoy	9
Griffiths	4

Final

Player	Score
Mountjoy	16

Losers: £1,750   Losers: £3,875   Losers: £6,000   Losers: £12,000   Losers: £24,000   Loser: £48,000   Winner: £80,000

High break: 131 – D. Mountjoy £8,000

Hendry then felt the full power of Mountjoy's amazing snooker rehabilitation. All seven frames in the afternoon went Mountjoy's way and he finished the session off with a best-of-tournament 131, followed immediately by a 106. Hendry, 14–7 behind, said: 'Doug punished every mistake I made. He was superb.'

After the twenty-minute break Mountjoy promptly knocked in a 124. That equalled Davis' world record of three tournament centuries in a row and, even more importantly, put him one frame away, at 15–7, from the £80,000 first prize.

Hendry then decided that there was only one way to win and that was by going for his shots. Remarkably, he started to pull the frames back and in frame 27 there was an outstanding incident when the black, hanging over the top corner pocket, was surrounded by the last five reds. Somehow these two top-class players managed to play for eighteen minutes without fouling the black, but then referee John Street re-racked the frame which Hendry promptly won to pull up to 15–12.

Now it was Mountjoy's turn to worry, but in the twenty-eighth frame he finally kept his nerve, knocked in a break of 39 and enjoyed the most important day of his snooker life.

Previous Years' Results

YEAR	WINNER	RUNNER-UP	SCORE
1977	(Super Crystalate) P. Fagan (Rep Ire)	D. Mountjoy (Wales)	12–9
1978	(Coral) D. Mountjoy (Wales)	David Taylor (Eng)	15–9
1979	(Coral) J. Virgo (Eng)	T. Griffiths (Wales)	14–13
1980	(Coral) S. Davis (Eng)	A. Higgins (NI)	16–6
1981	(Coral) S. Davis (Eng)	T. Griffiths (Wales)	16–3
1982	(Coral) T. Griffiths (Wales)	A. Higgins (NI)	16–15
1983	(Coral) A. Higgins (NI)	S. Davis (Eng)	16–15
1984	(Coral) S. Davis (Eng)	A. Higgins (NI)	16–8
1985	(Coral) S. Davis (Eng)	W. Thorne (Eng)	16–14
1986	S. Davis (Eng)	N. Foulds (Eng)	16–7
1987	S. Davis (Eng)	J. White (Eng)	16–14

EVEREST WORLD MATCHPLAY

Steve Davis picked up snooker's then biggest first prize of £100,000 and paid tribute to veteran Ray Reardon as the inspiration behind his success in the £250,000 Everest World Matchplay at the International Hall in Brentwood.

Davis, who lives only four miles down the road from the venue, made it seven wins in a row over John Parrott in the final as he won the match 9–5. He said: 'I remember the 1970s when Ray was at his best and I don't think he would have been pleased with my displays in the Canadian Masters and the Tennents UK Open. Ray used to go out and be in total control of matches. He could just dominate players and that's something I had failed to do in recent matches. If you can control yourself, you can control the table, and I was more like that against John. It was very important for me to win again, because if you have to prove something there is no better way than winning.'

The final started badly for Parrott as he found himself 6–0 down but he cheered himself up by taking three frames in a row, including a break of 135 in the ninth frame that earned him £10,000 for the high

At the double: John Parrott and Steve Davis pose before the start of the Everest World Matchplay.

break. He was also £40,000 richer for finishing runner-up.

The Everest was a new event on the calendar and boasted, at that time, the game's biggest first prize – though, of course, it was overtaken by the £105,000 on offer for the winner of the 1989 Embassy World Championship. The tournament featured the top twelve players in the world based on performances in the 1987/88 season.

In the semi-finals Davis beat Jimmy White 9–5 while Parrott, 3–0 ahead and then 6–5 behind, found himself in trouble against Stephen Hendry. But Hendry lost the twelfth frame and the interval allowed Parrott to re-think his game, come out to take three successive frames and go through 9–6.

The tournament had started with two near-147s as Joe Johnson beat Cliff Thorburn 9–4. Johnson knocked in fifteen reds and fifteen blacks, but then got an appalling kick on the yellow. In the same match Thorburn knocked in thirteen reds and blacks only to fail on the fourteenth red.

Everest World Matchplay Results

FIRST ROUND		QUARTER-FINALS		SEMI-FINALS		FINAL	
		S. Davis (Eng)	9				
M. Hallett (Eng)	9	v		S. Davis	9		
v		Hallett	2				
W. Thorne (Eng)	8					S. Davis	9
				v			
T. Griffiths (Wales)	9	Griffiths	5				
v		v		White	5		
P. Francisco (SA)	7	J. White (Eng)	9				
						v	
		J. Parrott (Eng)	9				
C. Thorburn (Can)	4	v		Parrott	9		
v		Johnson	7				
J. Johnson (Eng)	9					Parrott	5
				v			
A. Knowles (Eng)	7	Dennis Taylor	7				
v		v		Hendry	6		
Dennis Taylor (NI)	9	S. Hendry (Scot)	9				
Losers: £5,000		Losers: £10,000		Losers: £20,000		Loser: £ 40,000	
						Winner: £100,000	
High break: 135 – J. Parrott £10,000							

NORWICH UNION EUROPEAN GRAND PRIX

Snooker in the UK is often considered to be a late-night television sport to be watched and enjoyed while sitting around a warm fire in the depths of winter. The final of the Norwich Union European Grand Prix had a distinctly different flavour that produced one of the game's most memorable matches. It was being staged at the Beach Plaza Hotel in Monte Carlo in the presence of Prince Albert of Monaco. Outside, a stone's throw away, the warm waters of the Mediterranean were washing gently over the silver sand.

Inside the hotel's Sea Club, Steve Davis and Jimmy White were putting on a remarkable show. White, in control, looked to have the match in his grasp as he led Davis 4–1, needing just one frame to collect the £50,000 first prize.

In those first five frames Davis had won only one – and he did that with a 136 break, the highest of the tournament. But from this position of power White saw the match slowly start to ebb away. Davis took the next two frames before an eighth frame of brilliant snooker and high drama.

White moved into a 55–40 lead with pink and black left and his opponent needing a snooker. Davis managed to hide the cue ball three times in a row behind the black and each time White somehow got out of trouble. Then Davis made his first mistake and left White the chance of a long pink. White went for it, potted it and then watched agonisingly as the cue ball bounced off two cushions and rolled diagonally down the table to drop into a corner pocket. Davis took that frame to make it 4–4, but even so there was still more excitement to come.

In the decider White, 41–25 in front, lined up a pink that would surely clinch him the game. He got a kick, and a disbelieving Davis returned to the table to clear up with a break of 35 to win. Davis said: 'I was down and out and Jimmy should have buried me. It was a match I had no right to win. After the world final against Dennis in 1985 that was the second most exciting match I have played in.'

The Grand Prix was played off by the eight Matchroom players and featured qualifying rounds in Brussels, Paris, Madrid and Milan. Davis, White, Dennis Taylor and Terry Griffiths fought through to the finals and they arrived in spectacular style – by helicopter. It was Davis who whirled away with the £50,000 first prize.

Norwich Union European Grand Prix Results

<u>SEMI-FINALS:</u> S. Davis (Eng) bt Dennis Taylor (NI) 3–1; J. White (Eng) bt T. Griffiths (Wales) 3–1
           Losers: £12,500
<u>FINAL:</u>   S. Davis bt White 5–4
           Loser: £25,000
           Winner: £50,000

High break: 136 – S. Davis   Weekend in Monte Carlo for two

MERCANTILE CREDIT CLASSIC

When Doug Mountjoy arrived at the Norbreck Castle Hotel in Blackpool, he knew that many critics were saying his success in the previous ranking tournament – the Tennents UK Open – had been a one-off, a never-to-be-repeated feat. Two weeks later Mountjoy was proving them totally wrong as he beat Wayne Jones 13–11 in the final

Mercantile Credit Classic Results

FOURTH ROUND		FIFTH ROUND		QUARTER-FINALS		SEMI-FINALS		FINAL	
A. Chappel (Wales)	5								
v		Chappel	1						
A. Harris (Eng)	1			Browne	3				
P. Browne (Rep Ire)	5								
v		Browne	5						
S. James (Eng)	4					Mountjoy	9		
N. Terry (Eng)	4								
v		Mountjoy	5						
D. Mountjoy (Wales)	5			Mountjoy	5				
A. Knowles (Eng)	5								
v		Knowles	4						
D. Reynolds (Eng)	4							Mountjoy	13
C. Thorburn (Can)	5								
v		Thorburn	5						
G. Cripsey (Eng)	1			Thorburn	5				
J. Virgo (Eng)	5								
v		Virgo	3						
R. Chaperon (Can)	1					Thorburn	5		
Dennis Taylor (NI)	4								
v		Newbury	1						
S. Newbury (Wales)	5			Hendry	4				
S. Hendry (Scot)	5								
v		Hendry	5					v	
R. Reardon (Wales)	4								
N. Foulds (Eng)	4								
v		Clark	5						
M. Clark (Eng)	5			Clark	4				
J. Johnson (Eng)	5								
v		Johnson	3						
A. Higgins (NI)	0					Thorne	4		
W. Thorne (Eng)	5								
v		Thorne	5						
D. O'Kane (NZ)	3			Thorne	5				
T. Griffiths (Wales)	5								
v		Griffiths	1						
A. Drago (Malta)	0							W. Jones	11
J. Parrott (Eng)	5								
v		Parrott	5						
J. Wright (Eng)	2			Parrott	4				
S. Francisco (SA)	5								
v		S. Francisco	1						
A. Meo (Eng)	1					W. Jones	9		
C. Wilson (Wales)	3								
v		David Taylor	3						
David Taylor (Eng)	5			W. Jones	5				
W. Jones (Wales)	5								
v		W. Jones	5						
E. Hughes (Rep Ire)	1								

Losers: £2,664.06	Losers £4,125	Losers £8,250	Losers: £16,500	Loser: £33,000
				Winner: £55,000

High break: 137 – W. Jones £5,500

to collect the £55,000 first prize. Mountjoy had achieved a tremendous ranking tournament double.

In fact, the whole tournament was a remarkable success for Welsh snooker. Not only did Wales provide both finalists in Mountjoy and Jones, but Tony Chappel caused the upset of the season when, after losing the first two frames, he crushed Steve Davis 5–3 in the third round.

Even Ray Reardon, a Welsh 'golden oldie', got in on the act by almost beating Stephen Hendry in the fourth round. Hendry had to knock in a break of 72 to secure a 5–4 victory. To complete the Welsh success, Steve Newbury beat Dennis Taylor 5–4 in the fourth round – it was quite a tournament for the boys from the valleys.

It was the first all-Welsh ranking tournament final, and at the end of the first day the score was 7–7. The match was never a classic because both men knew each other's game so well. When Jones went 11–9 in front, it seemed that Mountjoy was going to have to take a back seat. But Mountjoy then called on his years of experience, and at 11–11 it was Jones who was looking worried. Two frames later the match was over and Mountjoy was, unbelievably, a champion yet again. He said: 'I just can't believe this is all happening. The UK was a fairy tale, but you can't have two fairy tales, can you?'

Mountjoy became only the second player ever (Davis was the first) to win two consecutive ranking tournaments, but he said honestly: 'I was lucky to have even

Good mates: Doug Mountjoy and Wayne Jones after the final of the Mercantile Credit Classic.

got this far. I could have lost my opening match with Nick Terry.'

There were tears yet again afterwards as Mountjoy talked about his close relationship with Jones. 'It was terrible out there, because Wayne is like a son to me,' he said. Jones was just delighted with his first ranking tournament final, a £33,000 cheque and a £5,500 bonus for scoring the highest break of 137.

And, of course, Jones had scored one of the great victories of the tournament when he beat Jimmy White 5–3. On doing so he raised a fist in delight and then planted a kiss on White's cheek!

Jones comes from Abertysswg, which lies in the Rhymney Valley in South Wales. Incredibly, the Abertysswg Working Men's Club has produced four Welsh amateur champions – Jones, Mountjoy, Des May and Alwyn Lloyd. Jones used to be a bricklayer in this tiny mining village which has a population of less than 3,000.

Previous Years' Results

YEAR	WINNER	RUNNER-UP	SCORE
1980	(Wilsons Classic)		
	J. Spencer (Eng)	A. Higgins (NI)	4–3
1981	(Wilsons Classic)		
	S. Davis (Eng)	Dennis Taylor (NI)	4–1
1982	(Lada)		
	T. Griffiths (Wales)	S. Davis (Eng)	9–8
1983	(Lada) S. Davis (Eng)	W. Werbeniuk (Can)	9–5
1984	(Lada) S. Davis (Eng)	A. Meo (Eng)	9–8
1985	W. Thorne (Eng)	C. Thorburn (Can)	13–8
1986	J. White (Eng)	C. Thorburn (Can)	13–12
1987	S. Davis (Eng)	J. White (Eng)	13–12
1988	S. Davis (Eng)	J. Parrott (Eng)	13–11

BENSON AND HEDGES MASTERS

Stephen Hendry has spent his short but successful career breaking records. At the Wembley Conference Centre, snooker's biggest UK auditorium, he became, at twenty, the youngest winner of the Benson and Hedges Masters. It was the first time Hendry had been invited as a member of snooker's top sixteen to compete in the sport's longest-running sponsored event. 'I can't wait to get started because I have heard all about the atmosphere at Wembley. I have been told the arena is very big and very noisy, but I know that will only inspire me,' he said.

Hendry was certainly inspired as he beat Willie Thorne 5–2 in the first round, Terry Griffiths 5–3 in the quarter-finals and then overcame Steve Davis – the man he just loves beating – 6–3 in the semi-final. Included in that victory over Davis was a break of 119 which gave him a £6,000 bonus for the best break of the tournament.

In the other half of the draw John Parrott had overwhelmed Dennis Taylor 5–1 and then scored a first-ever victory – 5–4 – over Jimmy White in the quarter-final. Parrott remarked: 'My legs were like blancmange against Jimmy.' In the semi-finals Parrott had to go all the way again before beating Neal Foulds 6–5.

The final was fought out in front of more than 2,000 fans. Parrott kicked off with a break of 93 but it was Hendry who had moved into a 5–2 lead by the break. Hendry commented: 'I did the damage in that first session.'

Parrott, a battler through and through, came back to 5–4 before Hendry pulled away again to make it 7–4 with breaks of 42 and 78. Frame 12 was superb, with Parrott, trailing 58–16, coming back to win it on the black; then in frame 13 Hendry, in front again, opted for a difficult plant on a red and missed.

Parrott sensed that he could reduce the deficit to one frame and potted the five reds left on the table. But then he failed on the yellow to allow Hendry to move 8–5 ahead. The fourteenth frame went Parrott's way but in the fifteenth Hendry clinched it 9–6 with a brilliant shot on the pink along the cushion. Parrott, after losing the three finals he had so far contested, said: 'Stephen deserved it because he was the best player all week.'

Tony Knowles literally crashed out 5–0 against Davis in the quarter-finals. At the end of the fourth frame he angrily knocked the balls all over the table and, on the way back to the dressing room, a door swung back on him. He put out his foot to stop it – smashing it to pieces. 'I had lost my cool,

The final pair: Stephen Hendry (left) shakes hands with stablemate John Parrott before the start of the Benson and Hedges Masters final. Hendry won to become, at twenty, the youngest Master.

but it was an accident,' he said. 'You could say the door went through my foot.'

There had been another 'snooker betting storm' when bookmakers suspended betting in the first round match between Silvino Francisco and Terry Griffiths thirty-seven minutes before the start. The *Daily* *Mirror* stated that 'a flood of bets had been received on the correct score of 5–1'. That was how the match had finished and some bookmakers refused to pay out because of betting irregularities. Francisco dismissed the allegations as a 'complete fabrication' and the WPBSA promised a full inquiry.

Benson and Hedges Masters Results

FIRST ROUND		QUARTER-FINALS		SEMI-FINALS		FINAL	
S. Davis (Eng)	5						
v		S. Davis	5				
C. Wilson (Wales)	2			S. Davis	3		
M. Hallett (Eng)	3						
v		Knowles	0				
A. Knowles (Eng)	5					Hendry	9
T. Griffiths (Wales)	5						
v		Griffiths	3				
S. Francisco (SA)	1			Hendry	6		
W. Thorne (Eng)	2						
v		Hendry	5				
S. Hendry (Scot)	5					v	
N. Foulds (Eng)	5						
v		N. Foulds	5				
P. Francisco (SA)	2			N. Foulds	5		
J. Johnson (Eng)	2						
v		Thorburn	2				
C. Thorburn (Can)	5					Parrott	6
J. Parrott (Eng)	5						
v		Parrott	5				
Dennis Taylor (NI)	1			Parrott	6		
J. Virgo (Eng)	2						
v		White	4				
J. White (Eng)	5						

Losers: £6,750   Losers: £13,000   Losers: £20,000   Loser: £36,000
                                                                                                        Winner: £62,000

High break: 119 – S. Hendry £6,000

Previous Years' Results

YEAR	WINNER	RUNNER-UP	SCORE
1975	J. Spencer (Eng)	R. Reardon (Wales)	9–8
1976	R. Reardon (Wales)	G. Miles (Eng)	7–3
1977	D. Mountjoy (Wales)	R. Reardon (Wales)	7–6
1978	A. Higgins (NI)	C. Thorburn (Can)	7–5
1979	P. Mans (SA)	A. Higgins (NI)	8–4
1980	T. Griffiths (Wales)	A. Higgins (NI)	9–5
1981	A. Higgins (NI)	T. Griffiths (Wales)	9–6
1982	S. Davis (Eng)	T. Griffiths (Wales)	9–5
1983	C. Thorburn (Can)	R. Reardon (Wales)	9–7
1984	J. White (Eng)	T. Griffiths (Wales)	9–5
1985	C. Thorburn (Can)	D. Mountjoy (Wales)	9–6
1986	C. Thorburn (Can)	J. White (Eng)	9–5
1987	Dennis Taylor (NI)	A. Higgins (NI)	9–8
1988	S. Davis (Eng)	M. Hallett (Eng)	9–0

ICI EUROPEAN OPEN

French Connection: John Parrott after his first ranking tournament success in the ICI European Open in Deauville, France.

The Deauville Casino, in its chandeliered majesty, was the most luxurious setting that snooker had ever found for a major ranking tournament. But the ICI European Open will be remembered solely for John Parrott's first major success.

Parrott, now firmly established in the game's top flight, finally ended his losing streak when he beat Terry Griffiths 9–8 to capture the £40,000 first prize. It was just a pity that so few people were there to witness his inaugural success. But then the northern French coast in January is hardly the most inviting venue.

Parrott, sipping champagne, reflected: 'I have been very uptight about getting this first title under my belt because no one likes being called second best. It was a horrible feeling knowing people were pointing fingers at me saying I had no bottle. But they don't know what they are talking about. There are only a few people who have been in snooker finals. Now I can relax after proving I can be a winner.'

This was the first joint overseas promotion between the WPBSA and Mark McCormack's International Management Group. The first mistake was bringing sixty-four players – that was too many. It was also very expensive, though world champion Steve Davis was not there to find out: he had pulled out as he wanted a rest.

In terms of media coverage, however, the event was successful as there was always something happening. On the first day, because of an administrative mix-up, Tony Meo arrived at the time he was actually supposed to be playing and, unshaven and totally exhausted, was deducted two frames. He lost 5–1 against David Roe. Then, of course, there was Alex 'Hopalong' Higgins who arrived complete with crutches after falling out of a second-floor flat window in Manchester just a few days earlier. Somehow Higgins spent three hours hopping round the table with his left foot broken in many places and managed to beat Les Dodd 5–2. There was a humor-

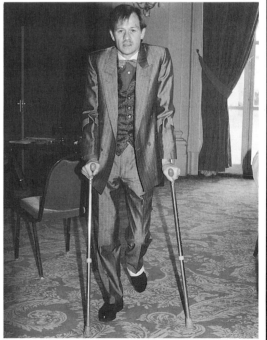

'Hopalong' Higgins: Alex Higgins limps into Deauville after breaking his left ankle in a fall from a second-floor window in Manchester.

ICI European Open Results

FOURTH ROUND

J. Chambers (Eng) 2
v
E. Charlton (Aust) 5

J. Virgo (Eng) 5
v
C. Edwards (Eng) 3

J. Campbell (Aust) 5
v
M. Bennett (Wales) 3

J. Parrott (Eng) 5
v
Gary Wilkinson (Eng) 2

D. Fowler (Eng) 5
v
T. Wilson (Eng) 2

J. Wych (Can) 5
v
M. Johnston-Allen (Eng) 4

M. Hallett (Eng) 5
v
P. Browne (Rep Ire) 4

S. Hendry (Scot) 5
v
S. Longworth (Eng) 0

M. Clark (Eng) 5
v
E. Hughes (Rep Ire) 1

J. Johnson (Eng) 5
v
D. Roe (Eng) 2

C. Wilson (Wales) 0
v
A. Robidoux (Can) 5

T. Griffiths (Wales) 5
v
A. Chappel (Wales) 2

C. Thorburn (Can) 5
v
M. Macleod (Scot) 1

Dennis Taylor (NI) 3
v
D. Mountjoy (Wales) 5

W. Thorne (Eng) 5
v
A. Higgins (NI) 1

J. White (Eng) 5
v
R. Williams (Eng) 2

FIFTH ROUND

Charlton 5
v
Virgo 4

Campbell 0
v
Parrott 5

Fowler 4
v
Wych 5

Hallett 5
v
Hendry 3

Clark 5
v
Johnson 4

Robidoux 3
v
Griffiths 5

Thorburn 5
v
Mountjoy 0

Thorne 3
v
White 5

QUARTER-FINALS

Charlton 1
v
Parrott 5

Wych 3
v
Hallett 5

Clark 1
v
Griffiths 5

Thorburn 3
v
White 5

SEMI-FINALS

Parrott 5
v
Hallett 4

Griffiths 5
v
White 4

FINAL

Parrott 9
v
Griffiths 8

Losers: £1,937.50

Losers: £3,000

Losers: £6,000

Losers: £12,000

Loser: £24,000
Winner: £40,000

High break: 116 – C. Thorburn, J. Parrott £4,000 (shared)

ous moment when Ireland's Eugene Hughes walking out in the interval was asked by a lady gambler if he would get her a drink. Hughes said: 'She thought I was a waiter.' Eddie Charlton's opening match was interrupted by a band in an adjoining room playing 'Happy Birthday', while the French air hostess on the flight over was convinced that Dennis Taylor's snooker cue was a fishing rod.

ANGLIAN WINDOWS BRITISH OPEN

Tony Meo, like Doug Mountjoy, also proved that it is foolish to write off good players. Welshman Mountjoy, dismissed as a snooker has-been, had already won the Tennents UK Open and the Mercantile Credit Classic; Meo, in danger of dropping out of the top thirty-two, came up trumps with a shock victory in the Anglian Windows British Open at Derby.

Meo had lived in the shadow of his Matchroom colleagues Steve Davis and Jimmy White for many years, but when he started the tournament at Derby he could have hardly believed that he was going to end up winning a major ranking tournament for the first time. True, there had been victories for Meo before, but always critics had tried to play down those successes. He won the World Doubles with Steve Davis on four occasions, the Winfield Masters in Australia and the English Professional Championship twice. But he had to win a ranking tournament to prove to the doubters that he was a great player.

Meo won the final 13–6 but his after-match celebrations were marred when opponent Dean Reynolds complained that the match had been 'boring'. Reynolds added: 'It wasn't my idea of snooker and I tried to make things happen, but in the end I was totally bored.'

Meo replied: 'Those comments are a bit silly. I was very nervous out there. I would like to win and knock in big breaks in every frame. But that's not snooker – that's called potting!'

Meo had given serious notice of his title intentions when he brushed aside Stephen Hendry 5–3 in the fifth round, while tour-nament favourite Steve Davis was another surprise departure the following night after a 5–1 beating by John Parrott. It was the first time Parrott had ever beaten the man he called the 'Guv'nor'.

The semi-finals produced some remarkable fighting snooker by both Reynolds and Meo. Reynolds, who had beaten Joe Johnson 5–4 from 4–2 behind in the quarter-finals, trailed Parrott 7–4. But he didn't worry, and won the match 9–8. Meo was in even more trouble as he was 8–6 down against Hallett and on two occasions needed snookers to stay alive. He got them and won the match, also with a score of 9–8.

Best of pals: Jimmy White (right) and Patsy Houlihan share a joke during the Anglian Windows British Open. A couple of days later, White withdrew with food poisoning.

Anglian Windows British Open Results

THIRD ROUND		FOURTH ROUND	FIFTH ROUND	QUARTER-FINALS	SEMI-FINALS	FINAL
S. Hendry (Scot)	5	Hendry 5	Hendry 3			
v		v	v			
C. Edwards (Eng)	0					
D. O'Kane (NZ)	5	O'Kane 2		Meo 5		
v		v		v		
A. Jones (Eng)	4					
Dennis Taylor (NI)	4	Roscoe 3	Meo 5		Meo 9	
v		v				
C. Roscoe (Wales)	5				v	
A. Meo (Eng)	5	Meo 5				Meo 13
v						
M. Bennett (Wales)	1					
P. Francisco (SA)	5	P. Francisco 5	P. Francisco 5			
v		v	v			
J. Campbell (Aust)	2					
R. Williams (Eng)	2	Roe 3		P. Francisco 3		
v		v				
D. Roe (Eng)	5					
A. Knowles (Eng)	5	Knowles 0	West 1			
v		v	v			
J. Wych (Can)	2					
B. West (Eng)	5	West 5				
v						
I. Graham (Eng)	1					
C. Thorburn (Can)	5	Thorburn 5	Thorburn 4			
v		v	v			
P. Browne (Rep Ire)	0					
E. Charlton (Aust)	3	Morgan 4		Hallett 5		
v		v		v		
D. Morgan (Wales)	5					
M. Hallett (Eng)	5	Hallett 5	Hallett 5		Hallett 8	
v		v				
N. Gilbert (Eng)	3					
S. Newbury (Wales)	3	Bales 0				
v						
R. Bales (Eng)	5					
J. Virgo (Eng)	5	Virgo 1	Clark 5			
v		v	v			
D. Fowler (Eng)	2					
David Taylor (Eng)	2	Clark 5		Clark 3		
v		v		v		
M. Clark (Eng)	5					
N. Foulds (Eng)	5	N. Foulds 5	N. Foulds 4			
v		v	v			
R. Reardon (Wales)	1					
J. Spencer (Eng)	1	Robidoux 1				
v						
A. Robidoux (Can)	5					

Tournament draw (read left to right):

Round 1

Player	Score		Round 2		Round 3		Round 4		Semi-final		Final
J. White (Eng)	5	v	White								
P. Houlihan (Eng)	3				Reynolds 5						
D. Reynolds (Eng)	5	v	Reynolds w/o	v		v					
L. Dodd (Eng)	2						Reynolds 5				
C. Wilson (Wales)	5	v	C. Wilson 5					v			
J. Rea (Scot)	2			v	C. Wilson 0					Reynolds 9		
S. James (Eng)	3	v	Chappel 3								v	
A. Chappel (Wales)	5											Reynolds 6
J. Johnson (Eng)	5	v	Johnson 5									
T. Whitthread (Eng)	2			v	Johnson 5							
A. Drago (Malta)	5	v	Drago 3			v	Johnson 4					
J. Bear (Can)	2											
T. Griffiths (Wales)	1	v	Johnston-Allen 5									
M. Johnston-Allen (Eng)	5			v	Johnston-Allen 2							
E. Hughes (Rep Ire)	5	v	E. Hughes 2									
W. Jones (Wales)	2											
J. Parrott (Eng)	5	v	Parrott 5									
J. Wright (Eng)	1			v	Parrott 5							
S. Longworth (Eng)	5	v	Longworth 1			v	Parrott 5					
K. Owers (Eng)	1											
S. Francisco (SA)	4	v	Macleod 0					v				
M. Macleod (Scot)	5			v	Mountjoy 2				Parrott 8			
D. Mountjoy (Wales)	5	v	Mountjoy 5									
M. Gauvreau (Can)	0											
W. Thorne (Eng)	5	v	Thorne 5									
Gary Wilkinson (Eng)	1			v	Thorne 0							
R. Chaperon (Can)	2	v	Marshall 1			v	Davis 1					
R. Marshall (Eng)	5											
S. Davis (Eng)	5	v	S. Davis 5									
G. Cripsey (Eng)	1			v	Davis 5							
A. Higgins (NI)	5	v	Higgins 0									
R. Foldvari (Aust)	1											

Losers: £1,531.25   Losers: £3,390.62   Losers: £5,250   Losers: £10,500   Losers: £21,000   Loser: £42,000   Winner: £70,000

High break: 140 - M. Johnston-Allen £7,000

Previous Years' Results

YEAR	WINNER	RUNNER-UP	SCORE
1980	(British Gold Cup)		
	A. Higgins (NI)	R. Reardon (Wales)	5–1
1981	(Yamaha)		
	S. Davis (Eng)	David Taylor (Eng)	9–6
1982	(Yamaha)		
	S. Davis (Eng)	T. Griffiths (Wales)	9–7
1983	(Yamaha)		
	R. Reardon (Wales)	J. White (Eng)	9–6
1984	(Yamaha) Three-man play-off		
	D. Martin (Eng)	J. Dunning (Eng)	3–2
	S. Davis (Eng	J. Dunning	4–1
	S. Davis	D. Martin	3–0
	Winner – Davis		
1985	(Dulux)		
	S. Francisco (SA)	K. Stevens (Can)	12–9
1986	(Dulux)		
	S. Davis (Eng)	W. Thorne (Eng)	12–7
1987	(Dulux)		
	J. White (Eng)	N. Foulds (Eng)	13–9
1988	(MIM Britannia)		
	S. Hendry (Scot)	M. Hallett (Eng)	13–2

FERSINA WINDOWS WORLD CUP

The Fersina Windows World Cup had, wrongly, been looked upon as a 'lesser' event on the snooker calendar. The critics were made to eat their words, however, as last season's final produced one of the greatest finishes of all time.

The Bournemouth Conference Centre was packed as defending champions England went out to face the Rest of the World side. England, naturally, were the clear favourites, especially as they went into a 3–1 lead.

The England trio – Steve Davis, Jimmy White and Neal Foulds – looked certain to collect the £43,200 first prize. But the Rest of the World's captain, South Africa's Silvino Francisco, forgot his poor form to take three of the next four frames against White and sent the match into the interval at 4–4.

Malta's Tony Drago was enjoying an inspired tournament and already, by taking the first frame off Davis, set a new record run of eight straight frame victories – beating the previous best of seven set by Alex Higgins two years earlier.

At night Drago took the first frame off White to put the Rest of the World in front at 5–4. England, however, won four frames in a row to lead 8–5 and the Rest of the World's brave fight looked at an end. But Francisco scored the highest break of the tournament – a 96 – to win the fourteenth frame and that man Drago returned to beat Foulds 2–0 and send the match into a last-frame decider.

Davis was the man entrusted with winning it for England against New Zealand's Dene O'Kane. The atmosphere was incredible and, not surprisingly, both players felt the tension.

Eventually Davis squeezed into a 46–31 lead, but in the end it was O'Kane who knocked in the pink and black to force a re-spotted black – the first time this had happened in the last frame of a major final. One miss now would see the end of the match and it was O'Kane who left the black over a pocket. Davis sunk it to give a relieved England squad their second successive title.

While the Rest of the World went away

Only just: The England team of (left to right) Neal Foulds, Steve Davis and Jimmy White collect the trophy after their 9–8 final win over the Rest of the World in the Fersina Windows World Cup.

Fersina Windows World Cup Results

	QUARTER-FINALS		SEMI-FINALS		FINAL	
S. Davis J. White N. Foulds	England	5				
	v		England	5		
E. Hughes P. Browne A. Kearney	Republic of Ireland	1				
					England	9
			v			
Dennis Taylor A. Higgins T. Murphy	Northern Ireland	1				
	v		Canada	2		
C. Thorburn R. Chaperon K. Stevens	Canada	5				
						v
S. Francisco A. Drago D. O'Kane	Rest of the World	5				
	v		Rest of the World	5		
E. Charlton J. Campbell W. King	Australia	2				
					Rest of the World	8
			v			
T. Griffiths C. Wilson D. Mountjoy	Wales	5				
	v		Wales	3		
S. Hendry M. Macleod J. Donnelly	Scotland	3				

Losers: £8,100   Losers: £13,500   Losers: £27,000
                                                 Winners: £43,200

High break: 96 – S. Francisco £5,400 (shared by the team)

to commiserate, at least they had the satisfaction of knowing that they had the best man of the tournament. Drago had played thirteen frames and won eleven of them.

In the semi-finals England had dismissed Canada 5–2 while the Rest of the World had scored a brilliant 5–3 win over Wales.

Previous Years' Results

YEAR	WINNER	RUNNER-UP	SCORE
1979	(State Express) Wales	England	14–3
1980	(State Express) Wales	Canada	8–5
1981	(State Express) England	Wales	4–3
1982	(State Express) Canada	England	4–2
1983	(State Express) England	Wales	4–2
1985	(Guinness) Ireland A	England A	9–7
1986	(Car Care) Ireland A	Canada	9–7
1987	(Tuborg) Ireland A	Canada	9–2
1988	England	Australia	9–7

BENSON AND HEDGES IRISH MASTERS

The Benson and Hedges Irish Masters had never produced an Irish winner since this most enjoyable of tournaments had started

Well done: Alex Higgins gets a kiss from girlfriend Siobhan Kidd following his success in the Benson and Hedges Irish Masters.

in 1978. Last season there were three Irish hopefuls, but with Dennis Taylor out of form, Jack McLaughlin rated an outsider and Alex Higgins looking for his first title of any note since 1983, there seemed little likelihood of the Irish fans cheering a home-grown success. However, we had reckoned without the Hurricane, for Higgins then proceeded to produce four masterful performances to win the title with a quite remarkable 9–8 final victory over Stephen Hendry.

The final venue – a horse sales ring called Goffs in County Kildare – was full as Higgins, still limping after breaking his foot in an accident, stepped out to tackle Hendry. Even though Higgins had already disposed of three members of the top seven – Cliff Thorburn, Neal Foulds and John Parrott – most of the unbiased observers made Hendry a clear favourite.

Hendry quickly moved into a 4–0 lead, including a break of 105, though Higgins, spurred on by a wildly noisy and totally biased crowd, fought back to 2–5 by the interval. The evening session produced some of the best snooker ever seen in Ireland. With spectators literally hanging from every vantage point, Higgins took four frames in a row to lead 6–5. Hendry's 109 break, however, brought it back to 6–6. Hendry, looking for a Benson and Hedges double after winning the Masters at the Wembley Conference Centre, moved into an 8–6 lead and needed just one frame to win. That was when Higgins, carried along on a human tidal wave of emotion, knocked in breaks of 54, 33 and 62 to win 9–8. The noise was deafening, the atmosphere unbelievable and Higgins could hardly believe he had become a winner again for the first time since that epic 1983 Coral UK success when he came back from 7–0 down to beat Steve Davis 16–15.

Afterwards he said: 'Since that fall I have not had a drink for ten weeks. My mind was clear out there. A few people thought I was an easy touch as I dropped out of the top sixteen but I proved I am still a force to be reckoned with. I was the first Irishman to win the World Championship and now I am the first Irishman to win the Irish Masters. I am very proud.'

Hendry, who had likened the Goffs arena to a bull-ring, had scored his fourth win over Davis in one season when he beat him 6–4 in the semi-final after trailing 3–1. In the second frame Hendry knocked in the highest break of the tournament – a 136.

Higgins' victory over the in-form John Parrott had proved yet another memorable match. Higgins, 4–0 in front, was pulled back to 4–4 and then took the two frames he needed to go into the final 6–4.

There was a bizarre incident in Davis' 5–4 victory over Mike Hallett in the quarter-finals. It occurred when the scores were locked at 3–3, with Hallett leading 64–40, and only 18 points left on the table. Davis, who normally has a computer-like brain, was convinced that he needed only one

Two plus two: Steve Davis 'borrows' a calculator after miscounting the scores during his Benson and Hedges Irish Masters quarter-final win over Mike Hallett.

snooker. He got the snooker and then sunk the blue and pink, leaving himself on the black – and still 8 points behind. He could not believe it, but finally accepted that he was 4–3 down.

He rushed from the arena knowing that he had to turn the fun back on himself. So he took a calculator from the press room and returned to hold it up to the crowd. It did the trick and it was Hallett who felt the pressure as a grimly determined Davis knocked in breaks of 42 and 68 to win 5–4.

But the whole tournament belonged to Higgins. After his ten-week abstinence the Hurricane managed a sip of celebratory champagne but was quickly back on the non-alcoholic cider. Whatever he chose to drink that night, he thoroughly deserved it.

Benson and Hedges Irish Masters Results

FIRST ROUND		QUARTER-FINALS		SEMI-FINALS		FINAL	
		S. Hendry (Scot)	5				
T. Griffiths (Wales)	5	v		Hendry	6		
v		Griffiths	2				
J. McLaughlin (NI)	4						
						Hendry	8
A. Knowles (Eng)	0						
v		Hallett	4				
M. Hallett (Eng)	5	v		S. Davis	4		
		S. Davis (Eng)	5				
						v	
Dennis Taylor (NI)	1						
v		Parrott	5				
J. Parrott (Eng)	5	v		Parrott	4		
		J. White (Eng)	1				
						Higgins	9
A. Higgins (NI)	5						
v		Higgins	5				
C. Thorburn (Can)	4	v		Higgins	6		
		N. Foulds (Eng)	2				

Losers: £4,191.11	Losers: £6,705.78	Losers: £11,316.01	Loser: £16,764.46
			Winner: £27,242.25

High break: 136 – S. Hendry £2,933.78

Previous Years' Results

YEAR	WINNER	RUNNER-UP	SCORE
1978	J. Spencer (Eng)	D. Mountjoy (Wales)	5–3
1979	D. Mountjoy (Wales)	R. Reardon (Wales)	6–5
1980	T. Griffiths (Wales)	D. Mountjoy (Wales)	9–8
1981	T. Griffiths (Wales)	R. Reardon (Wales)	9–7
1982	T. Griffiths (Wales)	S. Davis (Eng)	9–5
1983	S. Davis (Eng)	R. Reardon (Wales)	9–2
1984	S. Davis (Eng)	T. Griffiths (Wales)	9–1
1985	J. White (Eng)	A. Higgins (NI)	9–5
1986	J. White (Eng)	W. Thorne (Eng)	9–5
1987	S. Davis (Eng)	W. Thorne (Eng)	9–1
1988	S. Davis (Eng)	N. Foulds (Eng)	9–4

PROFESSIONAL PLAYERS TOURNAMENTS

The WPBSA allocated £75,000 for three Professional Players Tournaments for members who had been knocked out in the early rounds of certain ranking tournaments. The object of the exercise, according to the WPBSA, was to give the lower-ranked players extra prize money and top-level match practice.

The first of these events was held at Marco's Leisure Centre in Glasgow when Gary Wilkinson came back from 2–0 and 4–3 down to take the £5,000 first prize by beating Alex Higgins 5–4 in the final.

The second Professional Players event took place at Pontin's St Mary's Bay holiday village in Devon where Paddy Browne earned his first professional title with a 5–1 final defeat of world number 14 Peter Francisco.

Despite the success of the first tournament, some of the professionals didn't turn up at Pontin's and the same problem occurred in the third tournament, sponsored by Appleyard Rippon, when David Taylor thrashed Steve Meakin 9–1 in the final in Leeds.

MATCHROOM LEAGUE

Steve Davis collected £70,000, took his season's earnings to a record £661,490 and didn't have to pot a ball to clinch his third successive Matchroom League title.

Davis was at home relaxing when the news came through that Parrott, the only person who could catch him, had been held to a 4–4 draw by Jimmy White in Bath. That result settled the destination of the trophy, but there was still plenty left to play for as the final matches unfolded.

The Matchroom League has been one of snooker's biggest successes, with 'live' matches all over the UK and Europe. Last season there was a first-time game in Iceland and Terry Griffiths discovered the jet-set life when he took part in matches in Finland and Monaco in the space of twenty-four hours. After beating Cliff Thorburn 5–3 in Finland, Griffiths caught three planes and a helicopter, only to be hammered 7–1 by Davis in Monte Carlo.

Parrott, in his first League season, finally clinched second spot when he battered Cliff Thorburn 7–1 in Marseilles, which left the final end-of-season drama at the bottom of the table where any one of five players could have joined Alex Higgins in being relegated last season. In the end, it was all down to the last match in Brentwood, Essex, where Jimmy White had to end Davis's 100 per cent League record if he was to save his place. White did just that and thrashed Davis 6–2, which meant that Terry Griffiths, a spectator at the match, was axed from this season's League.

Snooker history was also made in the League match at Crawley, Sussex, when Thorburn became the first man to score *two* 147s in competitive play. His first had come during the 1983 World Championship while the record-breaker at Crawley was knocked in during the fourth frame of his match with White. The League also held the distinction of being the first tournament to feature two 147s – Tony Meo having achieved the first in 1988.

'After the second black, I went into the pack and the reds split perfectly. It was a great feeling when they all went in – I was very proud,' said Thorburn, who earned £5,000 for his high break performance. But there was no celebration for the Canadian – he was driving and had to wait until he returned home to open a can of beer! Remarkably, White nearly followed with a 147 in the final frame against Thorburn but missed a tenth red. Neal Foulds came even closer a couple of days later when he scored 125 against John Parrott in Watford only to fail on an easy brown.

The League's third season ended in a lavish ball at the Cafe Royal where Matchroom chairman Barry Hearn announced the new format for the 1989/90 season. The Matchroom League, to be sponsored by StormSeal, will be based solely in the UK with ten players competing in forty-five matches. A new Matchroom International Division has been created with six players taking part in fifteen overseas games. Doug Mountjoy and Dennis Taylor were the players invited to take the place of Higgins and Griffiths in the home-based League, while Davis, White, Griffiths, Mike Hallett, Meo and Higgins will this season battle it out in the International Division.

Matchroom League Results

J. Parrott 5, T. Griffiths 3; S. Davis 5, N. Foulds 3; C. Thorburn 5, S. Hendry 3; J. White 4, W. Thorne 4; Thorburn 4, A. Meo 4; Meo 5, Griffiths 3; Parrott 5, Thorne 3; Thorburn 7, White 1; Parrott 5, Foulds 3; White 5, A. Higgins 3; White 5, Griffiths 3; Thorne 4, Foulds 4; Thorburn 5, Higgins 3; Parrott 6, Meo 2; Davis 6, Meo 2; Thorne 5, Griffiths 3; Hendry 4, Foulds 4; Davis 7, Thorne 1; Hendry 5, Parrott 3; Foulds 7, White 1; Thorne 5, Higgins 3; Davis 5, Hendry 3; Davis 6, Thorburn 2; Hendry 5, Meo 3; Foulds 4, Meo 4; Meo 5, White 3; Davis 5, Parrott 3; Foulds 5, Higgins 3; Parrott 7, Higgins 1; Griffiths 5, Thorburn 3; Hendry 5, Thorne 3; Hendry 5, Higgins 3; Davis 7, Griffiths 1; Thorburn 5, Foulds 3; Higgins 4, Meo 4; White 4, Parrott 4; Hendry 6, White 2; Hendry 6, Griffiths 2; Griffiths 5, Higgins 3; Thorburn 5, Thorne 3; Thorne 4, Meo 4; Davis 5, Higgins 3; Griffiths 6, Foulds 2; Parrott 7, Thorburn 1; White 6, Davis 2.

Matchroom League: Final Table

	P	W	D	L	F	A	Pts	Prize Money (£)
Steve Davis (Eng)	9	8	0	1	48	24	24	70,000
John Parrott (Eng)	9	6	1	2	45	27	19	30,000
Stephen Hendry (Scot)	9	6	1	2	42	30	19	25,000
Cliff Thorburn (Can)	9	5	1	3	37	35	16	20,000
Jimmy White (Eng)	9	3	2	4	31	41	11	17,000
Tony Meo (Eng)	9	2	4	3	33	39	10	15,000
Neal Foulds (Eng)	9	2	3	4	35	37	9	13,000
Willie Thorne (Eng)	9	2	3	4	32	40	9	11,000
Terry Griffiths (Wales)	9	3	0	6	31	41	9	9,000
Alex Higgins (NI)	9	0	1	8	26	46	1	5,000

High break: 147 – Cliff Thorburn £5,000

CONTINENTAL AIRLINES LONDON MASTERS

Take a dinner-jacketed audience of 400, throw in the splendour of London's Cafe Royal in the heart of Theatreland, select the best snooker players in the world and you have the perfect recipe for a great night out. That was the format for the £60,000 Continental Airlines London Masters – snooker's first major 'dine and watch' snooker tournament.

The £25,000 first prize ended up in the hands of Stephen Hendry who, despite taking antibiotics for a serious viral ailment, came from 2–1 down in the final to beat stablemate John Parrott 4–2.

Hendry said: 'I was really groggy. I had hardly eaten for three days, my glands were swollen, I had headaches and I had been sick.' Even so, he was smiling after his second victory of the season and he also picked up £3,000 for the high break of 89. The victory took his prize money through the £300,000 barrier.

In the semi-finals Hendry crushed Steve Davis 4–1 – his third win in a row over the world number 1 – while Parrott destroyed White 4–0. Seats at the Masters cost £50 and all the matches, which took place at approximately monthly intervals, were sell-outs.

The event was promoted by Barry Hearn and In Style, a promotions company with Bob Willis, the former England Test crick-

eter, in their ranks. Willis said: 'Major companies love the format – it's a great way for them to entertain their clients throughout the season.'

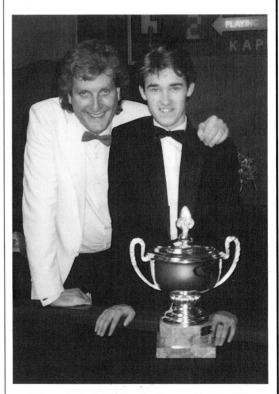

Well batted: Bob Willis, the former England Test cricketer, congratulates Stephen Hendry after his victory in the first Continental Airlines London Masters in the splendid surroundings of the Cafe Royal.

Continental Airlines London Masters Results

FIRST ROUND: S. Hendry (Scot) 4, T. Griffiths (Wales) 0; J. White (Eng) 4, T. Drago (Malta) 1; J. Parrott (Eng) 4, Dennis Taylor (NI) 2; S. Davis (Eng) 4, N. Foulds (Eng) 0
Losers: £2,500

SEMI-FINALS: Hendry 4, S. Davis 1; Parrott 4, White 0
Losers: £6,000

FINAL: Hendry 4, Parrott 2
Loser: £10,000   Winner: £25,000

High break: 89 – S. Hendry £3,000

EMBASSY WORLD CHAMPIONSHIP

Steve Davis, dressed in T-shirt and jeans, arrived unannounced at Sheffield's Crucible Theatre the day before the Embassy World Championship got under way. He took a seat in the still-to-be-finished arena and soaked up the atmosphere.

Seventeen days later, Davis collected the famous trophy for a record-equalling sixth time, accepted the cheers of a sell-out audience and handed the £105,000 winner's cheque to manager Barry Hearn. Davis, sport's supreme professional, had finished work. 'I always drive into Sheffield the day before the tournament starts – just to get the flavour,' he said. 'It's something I do every year. As soon as I see the Crucible, my stomach starts churning over. The butterflies have arrived.'

Davis met John Parrott in the final – a fitting conclusion to a season in which Parrott had jumped up from number 7 to number 2 in the rankings. And Parrott was certainly not going into the final in awe of Davis as he had handed out a 5–1 beating to the world number 1 in the quarter-final of the British Open just the previous month.

But Davis had other ideas. On day 1 Parrott managed to win only three frames as Davis finished 13–3 ahead. Davis had clinically taken apart the second best player in the game. He had destroyed Parrott with a series of telling breaks and immaculate safety play. There was nowhere for Parrott to hide as Davis, without mercy, ground towards a hat-trick of world titles.

Pass the caviar: Steve Davis prefers a sausage sandwich after winning the Embassy World Championship.

On day 2, Bank Holiday Monday, millions watched on television wondering whether Parrott could conjure up a miracle escape. Davis, determined and resolute, won five frames in a row in a mere ninety-one minutes to coast home 18–3 – the biggest margin of victory in Embassy World Championship history. It was snooker of the highest quality, snooker that even surprised Davis' fans.

Yet, Davis revealed, his snooker had been far from World Championship material before a ball was struck at the Crucible. He said: 'I was more vulnerable

Choker (1): Stephen Hendry after losing 16–9 to Steve Davis in the World semi-final.

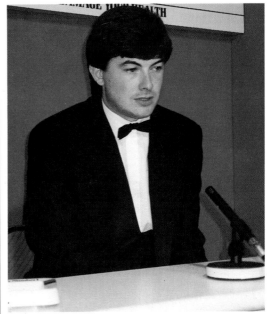

Choker (2): John Parrott who was hammered 18–3 by Steve Davis in the World final.

before this tournament than ever before. My snooker a month ago was not good enough to win the world title. Now I have played the best snooker of my career. I have reached a standard of play that I did not think possible. I did my job very well.'

Davis won three of his matches with a session to spare. It was snooker, at times, without a flaw. Six hours' practice a day with his dad, Bill, had honed the Davis snooker knife to absolute perfection.

Parrott had been looking forward to his first world final after a season in which he had won his first major tournament. The final ended in humiliation but the Liverpudlian, honest as ever, said: 'I played like a slow puncture. I started badly and got worse. I have not played anything like my best and Steve has played exceptionally well. That's a recipe for 18–3.'

But as the champagne flowed into the early hours at the traditional after-match party many people's thoughts were still with the bereaved of the Hillsborough soccer tragedy which happened on the first day of the Embassy. As the tournament got

under way details were coming through to the press room of the rising death toll from the stadium less than three miles away where Liverpool were playing Nottingham Forest in an FA Cup semi-final. The final death toll was to be ninety-five. Of course, everybody was affected by the waste of human life – none more so than Parrott, a Merseyside football fan since he was a small boy.

In the semi-final Stephen Hendry came from 10–2 down against Davis with one of the most inspired sessions in the Championship's history. He finished the second session 13–9 behind after a series of breathtaking frames. Davis' answer the next day was to win the three frames he needed in just thirty-three minutes.

Controversy came in the Dean Reynolds' quarter-final defeat by Tony Meo when referee John Williams warned Reynolds for slow play while he was in the middle of a break. An hour before the match got under way, WPBSA chairman John Virgo had been on TV saying that referees had the power to warn slow

Embassy World Championship Results

FIRST ROUND

S. Davis (Eng) — 10
v
S. Newbury (Wales) — 5

C. Wilson (Wales) — 1
v
S. Duggan (Eng) — 10

M. Hallett (Eng) — 10
v
D. Mountjoy (Wales) — 7

A. Knowles (Eng) — 6
v
D. Roe (Eng) — 10

T. Griffiths (Wales) — 10
v
R. Chaperon (Can) — 6

S. Francisco (SA) — 10
v
J. O'Boye (Eng) — 6

W. Thorne (Eng) — 10
v
P. Browne (Rep Ire) — 5

S. Hendry (Scot) — 10
v
Gary Wilkinson (Eng) — 9

N. Foulds (Eng) — 9
v
W. Jones (Wales) — 10

P. Francisco (SA) — 7
v
D. Reynolds (Eng) — 10

J. Johnson (Eng) — 5
v
A. Meo (Eng) — 10

C. Thorburn (Can) — 9
v
E. Charlton (Aust) — 10

J. Parrott (Eng) — 10
v
S. James (Eng) — 9

Dennis Taylor (NI) — 10
v
E. Hughes (Rep Ire) — 3

J. Virgo (Eng) — 10
v
D. Morgan (Wales) — 4

J. White (Eng) — 10
v
D. O'Kane (NZ) — 7

SECOND ROUND

S. Davis — 13
v
Duggan — 3

Hallett — 13
v
Roe — 12

Griffiths — 13
v
S. Francisco — 9

Thorne — 4
v
Hendry — 13

W. Jones — 3
v
Reynolds — 13

Meo — 13
v
Charlton — 8

Parrott — 13
v
Dennis Taylor — 10

Virgo — 12
v
White — 13

QUARTER-FINALS

S. Davis — 13
v
Hallett — 3

Griffiths — 5
v
Hendry — 13

Reynolds — 9
v
Meo — 13

Parrott — 13
v
White — 7

SEMI-FINALS

S. Davis — 16
v
Hendry — 9

Meo — 7
v
Parrott — 16

FINAL

S. Davis — 18
v
Parrott — 3

Losers: £4,429.68

Losers: £7,875

Losers: £15,750

Losers: £31,500

Loser: £ 63,000
Winner: £105,000

High break: 141 – S. Hendry £10,500

Giantkiller: Darren Morgan, the first-year professional, who beat Alex Higgins 10–8 in the final qualifying round of the Embassy World Championship.

So close: Gary Wilkinson can still manage a smile despite losing 10–9 to Stephen Hendry in the first round of the World Championship.

players – a follow-up to the Cliff Thorburn –Eddie Charlton first-round match which had finished at 2.39 in the morning, the second latest ending to a match at the Crucible. Charlton won 10–9 with forty-eight diehard spectators, albeit five of them asleep, still watching!

The Embassy always has its share of shocks and surprises but this is *the* tournament where the form-horses usually bring forth the goods. The quarter-finals produced the top six players on the 1989/90 rankings – Davis, Parrott, Hendry, White, Terry Griffiths and Mike Hallett – and the two players who reached the final of the British Open, Meo and Reynolds. But, in the final analysis, the famous trophy ended up in the hands of the greatest player the game has ever produced – Steve Davis, MBE.

World Championship Roll of Honour 1927–87

YEAR	WINNER	RUNNER-UP	SCORE	VENUE
1927	J. Davis (Eng)	T. Dennis (Eng)	20–11	Camkin's Hall, Birmingham
1928	J. Davis (Eng)	F. Lawrence (Eng)	16–13	Camkin's Hall, Birmingham
1929	J. Davis (Eng)	T. Dennis (Eng)	19–14	Lounge Billiard Hall, Nottingham
1930	J. Davis (Eng)	T. Dennis (Eng)	25–12	Thurston's Hall, London
1931	J. Davis (Eng)	T. Dennis (Eng)	25–21	Lounge Billiard Hall, Nottingham
1932	J. Davis (Eng)	C. McConachy (NZ)	30–19	Thurston's Hall, London
1933	J. Davis (Eng)	W. Smith (Eng)	25–18	Joe Davis Billiards Centre, Chesterfield
1934	J. Davis (Eng)	T. Newman (Eng)	25–23	Lounge Billiard Hall, Nottingham
1935	J. Davis (Eng)	W. Smith (Eng)	25–20	Thurston's Hall, London
1936	J. Davis (Eng)	H. Lindrum (Aust)	34–27	Thurston's Hall, London
1937	J. Davis (Eng)	J. Lindrum (Aust)	32–29	Thurston's Hall, London
1938	J. Davis (Eng)	S. Smith (Eng)	37–24	Thurston's Hall, London
1939	J. Davis (Eng)	S. Smith (Eng)	43–30	Thurston's Hall, London
1940	J. Davis (Eng)	F. Davis (Eng)	37–36	Thurston's Hall, London
1941–45	No tournament held			
1946	J. Davis (Eng)	H. Lindrum (Aust)	78–67	Horticultural Hall, London
1947	W. Donaldson (Scot)	F. Davis (Eng)	82–63	Leicester Square Hall, London
1948	F. Davis (Eng)	W. Donaldson (Scot)	84–61	Leicester Square Hall, London
1949	F. Davis (Eng)	W. Donaldson (Scot)	80–65	Leicester Square Hall, London
1950	W. Donaldson (Scot)	F. Davis (Eng)	51–46	Tower Circus, Blackpool
1951	F. Davis (Eng)	W. Donaldson (Scot)	58–39	Tower Circus, Blackpool

In 1952, a dispute between the Billiards Association and Control Council and the professional players led to a split and two tournaments were held.

The BA&CC tournament attracted just two players in Horace Lindrum and Clark McConachy, while the professionals organised the World Matchplay Championship in which Fred Davis met Walter Donaldson in the final.

BA&CC Tournament

YEAR	WINNER	RUNNER-UP	SCORE	VENUE
1952	H. Lindrum (Aust)	C. McConachy (NZ)	94–49	Houldsworth Hall, Manchester

World Matchplay Championship

YEAR	WINNER	RUNNER-UP	SCORE
1952	F. Davis (Eng)	W. Donaldson (Scot)	38–35
1953	F. Davis (Eng)	W. Donaldson (Scot)	37–34
1954	F. Davis (Eng)	W. Donaldson (Scot)	39–21
1955	F. Davis (Eng)	J. Pulman (Eng)	37–34
1956	F. Davis (Eng)	J. Pulman (Eng)	38–35
1957	J. Pulman (Eng)	J. Rea (NI)	39–34

Between 1958 and 1963 no matches took place. From 1964 the title was decided on a challenge basis which meant that there was often more than one event per year.

YEAR	WINNER	RUNNER-UP	SCORE	VENUE
1964	J. Pulman (Eng)	F. Davis (Eng)	19–16	Burroughes Hall, London
	J. Pulman (Eng)	R. Williams (Eng)	40–33	Burroughes Hall, London
1965	J. Pulman (Eng)	F. Davis (Eng)	37–36	Burroughes Hall, London
	J. Pulman (Eng)	R. Williams (Eng)	25–22	Match series in South Africa
	J. Pulman (Eng)	F. van Rensburg (SA)	39–12	South Africa
1966	J. Pulman (Eng)	F. Davis (Eng)	5–2	Match series at St George's Hall, Liverpool
1967	No tournament held			
1968	J. Pulman (Eng)	E. Charlton (Aust)	39–34	Co-operative Hall, Bolton
1969	Championship again organised on a knockout basis (Players No. 6)			
	J. Spencer (Eng)	G. Owen (Wales)	37–24	Victoria Hall, London
1970	(Players No. 6)			
	R. Reardon (Wales)	J. Pulman (Eng)	37–33	Victoria Hall, London
1971	(actually held Nov 1970 as a round robin)			
	J. Spencer (Eng)	W. Simpson (Aust)	37–29	Sydney, Australia
1972	(reverted to knockout basis)			
	A. Higgins (NI)	J. Spencer (Eng)	37–32	Selly Park British Legion, Birmingham
1973	(Park Drive)			
	R. Reardon (Wales)	E. Charlton (Australia)	38–32	City Exhibition Hall, Manchester
1974	(Park Drive)			
	R. Reardon (Wales)	G. Miles (Eng)	22–12	Belle Vue, Manchester
1975	R. Reardon (Wales)	E. Charlton (Aust)	31–30	Melbourne, Australia
1976	(Embassy until present day)			
	R. Reardon (Wales)	A. Higgins (NI)	27–16	Town Hall, Middlesbrough, and Wythenshawe Forum, Manchester
1977	J. Spencer (Eng)	C. Thorburn (Can)	25–12	Crucible Theatre, Sheffield
1978	R. Reardon (Wales)	P. Mans (SA)	25–18	Crucible Theatre, Sheffield
1979	T. Griffiths (Wales)	Dennis Taylor (NI)	24–16	Crucible Theatre, Sheffield
1980	C. Thorburn (Can)	A. Higgins (NI)	18–16	Crucible Theatre, Sheffield
1981	S. Davis (Eng)	D. Mountjoy (Wales)	18–12	Crucible Theatre, Sheffield
1982	A. Higgins (NI)	R. Reardon (Wales)	18–15	Crucible Theatre, Sheffield
1983	S. Davis (Eng)	C. Thorburn (Can)	18–6	Crucible Theatre, Sheffield
1984	S. Davis (Eng)	J. White (Eng)	18–16	Crucible Theatre, Sheffield
1985	Dennis Taylor (NI)	S. Davis (Eng)	18–17	Crucible Theatre, Sheffield
1986	J. Johnson (Eng)	S. Davis (Eng)	18–12	Crucible Theatre, Sheffield
1987	S. Davis (Eng)	J. Johnson (Eng)	18–14	Crucible Theatre, Sheffield
1988	S. Davis (Eng)	T. Griffiths (Wales)	18–11	Crucible Theatre, Sheffield

English Championship Results

FIRST ROUND		SECOND ROUND		QUARTER-FINALS		SEMI-FINALS		FINAL	
D.Reynolds	5								
v		Reynolds	4						
A. Harris	1			Rowswell	1				
D. Martin	2								
v		Rowswell	5						
B. Rowswell	5			v		Wilkinson	3		
R. Williams	3								
v		Graham	1						
I. Graham	5			v					
J. Virgo	3			Wilkinson	5				
v		Wilkinson	5						
Gary Wilkinson	5					v		Hallett	9
M. Hallett	5								
v		Hallett	5						
P. Houlihan	2			v					
David Taylor	1			Hallett	5				
v		Price	4						
M. Price	5			v		Hallett	5		
S. Longworth	5								
v		Longworth	5						
R. Marshall	3			v					
A. Knowles	5			Longworth	1				
v		Knowles	4					v	
I. Williamson	2								
J. Parrott	5								
v		Parrott	5						
G. Miles	3			v					
A. Meo	3			Parrott	5				
v		Fowler	4						
D. Fowler	5			v		Parrott	5		
J. Spencer	1								
v		Edwards	0						
C. Edwards	5			v					
J. Johnson	5			Johnson	4				
v		Johnson	5						
D. Gilbert	2					v		Parrott	7
W. Thorne	5								
v		Thorne	5						
M. Clark	1			v					
B. West	4			Thorne	3				
v		Roe	1						
D. Roe	5			v		Foulds	4		
S. James	3								
v		Cripsey	1						
G. Cripsey	5			v					
N. Foulds	5			Foulds	5				
v		Foulds	5						
P. Medati	3								

Losers: £575   Losers: £1,250   Losers: £2,500   Losers: £5,000   Loser: £10,000
                                                                               Winner: £15,500

High break: 130 – J. Parrott £1,300

NATIONAL CHAMPIONSHIPS

ENGLISH CHAMPIONSHIP

There must be something in the Grimsby air that helps breed English champions. Dean Reynolds took the title in 1988 and Mike Hallett captured it twelve months later in front of a sell-out crowd at Redwood Lodge in Bristol.

If no sponsor is found, this will be the last English Championship as the WPBSA channels funds into different tournaments. That seems a sad decision, because there is still a special feeling about being national champion in any sport. Just ask Hallett, who had waited ten years for this first major tournament triumph. The world number 9 had been in two important finals the previous season and had been thrashed in both. This time he made no mistake as he hung on to beat his Cuemasters stablemate, John Parrott.

It was a breathtaking final with Hallett running in three century breaks. He took a 6–2 lead, watched Parrott come back to 7–7 and then captured the last two frames, though he was helped by a fluke on a red when snookered in the final frame. He said: 'I have waited a long time for this. It is a great feeling. The fact that Steve Davis

At last: A happy Mike Hallett after winning his first major title, the English Professional Championship.

and Jimmy White did not enter did not devalue the tournament at all. I was delighted to keep the title in Grimsby.'

Hallett went home a winner and £15,500 richer. The money was nice; the trophy was even nicer.

SENATOR WINDOWS WELSH CHAMPIONSHIP

Doug Mountjoy had enjoyed a most remarkable season, winning two ranking tournaments when his career seemed destined to go steadily downhill. He then made it three wins in one season with a tremendous 9–6 final victory over Terry Griffiths in the Senator Windows Welsh Championship in Newport.

Mountjoy's run of success looked to have come to an end as he trailed 5–2 to his good friend Griffiths. But there was no stopping him as he ran away with frame

after frame to take his fifth Welsh title in ten years. Afterwards Mountjoy said: 'It makes me very proud to be Welsh champion again and that is probably as well as I have played all season.' Griffiths paid the following tribute to his fellow Welshman's success: 'That is the most consistent playing of snooker I have seen from Doug. There was nothing I could do to stop him.'

In the earlier rounds first-year professional Darren Morgan overcame Tony Chappel and then he made Griffiths fight all the way through to the final pink before losing 6–5 in the quarter-final.

The Welsh event was certainly hard fought and Wayne Jones, a runner-up in the Mercantile Credit Classic, lost to Steve Newbury 6–5 in a five-hour battle after at one stage trailing 5–1.

In the semi-finals Griffiths captured four of the last five frames to beat Newbury 9–7 and Mountjoy knocked out Mark Bennett 9–5.

Ticket sales were up by 50 per cent and nearly 4,000 spectators visited the venue in the six days' play.

Welsh Wizard: Doug Mountjoy receives his Senator Windows Welsh Professional trophy.

Senator Windows Welsh Championship Results

FIRST ROUND		QUARTER-FINALS		SEMI-FINALS		FINAL	
		T. Griffiths	6	Griffiths	9		
A. Chappel	5	v					
v		D. Morgan	5			Griffiths	6
D. Morgan	6			v			
		S. Newbury	6	Newbury	7		
		v					v
		W. Jones	5				
		D. Mountjoy	6	Mountjoy	9		
		v					
		R. Reardon	3	v		Mountjoy	9
M. Bennett	6						
v		M. Bennett	6	Bennett	5		
C. Roscoe	3	v					
		C. Wilson	1				
Losers: £150		Losers: £750		Losers: £2,500		Loser: £6,000	
						Winner: £10,500	

High break: 124 – D. Mountjoy £1,200

SCOTTISH CHAMPIONSHIP

John Rea made snooker history when he knocked in a 147 maximum break during the Scottish Championship final. But he didn't make a lot of money!

There was no high break prize on offer as Rea became the first Scot to score the magic maximum in tournament play. He had to make do with a £500 special payment from the WPBSA. Just for good measure Rea, a Clydebank professional, went on to take the title and the £2,000 top prize at Marco's Leisure Centre in Glasgow. The 147 came during his quarter-final match with Ian Black when he was trailing 3–2. Rea said: 'I knew the 147 was on after I had scored 72. There was just one difficult red on the cushion. It was a tremendous feeling when the black went in and the crowd of about 100 went wild. They gave me a standing ovation. In the three previous years there had been a car on offer for a 147 – this time there was nothing. That's just my luck.'

After that Rea beat Jim Donnelly 5–1 in the semi-final and, just to prove the 147 was no fluke, he fired in a 142, 'It must be some kind of record,' said a smiling Rea. 'Two 140-plus breaks in one tournament.'

Maximum man: Scottish champion John Rea who became the first Scot to score a 147 in tournament play and the first player to score a maximum during a national championship.

Scottish Championship Results

QUARTER-FINALS		SEMI-FINALS		FINAL	
M. Macleod	5				
v		Macleod	5		
E. McLaughlin	0				
		v		Macleod	7
E. Sinclair	4				
v		Gibson	1		
M. Gibson	5				
				v	
John Rea	5				
v		Rea	5		
I. Black	4				
		v		Rea	9
J. Donnelly	5				
v		Donnelly	1		
B. Demarco	1				
Losers: £312.50		Losers: £750		Loser: £1,250	
				Winner: £2,000	
High Break: 147 – J. Rea					

IRISH CHAMPIONSHIP

Dennis Taylor, who had dominated the Irish Championship, decided not to compete in the 1989 event at the Antrim Forum. That left the way clear for Alex Higgins (nicknamed 'Hopalong' following a frightening accident at the start of the year when he cut his head and broke his left foot in many places) to dominate the proceedings and win the title with a 9–7 final victory over defending champion Jack McLaughlin. Despite his handicap, Higgins was determined to play in Ireland and the fans responded by packing the venue every time he appeared.

Higgins beat Paul Watchorn 5–2 in the quarter-final and then saw off Eugene Hughes 6–2. In the other half of the draw McLaughlin whitewashed Jack Rea 5–0 and then beat Paddy Browne 6–3.

In the final Higgins lost the first three frames but finished the first session 4–3 ahead. At night McLaughlin failed to cope with Higgins' superb safety play which helped the Hurricane chalk up another success.

Hurricane force: Alex Higgins after winning the Irish Professional Championship.

Irish Championship Results

FIRST ROUND		QUARTER-FINALS		SEMI-FINALS		FINAL	
		J. McLaughlin	5				
Jack Rea	w/o	v		McLaughlin	6		
v		Jack Rea	0				
P. Fagan				v		McLaughlin	7
		T. Murphy	4				
P. Browne	5	v		Browne	3		
v		Browne	5				
D. Sheehan	2					v	
		E. Hughes	5				
A. Kearney	5	v		E. Hughes	2		
v		Kearney	1				
B. Kelly	2			v		Higgins	9
		A. Higgins	5				
P. Watchorn	5	v		Higgins	6		
v		Watchorn	2				
P. Burke	4						
Losers: £150		Losers: £450		Losers: £900		Loser: £2,500	
						Winner: £5,000	

High break: 84 – T. Murphy £300

CANADIAN CHAMPIONSHIP

Professional new boy Alain Robidoux shocked the Canadian snooker fans when he won the Canadian professional title – at his very first attempt. Robidoux, a French-Canadian from Montreal, showed few signs of nerves as he scored an 8–4 win over Jim Wych in the final. Then aged twenty-eight, he started the season ranked 102 in the world, but he had already proved his pedigree by winning the Canadian amateur title on three occasions.

He said: 'Of course I was surprised – I

just went into this tournament determined to do well. I knew in my heart that I could beat some of the players, but I did not expect to win it overall. But you will always have to remember that these players are only human and therefore beatable. You watch players like Cliff Thorburn and Kirk Stevens on television and they just show you the good shots and the best frames so you can end up thinking they are superhuman.'

The tournament was held at the outstanding Westbury Club in Kitchener, Ontario – certainly an impressive venue.

Canadian Championship Results

FIRST ROUND		QUARTER-FINALS		SEMI-FINALS		FINAL	
F. Jonik	w/o	C. Thorburn	6				
v		v		Thorburn	5		
G. Rigitano		Jonik	4				
				v		Wych	4
J. Wych	6						
v		Wych	6				
P. Thornley	5	v		Wych	7		
M. Morra	6						
v		Morra	4				v
G. Watson	2						
A. Robidoux	6						
v		Robidoux	6				
B. Chaperon	3	v		Robidoux	7		
J. Caggianello	6						
v		Caggianello	4				
J. Bear	3			v		Robidoux	8
B. Mikkelsen	6						
v		Mikkelsen	6				
M. Gauvreau	2	v		Mikkelsen	3		
		K. Stevens	5				

Losers: £595.24   Losers: £1,071.43   Losers: £1,904.76   Loser: £3,571.43
                                                                              Winner: £6,428.57

High break: 125 – M. Morra £476.19

AUSTRALIAN CHAMPIONSHIP

John Campbell captured the Australian Championship after a 9–7 defeat of Rob Foldvari at the Returned Soldiers' Club in Sydney – a match that lasted ten hours, seventeen minutes.

The match was stamina-draining, with Campbell making sure of every shot and Foldvari, a former world billiards champion, determined not to give anything away. Foldvari battled to stay with Campbell until Campbell took the lead with two frames left. Then Foldvari went in off in the sixteenth frame and Campbell mopped up the colours to clinch the title.

Foldvari had accounted for title holder Warren King 8–4 in the semi-finals while Campbell overcame veteran Australian Eddie Charlton 8–6.

In the quarter-finals Charlton had whitewashed Greg Jenkins 5–0 and King came through to win 5–4 on the final black against Sam Frangie. Wally Potasnik came from 3–0 down against Foldvari to level at 3–3 before Foldvari pulled away to win.

Australian Championship Results

FIRST ROUND		SECOND ROUND		QUARTER-FINALS		SEMI-FINALS		FINAL	
		S. Frangie	5						
		v		Frangie	4				
		L. Condo	2	v		King	4		
W. Potasnik	5			W. King	5				
v		Potasnik	5			v		Foldvari	7
Edward Charlton	1	v		Potasnik	3				
		Glen Wilkinson				Foldvari	8		
			3	R. Foldvari	5				
		I. Anderson	5	Anderson	0				v
		v		v		J. Campbell	8		
		J. Giannaros	2	J. Campbell	5			J. Campbell	9
		G. Jenkins	5	Jenkins	0	v			
		v		v		Eddie Charlton	6		
		P. Morgan	3	Eddie Charlton	5				
		Losers: £190.48		Losers: £476.19		Losers: £714.29		Loser: £1,047.62	
								Winner: £1,904.76	

High break: 124 – R. Foldvari £142.86

SOUTH AFRICAN CHAMPIONSHIP

Perrie Mans has opted out of the world-wide snooker circuit but that did not stop him regaining his South African professional title with an 8–5 triumph over Robbie Grace in the final at Sturrock Park in Johannesburg.

Mans was once a major force in the world game, finishing runner-up in the World Championship in 1978 and taking the Benson and Hedges Masters title the following year. From 1965 to 1979 he dominated the South African scene; now he was South African champion again.

Mans, seeded number 4, destroyed Derek Mienie 5–0 and then overcame Mike Hines 6–4 in the semi-final. In the other half of the draw Grace beat Lucas Blighnaut 5–3 and then overcame Vic Blighnaut 6–2 in the semi-final.

South African Championship Results

FIRST ROUND		QUARTER-FINALS		SEMI-FINALS		FINAL	
		F. Ellis	1				
M. Hines	5	v		Hines	4		
v		Hines	5			Mans	8
R. Amdai	2			v			
		P. Mans	5	Mans	6		
		v					
		D. Mienie	0				v
		R. Grace	5	Grace	6		
		v				Grace	5
		L. Blighnaut	3	v			
		J. van Rensburg	4	V. Blighnaut	2		
		v					
		V. Blighnaut	5				
Losers: £127		Losers: £760		Losers: £1,266		Loser: £3,038	
						Winner: £5,063	

High break: 66 – P. Mans £127

OTHER TOURNAMENT RESULTS

Winfield Masters

YEAR	WINNER	RUNNER-UP	SCORE
1983	C. Thorburn (Can)	W. Werbeniuk (Can)	7–3
1984	A. Knowles (Eng)	J. Virgo (Eng)	7–3
1985	A. Meo (Eng)	J. Campbell (Aust)	7–2
1986	S. Davis (Eng)	Dennis Taylor (NI)	3–2
1987	S. Hendry (Scot)	M. Hallett (Eng)	371–226 (5-frame agg.)

Kit-Kat Break for World Champions

YEAR	WINNER	RUNNER-UP	SCORE
1985	Dennis Taylor (NI)	S. Davis (Eng)	9–5

BCE Belgian Classic

YEAR	WINNER	RUNNER-UP	SCORE
1986	T. Griffiths (Wales)	K. Stevens (Can)	9–7

Foster's World Doubles

YEAR	WINNERS	RUNNERS-UP	SCORE
1982	(Hofmeister) S. Davis (Eng) A. Meo (Eng)	T. Griffiths (Wales) D. Mountjoy (Wales)	13–2
1983	(Hofmeister) S. Davis (Eng) A. Meo (Eng)	A. Knowles (Eng) J. White (Eng)	10–2
1984	(Hofmeister) A. Higgins (NI) J. White (Eng)	C. Thorburn (Can) W. Thorne (Eng)	10–2
1985	(Hofmeister) S. Davis (Eng) A. Meo (Eng)	A. Jones (Eng) R. Reardon (Wales)	12–5
1986	(Hofmeister) S. Davis (Eng) A. Meo (Eng)	S. Hendry (Scot) M. Hallett (Eng)	12–3
1987	(Foster's) S. Hendry (Scot) M. Hallett (Eng)	C. Thorburn (Can) Dennis Taylor (NI)	12–8

Langs Supreme Scottish Masters

YEAR	WINNER	RUNNER-UP	SCORE
1981	J. White (Eng)	C. Thorburn (Can)	9–4
1982	S. Davis (Eng)	A. Higgins (NI)	9–4
1983	S. Davis (Eng)	A. Knowles (Eng)	9–6
1984	S. Davis (Eng)	J. White (Eng)	9–4
1985	C. Thorburn (Can)	W. Thorne (Eng)	9–7
1986	C. Thorburn (Can)	A. Higgins (NI)	9–8
1987	J. Johnson (Eng)	T. Griffiths (Wales)	9–7

(Above) **Bouncy, bouncy:** Willie Thorne in action.

(Right) **Red nose day:** Stephen Hendry joins in the fun for Comic Relief.

Golden oldies: Former world champions Fred Davis (left) and John Pulman at the WPBSA awards dinner.

(Right) **Head up:** BBC commentator Ted Lowe gets a 'wigging' during the World Team Cup.

On dry land: Accident-prone Steve James (left) and former manager Ken Lowe pictured by the boat they fell out of twenty-four hours earlier in Stoke!

A GAME

(Right) **Post boy:** A cut-out Alex Higgins finds another role as a letter rack.

Wot, no hair? John Spencer impersonates the balding Willie Thorne during a light-hearted moment at the World Championship.

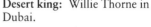

Desert king: Willie Thorne in Dubai.

(Left) **Down and out:** Steve Davis switches off.

THE 'M' MEN: MOUNTJOY AND MEO

DOUG MOUNTJOY
by Bob Holmes

On the face of it, they were unlikely candidates for stardom: Doug Mountjoy, a former miner who does not believe in fairy tales, and Frank Callan, a retired fishmonger who is sceptical about most things, let alone miracles. Yet between them they painstakingly fashioned the snooker story of the season, perhaps of the decade.

Players come to Callan, the game's most celebrated 'guru', from many sources. Superstars come for a 'Krypton' tuning, fallen idols plead with him to resurrect their game, while wealthy Asian eccentrics have flown around the world for him to sort out their waggles. Mountjoy only came from South Wales but it is always a difficult journey from the pit of despair.

Although the craggy smile had never left Mountjoy, the deft touch of the master craftsman had begun to miss some crucial shots. 'My confidence just slowly drained away,' he recalls. 'I didn't feel I had anything left to offer the game and there were times when I just wanted to get off the table.' Losing to Dave Martin in the Mercantile Credit Classic in 1988 finally persuaded the forty-six-year-old Welshman to call Callan. 'I knew Dave had seen him,' he reasoned, 'so I went to Preston and had a session with him. I learned more in those three hours than I had in the previous thirty-four years.'

Initially, Mountjoy had confined his ambitions to regaining the form that had established him as a card-carrying member of the world's elite. He had, after all, won the Welsh title three times in the 1980s, been runner-up to Steve Davis in the World Championship as recently as 1981 and a losing finalist to Cliff Thorburn in the Benson and Hedges Masters four years later. But a bad run had already forced the former coal-face worker to contemplate life among the lower seams. 'I was wondering if I could earn enough at the bottom end of the ladder to stay here,' he admitted as he gazed out over his beloved valleys from his superb bungalow near Pontypool. And suggestions that he had even dreamt of putting away his cue are swept away by the kind of look you might have expected from Salvador Dali if you had tried to snatch his brushes before he died. 'I'm a snooker player – what else would I do?' Mountjoy said.

That first afternoon at the Royale Club in Preston might have satisfied some

Cheers: Doug Mountjoy celebrates with a pint after winning the Tennents UK Open in Preston.

snooker players. 'Frank spotted one or two things right away,' remembers Mountjoy. 'But I knew he'd coached Steve Davis and I wanted more.' Gradually, over countless sessions, Callan rebuilt the Welshman's game. 'He changed my cue, my stance, taught me the pause – in fact there was not much he didn't change. Quite soon I began to feel superior as I realised what could be done with this method,' he admits. But the results still refused to come. 'I lost 13–1 to Neal Foulds in the World Championship and Wayne Jones told me: "You look brilliant – it's a pity you can't pot a ball." '

But Callan saw progress and told him: 'You should be in the top eight inside two years.' The coach had realised that Mountjoy's once-considerable natural talents were waning – but, crucially, were not beyond repair. By his own admission Mountjoy was 'an impetuous Jimmy White type', but he was not White's age. As Callan constantly reminded him: 'Your faculties begin to go at forty and you need to compensate.'

'Doug had the ability,' continues the guru, 'but there was no method to fall back on once he lost his sharpness. What the pause gives you is that extra fraction of a second to transfer your eye to the object ball.' What Callan had also given him was a pause for thought. He gratefully accepted both.

But it did not come easily. Mountjoy sighed: 'When you've been doing something one way all your life, adapting to another method takes some grasping. And after the World Championship, I knew I had a long summer ahead of me.' Callan concurred, using a phrase that indicates their fireproof bond, as he added: 'It took him a while but then he wouldn't win "Mastermind", now would he?'

Even before his long summer ended, however, before the still longer winter began, before he had won a game, Mountjoy admits to having a confidence 'that was something else'. He added: 'I just practised hour after hour and thought, "If it takes a couple of years, so what? I'll have a game at the end of it." ' He stuck at it all right, and, as the world knows, the only misjudgement he made was in the timing. But even Callan was a little too thin on that one.

The first hints of a Mountjoy revival were barely detected by the media. They came in a 5–1 win over Stephen Hendry – yes, the same Hendry – in the fourth round of the Rothmans Grand Prix. He followed that by taking a 4–0 interval lead over Alain Robidoux in the fifth round but, like daffodils in a March snowdrift, these signs of spring were soon enveloped in a 5–4 defeat. And so to Preston.

Callan, on his home ground, had talked about the problems players had in adapting to his controversial style after a lifetime of 'going down a different road'. 'There are no short cuts,' he said, and regarding what seemed then a mere upsurge in form

That's the way to do it: Frank Callan keeps a watchful eye on Mountjoy at a practice session.

> ### WHO SAID THAT?
> 'I thought my days at the top were over. I was going down the rankings and my only thought was that I would try to survive.'
> ▲
> – *Doug Mountjoy after winning the Tennėnts UK Open title.*

by a promising pupil added: 'Doug deserves everything he gets. He's put the work in – I can only advise.'

Among the travelling band that makes up the pro circuit there is no one more intimately involved with on-table happenings than Callan. Now sixty-seven, he failed his national coaching examination and was thirty-two before he made his first century break, but that inauspicious past has not prevented players from flocking to him like wealthy invalids to hot springs.

'I have had some poor fellas on the edge of despair,' he recalls, 'but I'll always try and help 'em out.' And he achieves as much satisfaction from assisting lesser lights as he does with the greats. 'I've had mentally handicapped people, young girls, old men, and if I can put something right, it means as much to me as watching Steve Davis.'

Davis, of course, is his most celebrated pupil and it was through helping 'the Nugget' that Callan established his reputation. 'Meeting Steve was one of the best things that happened to me,' he readily acknowledges, and if Davis now prefers to consult his father, Bill, many of the top pros recognise the debt the world champion owes to Callan by making their own pilgrimage to Preston.

But never has there been a more dramatic or sustained comeback than Mountjoy's. Facing a future as bleak as the Welsh coalfields, he and Callan effected an economic miracle. Yet, as the amiable boyo from the Rhymney Valley raised himself up the mineshaft and back to the promised land of the top sixteen, there were moments when, without the drill that

It's mine: Doug Mountjoy holds the Tennents UK Open trophy aloft and Frank Callan joins in the celebrations.

is now clasped to his consciousness like a safety-belt, he might have teetered into oblivion.

In spite of having subsided to Robidoux in the Grand Prix, Mountjoy's confidence was intact and he knew that in the Tennents UK Open he would have Callan by his side. Avenging that drubbing by Foulds (9–4 in the fourth round) was not a bad way to start, but he did not get carried away by it: 'It wasn't the same Neal,' he said. True, but it wasn't the same Doug either.

Nerves all but betrayed him against both Joe Johnson and John Virgo yet somehow, remembering the drill, he survived to appear 'as relaxed as I've ever felt' for his semi-final with Terry Griffiths. However, even a brilliant display that saw off his lacklustre compatriot 9–4 still left him very much the underdog in the final. Hendry, his opponent, had just given Davis the thrashing of his life in the other semi-final.

The Scottish genius justifiably felt he had done the hard part. 'With respect to Doug,' said Hendry's manager, Ian Doyle, 'the final was an anti-climax. For Stephen, beating Davis was the real final.' The way Hendry played on the first day, it looked as if Doyle was absolutely right. But when the bonnie prince of the baize won Saturday's final frame to level at 7–7, there was only one man who thought an upset was on the cards. That man was Doyle.

'I told his family that it was the worst thing that could have happened. Psychologically he needed to be behind going into that last day,' said the Stirling entrepreneur. That may have been true for the Scot but if, as the afternoon unfolded, Sigmund Freud had been holding his cue and Joe Davis playing the shots, it would not have stopped Mountjoy that day.

From the nervous foothills of a 9–7 lead, the Welsh wizard scaled a peak of excellence to which only the giants aspire. Easing himself into the form of his life, he went 12–7 and, as Hendry's hang-dog look lengthened, 222 points were slotted without reply. Three successive centuries were classically compiled, including one for the highest televised break. One more frame was required for his first ranking tournament victory – and a total of £88,000.

The view from Pontypool had never looked brighter and although Hendry's comeback temporarily obscured the happy vista, the Welshman eventually cleared this obstinate cloud of Scotch mist. Even through his tears of triumph, he did not forget the drill. 'I owe it all to Frank,' he stammered. 'I'm nothing without him.'

'This had to be the best he's ever played and the best result for me as a coach,' said Callan, who really came into his own. 'Reaching the final was like swimming the Channel, but winning it was like swimming the Atlantic!'

'It took a few days to sink in,' Mountjoy admitted, 'but I made sure all the cards of congratulations were down inside a week. My problem was keeping my feet on the ground and I didn't want to dwell on it – or become a one-tournament wonder. But

the trouble was Christmas came and then I won another title so we seemed to have some sort of good wishes up for quite a while.'

Not that these lingering reminders were ever likely to distract a down-to-earth character like Mountjoy. Just as he did before turning pro in 1976, he still 'clocks in for a shift' and, although the demands of his local club's green baize are less arduous than either coalfield or factory, his self-discipline makes the Dalai Lama seem like Alex Higgins.

'And to make sure I get enough work in during tournaments,' he explained, 'I get up at three or four in the morning. Then I have the practise table to myself for a few hours before going back to bed. But even this is no guarantee of peace,' he chuckled, 'as some of the younger lads are just coming in.' Mercifully, however, the maestro is rarely interrupted as they often have trouble finding their rooms, let alone their way around the table.

Mountjoy, of the boxer's face and hooker's build, is as reluctant to tell tales of his not-long-out-of-school colleagues as he is to accept more than a modest slice of acclaim. And it is impossible to be in his company for more than a few minutes without hearing – in reverential tones – the name of the man upon whom he heaps the lion's share. 'My game was in pieces when I went to Frank,' he is fond of saying.

What Callan does not know about snooker is not worth wiping off the cue ball and he has achieved for the rejuvenated Welshman what Superglue might have done for Humpty Dumpty. But the Royale Club is not the only academy of

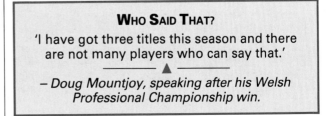

WHO SAID THAT?
'I have got three titles this season and there are not many players who can say that.'
▲
– *Doug Mountjoy, speaking after his Welsh Professional Championship win.*

which Mountjoy is a graduate. Abertysswg Working Men's Club had only one table and no licence in the early seventies, yet produced four Welsh champions with the credentials to take on the world. Mountjoy was one of them.

Yet it was only after a family break of maximum significance – 'taking the missus and kids to Pontin's', where he won a £1,000 tournament – that he turned pro. 'We bought Yvonne a hairdressing business and I looked after Andrew and Yvette during the day, playing snooker in the evenings,' he explained.

Previously the pit had given way to a factory foreman's job in Cardiff, but even though he was perhaps the brightest prospect in the Valleys since first picking up a cue at twelve, he admits: 'I never thought of playing snooker for a living. And even though I could beat most older fellas as a kid, there was no one to ferry me around Jimmy White-fashion. There just wasn't the money down in Wales.'

Indeed, a £10 fee for his first exhibition confirms that, like many Welsh sporting heroes, he was mined from a seam rich in resilience with a solid bedrock of family support. Both saw him through the rela-tively lean time in the mid-1980s and pro-vided a sturdy platform on which Callan could build. 'I may not have been happy with my game,' says Mountjoy, 'but I was a happy man.'

The Mountjoy miracle was almost with-out parallel, for he has not merely returned to the heights he once enjoyed, he has sur-passed them. He has won not one impor-tant tournament but three – each in a different manner. While the Tennents was an exhibition of champagne snooker, at the Mercantile he was inhibited by famili-arity against old pal Wayne Jones and relied on steady draughts of Pilsner – but he still possessed the greater will to win. In the Welsh Professional Championship, he came from behind to beat Terry Griffiths.

After the Mercantile, where the emotion was even greater than at Preston, he had said: 'I just can't believe this is all happen-ing. The UK was a fairy tale, but you can't have two, can you?' A swift look at his bank balance confirmed that he had experienced just that, and when his Welsh winnings brought his credit over £150,000 in three-and-a-half months, no one minded him saying: 'I've got a few bob now.' He could certainly afford to buy

A winner at last: Doug Mountjoy enjoys a joke with the press after winning the Tennents UK Open.

Yvonne the new TV and video he had promised if he got to the semi-final in Blackpool, but, more importantly, any threat to the family's continued residence in those beloved acres outside Pontypool was well and truly removed. 'It's been like a holiday since we came here,' he smiled.

Now that he is back where he belongs on the table too – among the world's elite – the future does indeed look more settled for Pontypool's most famous citizen since it lost its Front Row.

Luck was on his side when a late invitation to the Benson and Hedges Masters at the Drury Lane Theatre in 1977 launched his career in the best possible manner. A semi-final win over Higgins was followed by a 6–5 win over Ray Reardon

and the days of factory shifts and mine shafts were soon forgotten. Or were they?

Mountjoy is a graduate of a hard school, has a happy home life, natural talent and now arguably the game's finest tutor. A former gambler – it was a win on a horse that financed his epoch-making trip to Pontin's – today he leaves nothing to chance. 'I stopped practising with Wayne [Jones] because I thought it might resurrect bad habits,' he said.

And in a final tribute to the man responsible for his own re-emergence, he insists: 'I was re-built not re-born.' With the solidity of his own foundations and the design of his new architect, the renovated edifice will take some toppling. No, Doug, you're right – it's not a fairy tale.

TONY MEO
by Alex Clyde

Tony Meo, the 'born loser' who became a real champion, is a boxing buff. It is probably significant that Robert de Niro is his favourite actor. De Niro has portrayed plenty of tough characters on screen, but

they didn't come any tougher than boxer Jake LaMotta in 'Raging Bull'. Fighting back to win titles when you're on the ropes and all the odds are stacked against you was the name of the game for the gutsy

Flashback: Tony Meo keeps in trim during his early Matchroom days. Barry Hearn looks on.

LaMotta throughout his turbulent ring career. However, until Meo embarked on a memorable fortnight of snooker combat at Derby in February 1989, it was not the sort of approach that even his loyal family and close friends thought he was capable of producing.

But how wrong they were all delighted to be proved, because that is precisely what happened in the Anglian Windows British Open at the Derby Assembly Rooms. The dapper and enigmatic left-hander from South London with the Italian background confounded the snooker world with one of sport's grittiest and most heart-warming leaps from oblivion to glory. The tears of frustration and failure turned into an ocean of tears of victory.

Meo didn't have what it takes, his critics muttered. He was sliding fast down the ladder towards obscurity and would always be remembered as one of snooker's 'Nearly Men'. Okay, they conceded, he had won the English Championship a couple of times and he had been carried along by his mighty partner Steve Davis to four World Doubles titles. But he was never going to win a big one, was he? After all, look what had happened when he had Davis at his mercy in the 1984 Lada Classic final at Warrington. Meo had only to clear the colours to complete a glorious 9–8 victory and he went and fluffed a simple yellow. Excuses didn't matter. 'Bottled it,' they muttered darkly and shook their heads sadly. And wasn't he the man who told the world – to his eternal regret – 'I'm just a born loser' after crumpling to a first-round defeat against John Parrott in the Embassy World Championship in 1986?

Meo, his confidence battered, slipped sadly and painfully out of the elite top sixteen the following year, despite collecting plenty of prize money from non-ranking events that kept him in the top ten of the money list that season. Apart from all the other blows, his pride was badly dented because he was a member of the success-oriented Matchroom team which carried all before it under its voluble and highly competitive manager, Barry Hearn.

Results did not improve during a dismal 1987/88 season and Meo did not even manage to qualify for the final stages of the World Championship at Sheffield. He was in the wilderness, a humble number 31 in the rankings, and a vicious circle seemed to have set in. Confidence, such an important part of a player's game, was low and results were poor.

But Anthony Christian Meo kept plugging away, hoping that his form would pick up and that his self-belief, badly shaken and increasingly fragile, would return. As happens in all the best Hollywood film scripts, Meo reached rock

---

WHO SAID THAT?

'It wasn't my idea of snooker and I tried to make things happen but in the end I was totally bored. I expected more from a final. It's the worst thing that could have happened to Tony as he probably thinks he can win a tournament again playing like that.'

▲

– Dean Reynolds after losing 13–6 to Tony Meo in the final of the Anglian Windows British Open.

'Those comments are a bit silly. My highest break was only 84 but so what? I am the British Open champion. When I started playing, all I knew was to go for my shots. It's all right being a crowd pleaser, but if you don't win where does that get you?'

▲

– Tony Meo after winning the Anglian Windows British Open.

'Sport is about winning, not entertaining. I know a lot of entertaining boxers who are in hospital.'

▲

– Barry Hearn after Tony Meo had won the Anglian Windows British Open and was then criticised for a 'boring' match by beaten finalist Dean Reynolds.

bottom just a matter of weeks before he was destined to bounce back and hit the jackpot with the British Open trophy and £70,000 winner's cheque at Derby. The emotional little Italian was able to cry all the way to the bank after a glorious run of form which included a 5–3 defeat of the defending champion, Stephen Hendry, and a heart-stopping recovery from 6–8 down – 50 points adrift and needing two snookers – to pip Mike Hallett 9–8 in the semi-final, followed by a tactically astute 13–6 massacre of a bemused Dean Reynolds in the final battle of the left-handers.

Yet life had never looked so gloomy just a few short weeks earlier, when an administrative mix-up had seen him arrive in Deauville expecting to play David Roe the following day in the ICI European Open. Meo discovered to his horror that the match had already started and that he had been docked two frames. He rushed into the arena, unshaven and unprepared and duly lost 5–1.

'How can I sink any lower?' he thought on the long gloomy route home. Later he admitted: 'Sitting on the plane, I seriously thought about packing it all in. I must admit I felt really terrible, but I suppose Barry would have talked me out of it.'

That humiliating low point seemed to act as some sort of springboard. After venting his frustration on the practice table, he gritted his teeth and headed for Derby, fuelled by a grim determination to show the snooker world that Tony Meo was a force to be reckoned with, a man who could not be written off as a joke. He told himself that all the ability he possessed as one half of the White-Meo double act – 'the Tearaway Teenagers from Tooting' – could not just vanish. Despite all the knocks and setbacks, A. Meo Esquire, the one-time wonderboy who had lost his way, could still play. All that anger and frustration had to be channelled in the right direction for a change – on to the match table in a big tournament.

This time, everything went right. Comfortable victories over Mark Bennett and Colin Roscoe earned him a place in the last sixteen, but this looked like the end of the road – to everyone bar Meo and his closest friends. His fifth-round opponent was the defending champion, Stephen Hendry.

But Hendry was taken by surprise. Meo got it together and never let the Scot find his rhythm. The result? A thoroughly deserved 5–3 victory, a place in the quarter-finals and a surge of new-found confidence.

Meo recalls his feelings in that match: 'I just took off and, before Stephen knew what was happening, I was 3–1 up. I seemed to find that extra gear. I'm always searching for it but often it doesn't come out. If you could just switch it on like that, you'd be world champion, you'd be the best, you'd be like Davis. But, obviously, not everybody can do that. We can all play on the practice table but it's being able to produce that form in a match that counts.'

Meo's next opponent was fourteenth seed Peter Francisco but in truth his real opponent was himself. The Hendry result was history and he had to start afresh without allowing any reaction of the sort that often afflicts a lesser-ranked player after knocking out one of the top guns.

Meo held himself together well to beat Francisco 5–3 and his reward was a semi-final spot against the ninth seed, Mike Hallett. Meo was back in the groove, looking like his old confident self of four or five years ago, and, although he was concentrating purely on his own matches, his chances of going all the way had not been harmed by events around him.

The big two, Davis and White, were both back home in London. White scratched from his fourth-round match against Reynolds with food poisoning, while Davis had been surprisingly thrashed 5–1 by John Parrott. The euphoria of finally nailing Davis affected the young Liverpudlian who threw away an 8–6 lead and lost his semi-final against Reynolds.

At first Meo had looked a goner against his old rival Hallett. He was swaying on the ropes after trailing 5–2 and 8–6.

Let Meo take up the story of his remarkable fightback. 'I was 5–2 down at the interval and I couldn't complain. I hadn't played badly, but Mike was superb. But I came out for the evening session full of determination. It was a good feeling – different from the final against Reynolds or when I beat Hendry. It was powerful, like I should imagine Mike Tyson gets when he steps into the ring.

'I really felt that if I saw a ball, a half-chance, I could knock it in and clear up. There was no fear, none at all. You've always got that bit of fear – well, I have, anyway – and it makes you nervous. But this time I felt nothing. I just felt great, as if I could kill. It was great, like I could play to my full potential. I was getting aggressive – not with Mike, you understand – but like I could rip the table apart. I was so strong, so confident. Because of that, Mike started to collapse a bit.'

Meo, normally the most sporting and undemonstrative of players at the table – he insists on clapping his opponent's good shots – is not the type to make extravagant theatrical gestures (unlike some players, who shall be nameless). But as he left the arena after coming back from the dead to reach his first major final for over five years, he gave it the full treatment. He punched the air with both fists and the grin from ear to ear was directed at his knot of loyal supporters at the back of the hall.

'I don't normally give it all that,' he confessed sheepishly. 'But I suppose it was the adrenalin. It had worked for me instead of against me this time, and I felt so good.'

The final against Reynolds may have seemed like a bit of an anti-climax to some. It was not the most sparkling snooker match ever played and there were not many big breaks. But it was a triumph of

On the march: Tony Meo in action during the final of the Anglian Windows British Open.

tactics and temperament for Meo, who totally outmanoeuvred his opponent. His safety play was faultless, as was his nerve as he edged towards the finishing line. Reynolds was shut out of the game and foolishly showed himself up afterwards with his churlish remarks about 'a boring match'.

Meo stayed aloof from any sort of slanging match. He left his manager Hearn to fire the bullets, something Mr H. does uncommonly well. Meo contented himself with saying: 'It's no good going for everything and leaving the balls for the other fellow to clear up. Let's just say that Davis wins finals that way and I did it his way. If anyone wants to compare my performance with Davis', I won't be insulted, I'll be flattered.'

The tears and champagne flowed in Derby that night as the reality began to sink in. Great family man that he is, Meo was doubly delighted that his wife Denise, who normally stays at home with their three young children, was there to share in the celebrations. And the partying continued a week later, when their youngest child, Sonny, blew out three candles on his birthday cake. It was like Christmas and Easter rolled into one for Tony Meo, proud snooker champion and proud family man.

Barely twenty-four hours after his triumph, Meo heard these sweet words from the MC at a Matchroom League fixture against Terry Griffiths in Scarborough: 'Tony Meo, British Open champion', and he knew he had made it. He had won a major tournament, an honour no one could ever take away from him or devalue.

'All the hard work has paid off,' he reflected as we talked in the front room of his smart four-bedroom 'semi' in Morden, Surrey, surrounded by large colour photos of the family – Tony, Denise and Gina (then eight), Tony Junior (six) and Sonny.

He said: 'There were times when I got so low that I thought, "What's the point in practising?" I slowed down and only did

That's my man: Tony Meo is congratulated by his wife, Denise, after his victory in the Anglian Windows British Open.

an hour a day, but that was no good. I realise that now. I'm just pleased that I've proved myself – it's taken a big weight off my shoulders. Now, no matter what happens in the future, I have won a major tournament.

'I never felt I got the credit I deserved when I won things in the past. When I won the Australian Masters, they said, "Yes, but it's only a little overseas event." Then when we won the doubles, it was, "It's not a singles title and anyway Davis was carrying him." Then, when I won the English, they said, "It's not a ranking tournament and Davis probably wasn't trying when he beat him."

'Davis "not trying"? Do they know the man? If Davis enters anything, he's incapable of not trying 100 per cent till the blood comes out of his ears.

'That I retained the English was another hurdle. It was a big step and I was really proud. But the mistake I probably made was letting the comments of some people get to me. After I had beaten Les Dodd in my second English final, a couple of journalists had a go at me, saying it had been a scrappy final. For God's sake, I had just won a final and they come out with that. I won't forgive them for those remarks.

'I don't want this to sound like I was feeling all sorry for myself, but I didn't think I got the credit, the recognition I deserved. Every time I achieved something, it seemed to get devalued – but not any more.

'I know I've got to set my sights higher now, but I'm realistic. There are a lot of good players around and I'm not going to get silly and say I'll do this or that. The fact is that I never like to talk too much about targets. I go out and play, taking one match at a time. I do my best, and if I play well and get that feeling that I can move up a gear like I did at Derby, then I will win. That's all you can do.'

His manager Hearn, whose delight at his

Just chatting: Tony Meo talks it over with his Matchroom boss Barry Hearn.

player's triumph ended years of frustration, confessed, 'We have tried everything with Tony – keep-fit, shouting, screaming, crying, cuddling – but in the end he had to do it in his own way and in his own time. We knew when we signed him that Tony had it in him to win a major title, but I didn't expect it would take him seven and a half years.'

Meo is a proud man and he has not forgotten the hurt he felt when the Matchroom men were being introduced at a reception in Hong Kong last year. The speaker went through the other players, listing their achievements and titles, until he came to Meo. 'Then there's Tony Meo,' he told the audience. 'Well, Tony's got 500 Italian suits . . . and his pride and joy is his BMW car.'

'That really hurt,' Meo recalled. 'They could have at least have mentioned my two English titles or the doubles. But I wouldn't have minded so much if they had said my pride and joy was my family, my wife and children. I could have taken that, because it happens to be true. But all the suits and a car? That made me sound flash. I don't know what those people in Hong Kong must have thought of me. I had done a 147 in the League that year as well and

they could have mentioned that. Still, I won't have that problem next time, will I?' he grinned.

Like all good Italians, Meo loves his food and has fought a constant battle to keep his weight down to under 11 stone – he is 5 feet 7 inches tall – but it was a new lean Tony who romped to the first prize in the British Open. 'I know I've had a lean time on the table, but that's not the reason for my being slimmer.' he explained. 'We've had an extension built on the house recently and one of my ambitions was to have my own sauna. I've been making good use of it.'

That was a real slimline tonic, but in case his critics doubt that Meo really believed he could come back, let me quote the words he used when I interviewed him just after he slipped out of the top sixteen in May 1987: 'It's no good saying I'll work harder, because I've done all that, practised all day long. It's something upstairs. I've got to get the balance right. There are plenty of good years left in me and anyone who writes Meo off will be making a big mistake.'

To borrow boxing parlance again, it has been a Rocky road but he produced the big knock-out just when it mattered.

How Did a Chimney Sweep Become Known as the Ballcrusher? A Profile of Len Ganley

by Mark Taylor

Chorus:
Everybody's doing the Len Ganley stance,
Everybody's doing the Len Ganley stance. (*Repeat*)

Keep your arms as rigid as a juggernaut,
Clench your fist, point your knuckles straight ahead,
Do your best to look like a teddy bear,
Then try and pretend to look vertically dead.

Chorus

Praise the lord, you all look so beautiful,
Bulging waistcoats, thirty inch at neck,
Shine your shoes and head for the Crucible,
Brush the baize and keep the crowd in check.

From the album 'Back in the DHSS' by Half Man Half Biscuit, 1986.

If this song strikes you as unusual, just consider the subject matter. A glance at the record sleeve will also reveal a surprising inscription: 'Len Ganley – The Godfather of Punk!'

There can't be many top-class sportsmen, let alone referees, who have become the subject of musical folklore. But then, Len Ganley is no normal referee. He has also been seen crushing snooker balls in television advertisements.

On a par with Dickie Bird in cricket and Clive Thomas in football, Ganley has carved out a bigger name for himself than many of the players for whom he officiates. Ever since Ray Reardon first advised the big Irishman to take up full-time refereeing at a charity night in 1976, Ganley has been one of the most instantly recognisable figures on the circuit. Even that night of Rear-

don's suggestion in Tamworth had a sense of theatre about it. Ganley takes up the story:

'The proper referee hadn't turned up, so the organiser Stan Fiddler asked me to officiate. At one point the crowd was very quiet after Ray had just made a century break and he remarked to them that if it had happened in the World Championship, the place would be coming down with tremendous applause. The reply came back: "Have you seen the size of the so-and-so referee?" Ray looked at me, I looked at him and we both burst out laughing. That was when he advised me to take up refereeing professionally.'

It all seemed a long way from sweeping chimneys. Born on 27 April 1943, Ganley was the youngest of eleven children – four girls and seven boys – living in the small village of Castle-Lane in Lurgan near Belfast, Northern Ireland.

'There really was a castle at the end of the road,' remembers Len. 'My father was a chimney sweep and my mother had a little shop.' The young Ganley was himself a chimney sweep for a time. 'I did it when I was fifteen with another brother – and no, I didn't get stuck up one of the chimneys.

'It was a hard upbringing,' he reflects, but there was one salvation . . . snooker. 'I took up the game at the age of nine, following my brothers into the Catholic Association. Very soon I was one of the best players in the club.'

Len went on to play in the Lurgan, Lisburn and Belfast League and continued playing when, in 1971, he suddenly found himself living in Burton-on-Trent in England.

Suddenly? 'I was visiting my sister during a ten-day holiday in England and I have been there ever since,' he explained. By this time Len also had a wife, Rosaline, and five children. A sixth was born after the journey across the Irish Channel.

Ganley enjoyed a variety of different jobs during these years, including spells as a milkman and a bus conductor – but his first love was still snooker. He twice won the Burton and South Derbyshire title, and in thirty-five years of playing has scored five breaks of over 100 including a very creditable best of 136.

He had also been refereeing for several years before the move to England, but his qualifications were not officially recognised in this country. Nevertheless, following Reardon's advice, it did not take him long to gain his Grade A certificate from the Billiards and Snooker Control Council, and in 1979 he joined the Professional Referees' Association.

Since becoming a full-time referee, Ganley has refereed many major finals, including two Embassy World Championship finals at the Crucible Theatre, Sheffield. These were in 1983, when Steve Davis beat Cliff Thorburn, and in 1987, when Davis beat Joe Johnson.

Len is naturally proud of those two landmarks in his career, but reveals that two other matches were particularly mem-

Me and my mates: Len Ganley enjoys a game of cards with his fellow officials (left to right) Alan Chamberlain, John Street, John Williams and John Smyth.

orable for him in terms of personal enjoyment. 'The match that will always stand out in my mind more than any other has to be the 1983 Coral UK Championship final between Alex Higgins and Steve Davis.' Few who remember that final would argue. It was, of course, the match when Ganley's fellow countryman Alex Higgins pulled off the greatest Houdini act of his life to come back from 7–0 down to triumph 16–15.

The second match is slightly less well-known because it was never seen on television and was also more recent, coming last season in the final of the English Professional Championship between Mike Hallett and John Parrott. Hallett won 9–7 and Ganley remembers: 'The result wasn't important. It was the fact that class snooker was played to the limit with two players giving their all to an audience that appreciated every moment. There were four breaks over 100, one 90 and five over 60 in only a sixteen-frame match.'

Finals apart, Ganley's greatest pleasure in his job has been the travelling abroad. He says: 'I have travelled the world several

Happy Christmas: Len Ganley joins in the festive fun at one of his many charity appearances.

Helping out: Len Ganley helps out as the tables are fitted during a tournament in Hong Kong.

times with the Matchroom and I have enjoyed every moment. I have seen different people from all walks of life, especially in Thailand, Singapore and China.'

But Ganley's good fortune has not made him forget there are many many other people a lot less fortunate than himself. Virtually all of his spare time away from snooker is spent in charity work, arranging events and functions to raise money for multiple sclerosis, cancer research and many other charities. One of the projects towards which his fund-raising activities are directed is a riding school for the mentally handicapped in Shropton. He also assists the Snooker Golf Society, which raises money for handicapped children, and does a lot of work for the Variety Club of Great Britain.

'It gives me a great deal of pleasure just to see the kids' faces at the end of the golf days when they come from a push chair to a mobile chair that they can actually use themselves. It is the greatest feeling in the world,' he explained. 'I look forward to many more years helping people in this way. If any charities need help in any way, I'm the man.'

And a final memory? 'The best laugh I have had in years was when Jimmy White was in the sea just off one of the bays in Hong Kong. We were on the boat and Barry Hearn dared me to jump into the sea. "You must be joking," said Jimmy – so I immediately leapt overboard. Jimmy thought it was a white whale coming out of the sky!'

CAN YOU MAKE THE GANLEY GRADE?

How would you fancy yourself as a professional referee like Len Ganley? Can you see yourself officiating at a World Championship final at the Crucible? Try answering the questions set by Len below, and see how you match up to the Ganley grade. (Answers on page 135.)

1 At the start of a frame, a player breaks off using the yellow instead of the cue ball. Is this a foul? What happens next?

2 A player nominates the green as a free ball after a foul stroke on the yellow with only the colours remaining. He then mishits the shot and has a simultaneous strike on both green and yellow balls. Fair or foul?

3 After a foul stroke, there are two reds on the table – one is snookered by the yellow and the other one by the green, with the white in the middle. The player nominates the green as his free ball and rolls up behind to snooker his opponent on one red, leaving the second red snookered behind the yellow. Fair or foul?

4 A player has potted a red and nominates black. He hits the black very hard and it comes back off the cushion and bounces up on to the top of the pack of reds where it remains. Fair or foul? What happens next?

5 In a foursome, a player plays out of turn and it's not noticed until he is on the green ball. The foul is awarded on green but the next player is also partially snookered. What happens?

6 Player A has missed the black. The black has come to rest on the lip of a pocket and player A has left the table. As player B begins to play the stroke, the ball drops into the pocket. What's the ref's verdict?

7 What action does a referee take when he considers a player to be time wasting?

8 Player A gets down to break off and he misses the balls completely. The cue ball comes to rest immediately behind the pink and snookers player B on all the reds. What does the referee award?

9 A billiards question this time: In a game of 150-up, player A is sitting waiting while his opponent is at the table. Player A's score stands at 148 points and the red and his cue ball are in baulk. His opponent's white is in a pocket. Player B lifts the white out of the pocket and plays a safe miss. What is the situation now?

10 Player A is on a break and has got to the blue when he realises that he has missed out a red. What is the highest break that player B can achieve with the remaining balls?

KING OF THE CUES

by Bruce Beckett

Steve Davis was panic-stricken. His gleaming £30,000 Porsche had just careered off a greasy road and smashed into a brick wall. The car was a write-off, he and his driver were badly shaken, but Davis could think of only one thing – the stick of wood resting on the back seat.

'I could see the case was bent. I had to know whether the cue was broken,' he recalled. 'I could not have put a price on my cue in those days. It was obviously worth more to me than the Porsche.' Fortunately, it was still in one piece.

Times have changed since his lucky escape from that potentially fatal accident in October 1983. Davis has met John Parris – cue maker, cue doctor and the man to whom many of the stars turn when they need urgent surgery performed on their 'right (or left) arm'.

Davis has used the same cue since he was fourteen. 'It was given to me by an old boy at a club in Plumstead. It was his prized possession,' he recalled. Sadly, the man died a month later, so he never saw what good use the cue has been put to. Just like its present owner, it has changed with age. The most famous cue in snooker has suffered from dry rot and in 1987 had its heart broken in two! The ferrule snapped, splitting the top of the cue, during the Rothman's Grand Prix at Reading and, after consultation with Parris, it was decided that the only way to fully repair the damage was to turn it into a two-piece.

'I lost ⅜ inch at the top of the cue, which meant it was too short,' explained Davis. 'To have the butt lengthened would have upset the balance, so it had to be cut in two.' Parris performed the delicate operation and soon reunited Davis with his trusty cue.

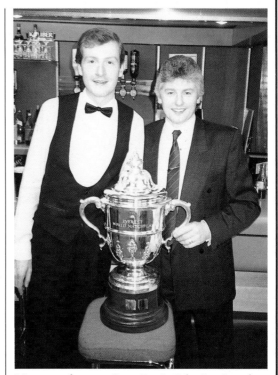

Master craftsmen: Steve Davis, John Parris and the Everest World Matchplay trophy.

If anyone were contemplating stealing the 'lance' used by snooker's knight of the rectangular table, he has some simple advice: 'Don't bother.' Davis has such faith in Parris now that he says: 'I wouldn't hesitate to change my cue if I was forced to. I have played with a few cues that John Parris has made, and if mine broke beyond repair, I would be confident of playing well in a short space of time with a new one. If anyone stole my cue in the belief that they would get a ransom for it, they would be disappointed. I would go straight to John and ask him to make me one similar.'

Parris used to keep a cheque for £200 from Davis on the wall of his workshop. 'People came from miles around just to look at his signature. I never bothered cashing it – it was worth more on the wall,' he said.

My vision of a cue maker was some wrinkled old man peering through horn-rimmed spectacles in a dusty workshop, but Parris hardly fits the bill. He's thirty-seven, married with two children, and looks more the executive type. So how did Parris Cues, advertised as 'The Ultimate in Cue Craftsmanship', get started?

'Basically, through my interest in snooker,' says Parris. 'I began messing around with my own cue, then a few people at my club in Bromley asked me whether I would do repairs and alterations for them. What began as a hobby turned into a full-time job. I was working as a joiner during the day, then staying up until two o'clock in the morning doctoring cues. In the end, one job had to go. I went full-time five years ago. Now I'm lucky if I get time to play snooker once a week!'

Parris converted the garage of his Bromley home into a workshop. But he soon ran out of space and a year ago moved to his present premises down a side street in Forest Hill, South East London. Now he has four people working for him and plans to employ more.

How did he learn his craft? 'Through blood, sweat and tears. There's nobody you can serve an apprenticeship with. Most people are in the mass-production industry, whereas most of our cues are made by eye and feel,' he said. 'I seem to have a knack, a gift for producing good cues. A lot of it is in the feel, sorting out the shafts for each cue. That's one of the longest jobs – putting the labels down on a table and matching the right shaft with the right person.'

Parris produces hand-made cues in batches of sixteen every two weeks, but still demand outstrips supply, as he explained: 'Sales have risen every year. As fast as I can make cues, they are selling. It must reach a peak soon, at least in this country.'

Hand-made cues are hardly cheap. They range in price from £150 to more than £250, but there are cheaper models for the less discerning. A hand-spliced cue will cost you around £140 and a hand-finished one about £80.

Price is no deterrent to the real snooker enthusiast. Parris is even thinking of bringing out a new, top-of-the-range cue, which he plans to call 'The Ultimate'. His cues sell worldwide. There have been orders from Iceland, Cyprus, Malaysia and the Middle East.

While many of the top professionals – Stephen Hendry, Dennis Taylor, Willie Thorne, Tony Drago and Kirk Stevens – play with maple cues, 90 per cent of those made by Parris are ash. 'Most players' first cue is made of maple. Some get used to it,' he explained. 'We make more maple cues for professionals than anyone else. Maple is quite a dense wood and you don't get as much feeling back through the cue.'

Parris buys in planks of ash and maple from England and North America, while the ebony for the splices comes from India and Sri Lanka. 'It's not so much the country of origin but finding a piece of straight-grained timber. We sling out 30 per cent of the wood as it comes off the lorry.' By the time the process is complete, around 70 per cent of the wood has been rejected. Mass producers can use the rejected wood for cheaper-range cues, but Parris throws it away.

He took me through the process of making a cue. Each plank of wood is cut into strips 6 feet long by 1½ inches square. They are then put aside for six months to give the wood time to settle. 'We reject another 20 per cent after that. If a cue is going to leave here with our name on it, each one has to reflect the quality we try to maintain. One bad cue could ruin our reputation,' he said.

The strip of wood is then planed down in four separate stages, spanning three

(Above left) **Plane sailing:** John Parris starts work on a chosen piece of ash. (Above right) **Glued up:** Trainee cue maker Craig Bishop sticks the splices in place. (Below right) **Tip top:** John Parris prepares the tip end of the cue for the ferrule.

months. 'There's still a certain amount of rejection after that. We may find a flaw or a blemish, or the wood just doesn't feel right. It's not until you have planed it down into the shape of a snooker cue that you know whether that particular piece of wood is going to become one of our cues.'

The cue stands for another month, then the moment arrives to match the shafts to individual requirements. 'That's probably the hardest job,' said Parris.

It's now time to cut the shaft to approximately the right length and hand-splice the butt with either ebony or rosewood. The next step is to cut the cue to the exact length and fit the appropriate brass ferrule. The shaft is given its final planing down to meet the exact specification, rough-sanded so that it is fairly smooth, and any final

weight adjustments are made. It might now become a two-piece or three-quarter cue. Seven different grades of sandpaper are used to get it down to a fully smooth finish and the grain is enhanced to bring out the lines – but don't ask how, because it's a trade secret! Linseed oil polish is put on the shaft, the ebony butts are burnished and the last task is to put on the leather tip and name plate. The whole process can take the best part of a year, and Parris says: 'We often get people ringing up to get a progress report on their cue.'

Hand-spliced and hand-finished cues subsidise those made entirely by hand. 'There's not a large profit margin on hand-made cues. When you take into account the amount of work that goes into a hand-made cue and the wastage involved, they

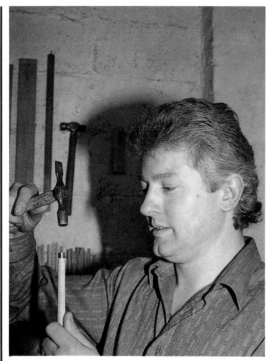

(Above) **Tap in:** John Parris makes sure the ferrule fits correctly.

(Right) **The end:** John Parris stands proudly in front of a case of his hand-made cues.

are actually inexpensive to buy,' he said. 'There's a vast difference between a hand-spliced and a hand-made cue. With the former, it's just a case of the four splices on the butt being done by hand rather than machine. The hand-made cue is exactly what it implies – made entirely by hand from start to finish.'

Parris has been commissioned to make cues by many of the leading professionals. Doug Mountjoy's new cue coincided with his extraordinary return to the snooker big time last season, and while his coach, Frank Callan, rightly took much of the credit, Parris said: 'I like to think the cue played a part in Doug's comeback.'

Parris measures up his customers just like a tailor – length, weight and the thickness of the butt are all important factors when choosing a cue. He explained: 'A lot of it is psychological, but you have to be happy in your own mind with a cue. You must feel confident that it will enable you to play a full range of shots and fulfil your aspirations in the game.'

Some customers are harder to please than others. Parris once spent a day taping weights to the outside of Alex Higgins' cue in an attempt to find the right balance, then returned to his workshop to insert them in the shaft. 'Alex is always seeking the ultimate cue. He will probably never find it,' says Parris.

But back to Davis, and Parris recalled: 'I virtually grabbed him by the throat and told him I was going to make him a cue. He must have thought I was a complete nut case!'

Most professional snooker players take great care of their cue. That was obvious during a bomb scare at Reading a few years ago. There was no time to get dressed when the alarm bell sounded in the early hours of the morning, yet almost every player emerged from the hotel carrying his cue case!

THE BIRTHPLACE OF SNOOKER – BUT THEY HAVE NEVER HEARD OF STEVE DAVIS!

by Chris Bradley

The barman of the Ooty Club unlocked the door. The walls were covered in hunting trophies and animal heads, but in the centre of this small room was what I had come to see – the original snooker table.

The fact that snooker was invented in India is interesting enough for many a quiz programme, but I wanted to know what was left of the birthplace of this great sport. To my surprise, it really was like stepping back a hundred years. Hardly anything has changed and I could imagine well-to-do officers of the British Army passing away idle summer days playing billiards and slowly inventing snooker.

A century ago pyramids, life pool and black pool were all gambling variations and are even played today in some clubs as alternatives to straight snooker. Initially these games relied more upon individual potting skills than later developments such as break building. But they all helped to shape the modern game of snooker, of which the acknowledged inventor was Sir Neville Chamberlain.

Chamberlain was stationed with the Devonshire Regiment at Jubbulpore, Central India. During his stint in 1875, he slightly altered black pool by adding another ball, and over the years different colours and values were also added. But what about the name of this new game?

A young subaltern visiting Chamberlain's regiment told him that a first-year cadet at the Royal Military Academy, Woolwich, was called a 'snooker' – itself a corruption of the French word *neux*, meaning raw or inexperienced. Later on,

Magnificent: The remarkable entrance to the Ooty Club.

during a game, one of the players prevented him from striking a red by laying the cue ball behind a colour and Chamberlain, remembering this new word, called out: 'Why, you're a regular snooker!' To soothe the feelings of the fellow and to explain the definition, he added that they were all, so to speak, snookers at the game. The name stuck.

Rules for this game of snookers, or snooker, were not developed until after 1881 when Chamberlain joined the Commander-in-Chief of the Madras Army for the annual migration from the unbearable summer heat of the Indian plains to Ootacamund (or Ooty, as it was popularly known). The entire town of Ooty in the Nilgiris (Blue Hills) was built by the British for the British. Clearing the jungle hilltop took many years – and many lives, as testified by the engravings on some of the early tombstones at St Stephen's church: 'Eaten by tiger'! Once the area had been cleared, the landscape was not unlike that of Yorkshire or Devon, and the pleasant climate made Ooty the jewel of hill stations. It was to this high-altitude paradise that the whole of Southern Army command moved from April to October.

The 'Snooty Ooty' residences had names like Willow Bank and Fernhill, there were point-to-point races across the rolling hillsides, and the Ooty Hunt met regularly to chase jackals. But it was the Ooty Club that was the centre of British society in 'Injah'. Chamberlain developed his new game of snooker, which gradually became a speciality of the club, and the first proper rules were posted in the billiards room. He spent three years there from 1882 to 1885, by which time news of the game had reached England via returning officers.

The well-respected billiards professional John Roberts, while giving some billiards lessons to the Maharajah of Cooch Behar in Calcutta, was introduced to Chamberlain, and brought these new rules back to England, where the game soon proved its popularity. The rest, as they say, is history.

I recently visited Ootacamund to look at snooker's play-pen. It lies about 150 miles south-west of Bangalore in the state of Tamil Nadu, and just to get there is quite an adventure. The narrow-gauge railway (featured in the film 'A Passage to India') that struggles up the mountain has operational problems that BR could only dream of. Not only is a rack-and-pinion system needed to get trains up the steep incline, but so too are hundreds of gallons of water for the thirsty old steam engines. Half-way there we had to abandon the train as elephants had drunk all the water in one of the mountain water tanks. Not only that, but the elephants were still crashing through the undergrowth when all the passengers were trying to find a path to the nearest road!

The town has been renamed Udagaman-

In play: The famous table which these days is seldom used.

dalam but, not surprisingly, everyone still refers to it as Ooty. The last of the British hangers-on after Indian Independence in 1947 have either joined their forebears in the graveyard or sold out and returned to the UK. Like most Indian towns, Ooty is crowded and colourful, dirty and decaying, but there's something missing. There is no urgency, no chaotic hustle and bustle of normal Indian life. However, it does retain one gem – the Ooty Club.

Immaculately set back into a hillside with long sweeping approaches and neatly clipped lawns up to the porticoed entrance, the club still has an atmosphere of grandeur. There are separate rooms for rummy and bridge, and the dining tables and lounge areas are all laid out for members and their guests. But where are they? Large stuffed fish and even larger tiger skins no longer gaze down on army generals from Secundderabad playing bridge with tea planters from Mysore.

At the rear of the club is the billiards room, approached by way of the Men's Bar where, even today, no women are allowed: equality in India still has a long way to go. The dimly lit room is seldom used, the cover remaining on the Burroughes and Watts eight-legged table for weeks at a time. On the walls are the heads of stags and leopards, and a few military prints and photographs. Alongside the original wooden scoreboard is a framed copy of the letter sent by Chamberlain in 1939 to substantiate Ooty's claim as the birthplace of snooker. In it he states that snooker 'never really made progress until it was played by members of the Ootacamund Club'.

In the corner is an open fireplace in which, the barman – who also acts as a marker – told me, a fire had not been lit for two weeks. With the rain hammering on the roof, the room was freezing. As you can imagine, the table is rather slow, with cushions as lively as soggy paper.

A musty silence lingers around the warping cues, smoke-stained wooden beams and fading photographs. What's left of the British Raj is only just alive.

The club secretary, Lieutenant Colonel K. P. Aiyappa (Retired), whose permission I required to get in, told me that the 'Indian only' membership is so strictly controlled that hardly anyone from Ooty is, or can be, a member. Most of the 320 members live in the large cities and have inherited membership from their rich fathers who bought up mansions from the disappearing Brits. As a round trip from Delhi is 2,500 miles, members think twice before nipping down the club!

Even in 'the season' of April and May, when some still follow the British tradition and head for the hill station, hardly anyone will play the green baize in the back room. Belonging to the Ooty Club is simply a status symbol that does not require use of the club itself. Lieutenant Colonel Aiyappa admitted that he had never heard of Steve Davis!

To liven (and warm) myself up, I headed across town to the Fernhill Palace. This former grand residence is now a busy hotel, despite being a little worn at the edges. On the indoor balcony is a poorly kept snooker table, and I wouldn't have been at all surprised to hear that Jack the Ripper had played there. A game on this table certainly keeps you on your toes as escaping balls from the torn pockets roll off the balcony and plunge 30 feet down on to unsuspecting German and American guests in the dining area below.

So next time you are waiting to get on a table at the local club, think of where it all started. You wouldn't have to wait long to get on to the original table today. But you probably couldn't find an opponent.

(Left) **Bygone age:** The billiard room at the Ooty Club with relics of yesteryear on the wall.
(Right) **What's the score?** The Ooty Club's old-fashioned scoreboard.

CHINESE SOAP OPERAS, A GOLFING 'OASIS' AND A SUPERSTAR WITH HIS FEET IN A BUCKET

by Terry Smith

Stephen Hendry sat at a press conference with his feet in a bucket of water, Jimmy White couldn't go fishing because the tide was out, Steve Davis dressed up as a jockey to play snooker and Dennis Taylor won a golf tournament in the middle of a desert! These were just some of the everyday happenings as snooker's travelling circus spent another season on the global road.

The highly paid international jet-setters kicked off the overseas season in New Zealand at the Lion Brown Masters in Wellington. That's where young Hendry attended a press conference with both feet in buckets of iced water. It was not a pretty sight but essential if he was to take part in a tournament that was being staged at one of snooker's most exclusive venues – the Legislative Council Chamber of the New Zealand Houses of Parliament.

But how did a budding world champion damage his feet? Hendry was relaxing in his hotel room and playing cards with stablemate Mike Hallett when he jumped off the bed, landed badly and twisted *both* ankles. He was whisked away to hospital where X-rays revealed nothing worse than bad bruising. Even so, the physiotherapist gave his considered opinion that Hendry shouldn't play snooker!

Hendry, however, decided he wasn't travelling to the other side of the world to pull out of a tournament. That's how he turned up at the press gathering to sit with his feet in a bucket of water – just to ease the swelling. But the pain of the injuries

meant that he couldn't even practise in a special room, normally used just by Kiwi MPs, that had been made available to the players.

Needless to say, it was Hendry who won in the end, thrashing Mike Hallett 6–1 in the final to collect the £11,250 top prize. With that, Hendry hopped (literally) back on a plane and returned to the UK.

Another excursion was much nearer home – to the millionaire's playground of Deauville on the Normandy coast of

Putting his feet in it: Stephen Hendry had to attend the Lion Brown press conference with his feet in a bucket of water following an accident. He went on to capture the title.

France. Jimmy White, the world number 2, was the centre of attraction as he prepared to take on giant American Steve Mizerak in the £50,000 Fiat Snooker/Pool Challenge with £33,000 to the winner.

Mizerak, all 21 stone of him, had already played world champion Steve Davis in a similar challenge encounter in St Moritz, Switzerland the previous year. Mizerak had won that battle and, with typical American modesty, he had stated: 'If I have beaten the world number 1, the number 2 has got no chance.'

The Challenge followed the lavish reopening of the Deauville Casino which had been attended by such celebrities as Roger Moore, Dustin Hoffman and Christopher Lee. A few millionaires, their wives dripping with gold and diamond adornments, completed the line-up.

The actual matches were held in the chandeliered splendour of the Casino. Here Mizerak won the straight pool 2–0, with White making just three visits to the table. Snooker was next and White knew he had to win 4–0 to stand any chance in the final discipline of eight-ball pool. It all went wrong as Mizerak won a frame with a break of 52, even though White took the

All aboard: Jimmy White and Steve Mizerak go afloat for a publicity shot at the Fiat Snooker/Pool Challenge won by Mizerak.

match 4–1. That made it 4–3 on aggregate to White, but the Mighty Yank won the eight-ball pool 3–0 to record a 6–4 overall success.

The secret in eight-ball is to knock hell out of the cue ball, which Mizerak duly did. 'I have never seen anyone hit a ball that hard,' admitted White. On one occasion a few years ago Mizerak had connected so hard that the ball broke in two!

And the fishing? The TV crews were keen to get out to sea for some 'atmosphere' shots while White and Mizerak did some fishing. Unfortunately the tide was out and the boat couldn't get out of harbour. They finally made the trip later but the fish escaped untouched!

Where next? It was back to Hong Kong, one of snooker's most fascinating and regular watering holes, for the LEP International Masters. There was no more popular winner than Jimmy White, who sent 3,200 Chinese fans totally mad as he beat Neal Foulds 6–3 in the final to earn £28,571.

The Whirlwind, by the very nature of his cheeky character and his attacking style, is adored by the Chinese snooker fraternity. But he had never before been able to produce his best form in the Queen Elizabeth II Stadium. That all changed last season.

It doesn't matter how many times you travel to this British colony, there is always an air of expectation as you fly in between the skyscrapers to land at Kai Tak International Airport. Each year the event proves just how well the local Chinese players are developing their game – just ask Willie Thorne who scraped home 3–2 against Kenny Kwok, a local Chinese soap opera star, and Tony Meo who beat Sunny Tong, a billiard hall manager, 3–2 after trailing 2–1 and 56–8.

Steve Davis was celebrating ten years as a professional while in Hong Kong and the predictable cake was cut while all the players were guests at the Foreign Correspondents' Club, an institution which, like its headquarters, is a real throwback to Britain's colonial past. Davis had no sooner blown out the candles on his cake than he was blown out of the event – 3–2 by Foulds.

And the jockey outfit? There is a traditional end-of-tournament 'race' in which the players try to achieve the quickest time in potting all the colours off their spots. Davis livened up the proceedings by wearing a 'totally over-the-top' dress shirt that made him look like a jockey!

The journey finished with a few holes of golf at the Royal Hong Kong Golf Club where membership costs a mere £100,000. The heat was almost unbearable and some members of the party stayed in the clubhouse while White managed to complete just one hole.

Golf also figured prominently on the next overseas sortie – to the oil-rich, money-no-object Middle East desert state of Dubai for the Dubai Duty Free Masters. And the man who ended up as the winner of the tournament – Neal Foulds – didn't even want to go! Foulds had been desperately disappointed at losing a qualifying round match for the Canadian Masters a day earlier. 'I was just shattered and did not want to play snooker for a while,' he said. But that was all forgotten as he played some of his best snooker for quite some time, culminating in a 5–4 triumph over Steve Davis in the final.

Dubai, which has less than 10 inches of rain a year, boasts what must surely be one of the modern marvels of the world – a championship golf course right slap-bang in the middle of the desert. It takes your breath away to see how they have managed to build this luxuriant green 'oasis' when just yards away nothing grows under the harsh, sweltering sun. The grass was specially imported from America and 750 sprinklers deposit one million gallons of water each day on the fairways and greens.

The Masters was held in the Al Nasr Stadium and the surrounding area was, liter-

(Above) **Happy anniversary:** Steve Davis celebrates ten years as a snooker professional.
(Right) **Taken for a ride . . .** but only on a camel, as Neal Foulds went on to win the Dubai Duty Free Masters.

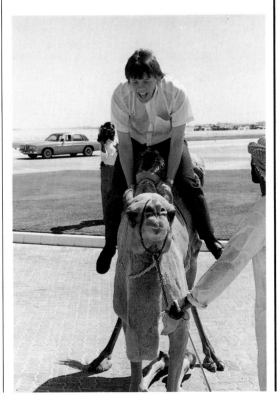

Desert delight: Neal Foulds holds aloft the Dubai Duty Free Masters trophy.

ally, transformed overnight when a local dignatory arrived and decided that the place was not up to scratch. A work party was summoned seemingly out of nowhere and by the next day there was a lawn, flowers and fully grown palm trees in place. Imagine that happening in the UK!

Again local players were used in the first round but, unlike in Hong Kong, they provided little opposition to the eight Matchroom stars. Just to prove the tournament was for real, Davis beat Attiq Qubesi, a student from Abu Dhabi, 2–0 in twenty-one minutes during which Qubesi failed to pot a single ball!

Worldwide travel is now an accepted part of a top snooker player's life – a life that looks like getting more and more hectic. It's hard work leaving home for so many days a year, but it is still a lot of fun – even if you do end up sitting down with your feet in a bucket of water!

Lion Brown New Zealand Masters Results

QUARTER-FINALS: S. Hendry (Scot) bt D. Morgan (Wales) 5–2; J. Johnson (Eng) bt D. Reynolds (Eng) 5–4; M. Hallett (Eng) bt D. O'Kane (NZ) 5–1; A. Knowles (Eng) bt W. King (Aust) 5–4

Losers: £2,600

SEMI-FINALS: Hendry bt Johnson 5–2; Hallett bt Knowles 5–3

PLAY-OFF FOR
THIRD PLACE: Johnson bt Knowles 5–4

Loser: £3,700; Winner: £4,440

FINAL: Hendry bt Hallett 6–1

Loser: £6,750; Winner £11,250

High break: 113 – J. Johnson £750

Fiat Snooker/Pool Challenge Results

S. Mizerak (USA) bt J. White (Eng) 6–4
(Straight pool – Mizerak won 2–0; snooker – White won 4–1; eight-ball pool – Mizerak won 3–0)

LEP International Masters Results

FIRST ROUND: S. Davis (Eng) bt M. Tak Man (Hong Kong) 3–0; N. Foulds (Eng) bt F. Chan (Hong Kong) 3–0; W. Thorne (Eng) bt K. Kwok (Hong Kong) 3–2; A. Meo (Eng) bt S. Tong (Hong Kong) 3–2; J. Parrott (Eng) bt L. Hon Man 3–0; Dennis Taylor (NI) bt I. Li 3–0; T. Griffiths (Wales) bt C. Chor Kwan (Hong Kong) 3–0; J. White (Eng) bt P. Sut Ming 3–1.

QUARTER-FINALS: Foulds bt Davis 3–2; Thorne bt Meo 3–0; Taylor bt Parrott 3–1; White bt Griffiths 3–1

Losers: £3,571

SEMI-FINALS: Foulds bt Thorne 5–4; White bt Taylor 5–2

Losers: £7,143

FINAL: White bt Foulds 6–3

Loser: £10,714; Winner: £28,571

High break: 118 – J. White £2,714

Dubai Duty Free Masters Results

FIRST ROUND: S. Davis (Eng) bt A. Qubesi (Dubai) 2–0; T. Griffiths (Wales) bt A. Marzoo (Dubai) 2–0; Dennis Taylor (NI) bt O. Khalifa (Dubai) 2–0; W. Thorne (Eng) bt G. Philip (Dubai) 2–0; N. Foulds (Eng) bt K. Abbas (Dubai) 2–0; C. Thorburn (Can) bt M. Mohammed (Dubai) 2–0; A. Meo (Eng) bt D. Luisie (Dubai) 2–0; J. White (Eng) bt K. bin Sulayem (Dubai) 2–0

QUARTER-FINALS: Davis bt Griffiths 3–2; Thorne bt Taylor 3–0; Foulds bt Thorburn 3–1; Meo bt White 3–2

Losers: £5,000

SEMI-FINALS: Davis bt Thorne 5–2; Foulds bt Meo 5–1

Losers: £8,000

FINAL: Foulds bt Davis 5–4

Loser: £12,000; Winner: £25,000

High break: 107 – W. Thorne £2,000

DID YOU MAKE GANLEY'S GRADE?
Answers to the questions on page 122

1 This is not a foul. The rule states that the game has not commenced until the tip of the cue comes into contact with the cue ball. The balls are re-racked and re-spotted. (*Score 4 points.*)

2 A simultaneous shot is classified as fair provided that one of the balls is the nominated ball. (*Score 5 points.*)

3 This is a fair shot. (*Score 6 points.*)

4 This is a foul shot, seven away, because the black has not come to rest on the bed of the table. The black is re-spotted and the game continues. (*Score 6 points.*)

5 All points gained in the break up to and including yellow are awarded and a free ball is given because of the partial snooker. (*Score 5 points.*)

6 The ball is determined to have dropped by vibration and is replaced. Player B has another attempt at the shot. (*Score 4 points.*)

7 The referee can warn the player that he is liable to be disqualified. (*Score 6 points.*)

8 He awards a foul and a free ball while player B could ask player A to play again from behind the pink. (*Score 5 points.*)

9 It is not a foul but a miss and player B forfeits 2 points. The game is determined to be over. (*Score 5 points.*)

10 34 including a free ball: two reds (including the free ball), two blacks and the blue, pink and black. (*Score 4 points.*)

How did you get on?
  0–10:   Oh dear, better try croquet!
11–20:   It's not easy, is it?
21–30:   Not bad – but could do with some more homework.
31–40:   Very good – are you after my job?
41–50:   Excellent – when are you refereeing the World final?

LADIES IN SNOOKER

by Gaye Jones

Allison Fisher re-established her position as the undisputed queen of ladies' snooker when she regained her world crown last season, beating defending champion Ann-Marie Farren 6–1 in the final. Such was her dominance of the event and her determination to win that Ann-Marie was the only player to take a frame off her during the entire week.

Allison's most notable performance on the way to her third World Championship final was her semi-final whitewash of long-time rival Stacey Hillyard. Stacey is the player Allison has been most wary of on the ladies' circuit since it was Stacey who beat her in the semi-finals of both the 1984 and 1987 World Championship, in each case coming from 1–3 behind.

A semi-final confrontation at the 1988 World Championship was, therefore, compulsive viewing. The whitewash score-line was actually unkind to Stacey and not indicative of the quality of the snooker and the narrow margin in two or three of the frame scores. What it did show was Allison's absolute determination that she was not going to let the title slip away from her again.

In an interesting paradox, Allison achieved her ambition of regaining the world crown but lost her total dominance of the tournament circuit. Between 1984 and 1988 Allison had not been beaten in any ladies' tournament she had entered apart from the two World Championship defeats by Stacey.

Last season she fell first to Ann-Marie Farren 3–2 in the final of the Hellerman Deutsch and then to Mandy Fisher 4–1 in the semi-final of the British Open. Mandy and Ann-Marie both admitted that, although they had played well themselves,

The Queen of Snooker: Ladies' world champion Allison Fisher.

they felt that Allison had been performing below par and given them an uncharacteristic number of chances.

An important product of these two victories is that Allison has since been taken to tight finishes by other players, but she has always scraped home because her opponents have 'bottled' on the crucial ball.

Like Steve Davis in the men's game Allison's absolute dominance of the ladies' circuit has created a psychological barrier among her opponents who go into matches expecting to get slaughtered and come out delighted to have pinched the odd frame or got close enough to still be able to win on the colours. Ann-Marie's and Mandy's victories have finally shown people that Allison is not infallible – everyone can have a bad day and even Steve Davis gets beaten sometimes!

Allison has also continued to pursue her ambition to become a WPBSA professional player. She competed in the pro-ticket tournaments for the second time and once again missed qualifying by two points.

Over the past year I have noticed a considerable change of attitude among snooker's *cognoscenti*, who now discuss the prospect of a lady professional as an acknowledged fact rather than an amusing pipe-dream. The ambition of Allison, Ann-Marie, Stacey and one or two other women to become part of the WPBSA has provoked much discussion on the merits of ladies aspiring to join the professional circuit. This is frequently referred to as the 'men's circuit', but I would suggest that it is only a men's circuit because there are, at present, no lady members.

After years and years of questioning the discriminatory tactics of many clubs and leagues, I find that many men are now also questioning the validity of banning women from playing snooker on the grounds of sex. The rise of Allison Fisher and other top lady players has stimulated a great deal of interest and discussion on the discrimination issue and whether the professional body would be prepared to accept a woman. I am delighted to say that the WPBSA had the good sense to state in print that if a lady were to qualify for professional status through the pro-ticket system on level terms alongside the men, she would, of course, be accepted should she subsequently qualify as a professional. If those at the top of the game are prepared to accept the fact that a woman could become a professional, how can so many club and league committees continue to retain their nineteenth-century attitudes towards the status of women?

Last season saw ladies' snooker extend its overseas appeal when Mandy Fisher made a trip to Dubai. Mandy continues to work on her thriving exhibition circuit of clubs throughout the UK and still maintains a remarkably high record of wins, even against one or two clubs who have imported 'ringers'! 'Sometimes I can tell they didn't expect me to win because the cheque is only made out for half the fee and they have to pay me the other half in cash,' she says with a wry smile! This season Mandy is scheduled to make more trips to countries abroad, including Japan and Singapore.

Allison Fisher played several exhibitions in Europe and she also jetted off to Canada two days after she had regained her World Championship crown last October. In a hectic twenty-three-day tour Allison managed charity events, challenge matches, coaching sessions and exhibition snooker – which included four century breaks, the highest of which, 117, was televised.

Recognition also came for Allison in the

Dynamic duo: Mandy Fisher, the British Open champion, teams up with John Lowe, the former world darts champion, during the Dart and Cue Exhibition in Manchester.

form of a contract with Barry Hearn's Matchroom League for whom she performed an exhibition match against a local player at each of the League's UK venues. The only hitch was the fact that a Matchroom exhibition prevented her competing in the UK Championship, a title she has held since its inception in 1984.

Having missed out on the chance to compete against the top players as a member of the League itself, Allison got her first real crack at one of the top professionals when she played a seven-frame exhibition agaist Mike Hallett in Edinburgh at the beginning of 1989.

Receiving a 14-point start, Allison proceeded to make a 100 break in the first frame, 87 in the second and 73 in the third, leaving Hallett wondering what had hit him. I doubt that he had expected to spend the first three-quarters of an hour sitting in his chair!

At the end of the first session Allison was 3–1 up and beat Hallett 5–2. 'I played really well,' she said, 'and I was especially pleased to have made a century break in the first frame I had ever played in Scotland.'

The WLBSA staged its first regional championship in 1988 with four players qualifying from each of four regional groupings to play off for the title of National Champion. The WPBSA, which had previously sponsored the B&SCC's Ladies' Snooker Championship which this tournament replaced, agreed to sponsor the WLBSA event to the tune of £2,000. This was a major step forward for ladies' snooker, allowing more players than ever to compete in a single event, encouraged

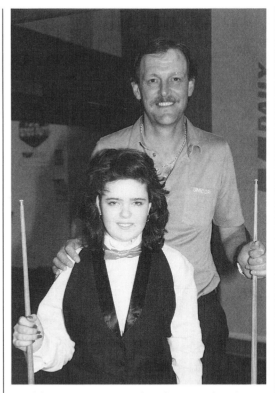

Double top: Lynette Horsburgh pictured with former world darts champion Bob Anderson.

by the fact that the sponsorship was sufficient to pay prize money to the last thirty-two players.

On finals day a little light relief was supplied by Lynette Horsburgh who was desperately trying to borrow a decent cue. She had left her cue out overnight and picked up the empty case as she left the house in the morning! Fortunately her bubbly personality could see the funny side of it and she was philosophical when she lost! The first National Championship title was taken by Allison Fisher who beat Stacey Hillyard 4–3.

RISING STARS

The undoubted sensation of the season was nineteen-year-old Tessa Davidson's victory in the UK Championship. Performing consistently all day and achieving a break of 84 in her semi-final match, Tessa reached her first ever ladies' final and faced

New girl: UK champion Tessa Davidson who made her mark on the ladies' circuit last season.

number 1 seed Stacey Hillyard. Refusing to be over-awed, she took the first two frames before Stacey rallied and looked set to make a match of it. Tessa had other ideas and stormed to a 4–1 victory and her first championship title.

Tessa had always been regarded as a good prospect by a number of players and observers, and in April 1988 she gained her first ranking points with a win over Mandy Fisher. Since then she has risen to number 10 in the WLBSA list and, incidentally, has played Mandy twice more and beaten her both times!

Tessa's husband Mark, himself a good player, said that they practise together quite a lot but ruefully admitted: 'She's better than me now.' Tessa had had a limited amount of coaching but much of what she knew she had learned for herself. 'She's a very deep thinker and she doesn't get upset about things,' he said.

A number of other new names appeared in the top twenty last season. June Banks and Margaret O'Driscoll both chose the 1987 World Championship as their first tournament and both made a considerable impact by taking out seeded players in the last thirty-two and playing each other in a remarkable match which June eventually won after being 2–0 down to take a place in the quarter-finals. Since then they have made steady progress and have recently gained places in the top sixteen. Lisa Gordon from Southend has also shown consistently good form throughout the year to establish herself at number 11 and Sharon Dick (Newport) and Sarah Smith (Sheffield) are also challenging the top players.

Sponsorship is improving too with Holiday Club Pontin's putting £10,000 into the 1988 and 1989 World Championships as well as liaising with the WLBSA to make the Ladies' Bowl Tournament at their Spring Festival a ranking tournament. For the past two years they have been the largest contributor to ladies' snooker and their support is based on their belief in the future of the ladies' game.

Many people now feel that the quality of the top women players justifies a greater input from sponsors in order to allow players to devote themselves to snooker full-time. This is the only route to greater success. But the 'Catch 22' situation of sponsorship requiring media coverage and media coverage not being available without sponsorship unfortunately still applies. Media coverage, particularly that of television, of the professional game is so great that it is almost impossible to gain an outlet for the ladies' game. This is compounded by the fact that few people are aware of the enormous improvement in ladies' snooker over the past two years. Allison Fisher is not the only woman who can play high-class snooker. She is undoubtedly the best, but there are others not far behind and catching up fast.

BILLIARDS

STRACHAN UK CHAMPIONSHIP

There is no doubt that Teesside's Mike Russell is the greatest young influence on the game of professional billiards. He proved that point emphatically with a crushing 7–0 whitewash of experienced player Bobby Close in the Strachan UK Championship final at the Marton Hotel and Country Club in Middlesbrough.

Russell, nineteen, had won the European Championship at the end of the previous season and there was no stopping him against Close as he compiled breaks of 69, 60, 70, 128, 121, 119 and 74 to demoralise his opponent completely.

In the semi-final Russell had crushed world champion Norman Dagley 4–0 to add to the 7–4 beating he gave him in that European final.

Dagley, accepting that Russell is the game's greatest young talent, said: 'I hardly made a mistake and yet I didn't win a frame. Mike never gave me a chance.'

Dagley had reached the last four with a tough 4–3 defeat of Peter Gilchrist, Russell's Teesside colleague. Dagley had then remarked: 'These youngsters are the future of our game.'

It was good to see India's Michael Ferreira reach the other semi-final but, despite a break of 109 in the second frame, Close came through 4–1.

Strachan UK Championship Results

FIRST ROUND		QUARTER-FINALS		SEMI-FINALS		FINAL	
I. Williamson (Eng)	4						
v		Williamson	0				
F. Davis (Eng)	1			Close	4		
R. Close (Eng)	4						
v		Close	4				
H. Griffiths (Wales)	0					Close	0
M. Ferreira (Ind)	4						
v		Ferreira	4				
M. Wildman (Eng)	2			Ferreira	1		
C. Everton (Wales)	w/o						
v		Everton	1				
R. Edmonds (Eng)							
R. Foldvari (Aust)	4						
v		Foldvari	1				
G. Thompson (Eng)	0			Russell	4		
M. Russell (Eng)	4						
v		Russell	4				
H. Nimmo (Scot)	0					Russell	7
P. Gilchrist (Eng)	4						
v		Gilchrist	3				
E. Charlton (Aust)	1			Dagley	0		
J. Karnehm (Eng)	0						
v		Dagley	4				
N. Dagley (Eng)	4						
Losers: £125		Losers: £500		Losers: £1,000		Loser: £2,000	
						Winner: £3,000	

YORKSHIRE BANK PROFESSIONAL PLAYERS' TOURNAMENT

There was no stopping Mike Russell in the second ranking tournament of the season – the Yorkshire Bank Professional Players' Tournament – at the Excelsior Club in Leeds. He collected £2,250 for a 7–2 beating of Ian Williamson, the former UK champion.

Russell looked on his way to his second successive whitewash victory in a final as he took a 5–0 lead, including breaks of 141, 101, 115 and 102.

After the interval Williamson pulled two frames back but Russell soon got into the groove again and, including a break of 133, ran out an easy winner.

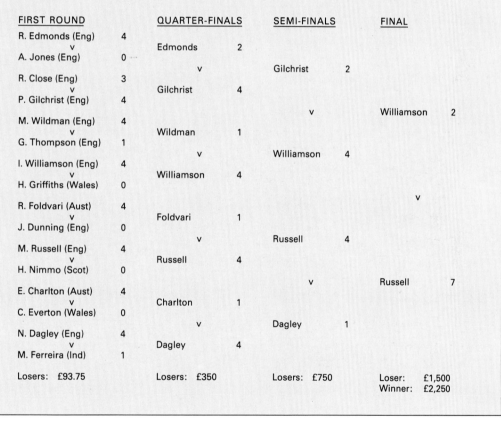

Yorkshire Bank Professional Players' Tournament Results

FIRST ROUND		QUARTER-FINALS		SEMI-FINALS		FINAL	
R. Edmonds (Eng)	4						
v		Edmonds	2				
A. Jones (Eng)	0						
				Gilchrist	2		
R. Close (Eng)	3						
v		Gilchrist	4				
P. Gilchrist (Eng)	4						
						Williamson	2
M. Wildman (Eng)	4						
v		Wildman	1				
G. Thompson (Eng)	1						
				Williamson	4		
I. Williamson (Eng)	4						
v		Williamson	4				
H. Griffiths (Wales)	0						
							v
R. Foldvari (Aust)	4						
v		Foldvari	1				
J. Dunning (Eng)	0						
				Russell	4		
M. Russell (Eng)	4						
v		Russell	4				
H. Nimmo (Scot)	0						
						Russell	7
E. Charlton (Aust)	4						
v		Charlton	1				
C. Everton (Wales)	0						
				Dagley	1		
N. Dagley (Eng)	4						
v		Dagley	4				
M. Ferreira (Ind)	1						
Losers: £93.75		Losers: £350		Losers: £750		Loser: £1,500	
						Winner: £2,250	

BRITISH OPEN CHAMPIONSHIP

Peter Gilchrist, yet another development from the Boys' Billiards League in the North East, won his first professional title when he stopped Mike Russell from achieving a grand slam in the British Open Championship at the Marton Hotel and Country Club in Middlesbrough. Russell was the favourite to beat Gilchrist, his old friend and rival, but it was Gilchrist who came through in the five-hour final 1489–974.

The normal format – best of seven 150

up – had been changed for this event to timed matches and Gilchrist slowed the final down. The plan worked a treat. After the first two-and-a-half-hour session, Gilchrist led 639–514 and in the evening he pulled away to lead 1021–655 by the interval. A break of 101 gave Russell fresh heart, though Gilchrist responded with two high century breaks. Russell's best break of the final – a 143 – pulled him closer, but Gilchrist's 122 enabled him to finish the match off.

Russell said: 'I was exhausted – I have never played a match this long before. I have learnt a lot about myself and I will be

Just champion: Peter Gilchrist is a happy man after winning the British Open.

British Open Championship Results

FIRST ROUND		QUARTER-FINALS		SEMI-FINALS		FINAL	
N. Dagley (Eng)	756						
v		Dagley	561				
E. Hughes (Rep Ire)	541			Close	576		
R. Close (Eng)	576						
v		Close	622				
F. Davis (Eng)	467					Russell	974
M. Russell (Eng)	888						
v		Russell	709				
J. Karnehm (Eng)	726			Russell	1054		
I. Williamson (Eng)	765						
v		Williamson	549				
H. Griffiths (Wales)	239						
						v	
R. Edmonds (Eng)	583						
v		Gilchrist	782				
P. Gilchrist (Eng)	702			Gilchrist	946		
E. Charlton (Aust)	461						
v		Ferreira	632				
M. Ferreira (Ind)	716					Gilchrist	1489
M. Wildman (Eng)	473						
v		Nimmo	449				
H. Nimmo (Scot)	647			Nimmo	518		
R. Foldvari (Aust)	340						
v		Everton	416				
C. Everton (Wales)	466						
Losers: £125		Losers: £500		Losers: £1,000		Loser: £1,500	
						Winner: £3,000	

High break: 250 – M. Russell £500

a better player in the timed matches in the future.'

Clive Everton, recovering from a knee operation, scored a remarkable 466–340

first-round win over the number 2 seed Rob Foldvari but was then edged out by 33 points by Hugh Nimmo in the quarter-final.

ROTHMANS WORLD MATCHPLAY

Mike Russell made it three wins out of four ranking tournaments when he thrashed Ian Williamson 6–1 to take the Rothmans World Matchplay title at the G-Mex Centre in Manchester.

The early rounds of the tournament were held at the Piccadilly Club in the same city, though the players were a little concerned about the lack of proper championship facilities. According to veteran Jack Karnehm, 'There were no tickets or pro-

grammes printed, no seating arrangements, no advertising and no spectators.

'The powers that be should be ashamed to have allowed a world-class tournament to be conducted in such an outrageous fashion. The Piccadilly Club itself was excellent and the generosity of the owners first-class, but the way in which the tournament was allowed to be organised must be the responsibility of the WPBSA officials concerned.'

Rothmans World Matchplay Results

FIRST ROUND		QUARTER-FINALS		SEMI-FINALS		FINAL	
N. Dagley (Eng)	4						
H. Griffiths (Wales)	0	Dagley	4				
				Dagley	3		
H. Nimmo (Scot)	1						
J. Karnehm (Eng)	4	Karnehm	0				
						Russell	6
M. Wildman (Eng)	4						
J. McLaughlin (NI)	0	Wildman	1				
				Russell	4		
M. Russell (Eng)	4						
B. Bennett (SA)	0	Russell	4				
							v
I. Williamson (Eng)	4						
C. Everton (Wales)	1	Williamson	4				
				Williamson	4		
B. Close (Eng)	4						
J. Dunning (Eng)	0	Close	1				
						Williamson	1
M. Ferreira (Ind)	4						
P. Burke (Rep Ire)	0	Ferreira	4				
				Ferreira	2		
R. Foldvari (Aust)	4						
P. Gilchrist (Eng)	0	Foldvari	1				
Losers: £125		Losers: £500		Losers: £1,000		Loser: £1,500	
						Winner: £3,000	

High break: 151 – N. Dagley £500

In the first round Rob Foldvari overwhelmed British open champion Peter Gilchrist 4–0, and the other top players came through safely to the last eight where the winners were Norman Dagley, Russell, Williamson and Ferreira.

Russell earned his final place after a 4–3 win over Dagley – taking the seventh frame with a break of 147, while Williamson beat Ferreira 4–2.

In the final the turning point came in frame four when Williamson, trailing 2–1, had a difficult shot to go level at 2–2. He missed and Russell ran out with a 147 unfinished to make it 3–1. After that there was only one winner – the impressive Russell.

WORLD PROFESSIONAL CHAMPIONSHIP

Mike Russell became, at twenty, the youngest winner of the World Professional Championship after a brilliant final victory over his fellow Teessider Peter Gilchrist in Leura, New South Wales.

Russell, with three wins in four previous tournaments, went into the final as the favourite but it was twenty-one-year-old Gilchrist who took an early 443–147 lead. By the end of the first session Gilchrist was

World Professional Championship Results

FIRST ROUND		QUARTER-FINALS		SEMI-FINALS		FINAL	
N. Dagley (Eng)	1422						
v		Dagley	1547				
H. Nimmo (Scot)	866			Dagley	1001		
B. Close (Eng)	1477						
v		Close	893				
G. Sethi (Ind)	984					Russell	2242
M. Russell (Eng)	2108			v			
v		Russell	1155				
H. Griffiths (Wales)	826			Russell	1685		
I. Williamson (Eng)	998						
v		Williamson	857				
M. Ferreira (Ind)	997						v
R. Edmonds (Eng)	1209						
v		Edmonds	766				
J. Karnehm (Eng)	973			Charlton	743		
E. Charlton (Aust)	889						
v		Charlton	1143				
S. Naisby (Eng)	844					Gilchrist	1347
M. Wildman (Eng)	851			v			
v		Gilchrist	1577				
P. Gilchrist (Eng)	1493			Gilchrist	1336		
R. Foldvari (Aust)	932						
v		Hughes	874				
E. Hughes (Rep Ire)	990						
Losers: £850		Losers: £1,200		Losers: £2,000		Loser: £3,400	
						Winner: £5,000	

High break: 593 – M. Russell £1,000

still in front 720-684, but then Russell turned on the style in spectacular fashion. He knocked in a break of 457 in twenty-seven minutes and went on to complete an outstanding 2242–1347 victory with a break of 593 that took thirty-five minutes. Russell's triumph earned him £5,000 and took his season's earnings to £16,250. That break of 593 also gave him the £1,000 high break bonus.

In the semi-finals Russell scored a 1685–1001 victory over defending champion Norman Dagley who had been looking for a hat-trick of world titles. In the other semi-final Gilchrist overcame Australia's Eddie Charlton 1336–743.

After a qualifying tournament in Leeds, six players joined the top ten to travel to Australia. The highlight of round 1 Down Under was Ian Williamson's 998–997 victory over India's Michael Ferreira. Williamson, 90 behind with eight minutes left, produced an unfinished break of 91 just as the time bell sounded. The biggest shock of the first round was the 990–932 victory by Eugene Hughes over Rob Foldvari, the number 2 seed.

Russell's name is now in the record books as the youngest professional billiards champion, beating the previous mark set by William Cook who was twenty-one when the inaugural tournament took place in 1870.

Billiards Prize Money 1989/90

	Strachan UK	Yorkshire Bank PPT	British Open	Rothmans World Matchplay	World Championship	TOTAL
1 M. Russell	3,000	2,250	1,500 HB 500	3,000	5,000 HB 1,000	16,250
2 P. Gilchrist	500	750	3,000	125	3,400	7,775
3 N. Dagley	1,000	750	500	1,000 HB 500	2,000	5,750
4 I. Williamson	500	1,500	500	1,500	1,200	5,200
5 R. Close	2,000	93.75	1,000	500	1,200	4,793.75
6 M. Ferreira	1,000	93.75	500	1,000	850	3,443.75
7 E. Charlton	125	350	125	–	2,000	2,600
8 R. Foldvari	500	350	125	500	850	2,325
9 H. Nimmo	125	93.75	1,000	125	850	2,193.75
10 M. Wildman	125	350	125	500	850	1,950
11 R. Edmonds	–	350	125	–	1,200	1,675
12 J. Karnehm	125	–	125	500	850	1,600
13 E. Hughes	–	–	125	–	1,200	1,325
14 H. Griffiths	125	93.75	125	125	850	1,318.75
15 C. Everton	500	93.75	500	125	–	1,218.75
16 G. Sethi	–	–	–	–	850	850
16 S. Naisby	–	–	–	–	850	850
18 F. Davis	125	–	125	–	–	250
19 J. Dunning	–	93.75	–	125	–	218.75
19 G. Thompson	125	93.75	–	–	–	218.75
21 J. McLaughlin	–	–	–	125	–	125
21 P. Burke	–	–	–	125	–	125
21 B. Bennett	–	–	–	125	–	125
24 A. Jones	–	93.75	–	–	–	93.75

WITH THE AMATEURS

WORLD AMATEUR CHAMPIONSHIP

Thailand's James Wattana left people in no doubt of his intentions as he went out to the Bicentennial World Amateur Championship in Sydney, Australia. 'I am going to win,' was the promise of the greatest amateur talent in the game.

Wattana, then eighteen and born in Bangkok, had learnt his snooker trade in Bradford. He ended his round-robin section on top of the table with five wins out of five, while his final opponent, English champion Barry Pinches, achieved a similar feat in his group.

In the final Pinches led 6–5 but was to win just two more frames as Wattana took the title 11–8. 'I am delighted for all the people in Bangkok who had set their hearts on this win,' he said.

There were other memorable moments in Sydney, including Canadian Brady Gollan's new championship record break of 135 which he knocked in against West Germany's Matthias Gutowski. That break had overtaken the 134 set by Malta's Jason Peplow just twenty-four hours earlier.

BCE ENGLISH AMATEUR CHAMPIONSHIP

Nigel Bond, of Matlock, already guaranteed a place as a professional this season, capped his amateur career in perfect style by clinching the BCE English Amateur title in Leeds.

Bond, twenty-three, finally came home a 13–11 winner over defending champion Barry Pinches, but he had had to survive a tremendous fightback by Pinches who had levelled at 11–11 after trailing 9–4 in a tense match.

Bond had produced one of the best performances of his career to win the Northern Area title as he beat world amateur champion James Wattana 8–4, while Pinches' second Southern title came with an 8–3 success over Dave Finbow.

Both players are expected to be leading lights on the professional circuit in years to come.

The champion: Nigel Bond after winning the English Amateur title.

WORLD JUNIOR CHAMPIONSHIP

Ken Doherty, nineteen, showed just why he is regarded as the best amateur to come out of the Republic of Ireland with a superb 11–5 victory over England's Jason Ferguson in the World Junior Championship final in Reykjavik, Iceland.

Dubliner Doherty plays most of his snooker in Ilford, Essex, with countryman and mentor Eugene Hughes, but said after his victory in Iceland: 'This is a great win for Ireland. It means more to win it for my country than for myself.'

Doherty's victory in Iceland – the Republic's first world snooker title – followed another first for the talented youngster. He was a leading member of the successful Ireland side that took the Junior Home International Championship title in Hemsby, Norfolk.

BENSON AND HEDGES CHALLENGE

Rutherglen's Drew Henry became the inaugural Benson and Hedges Challenge champion with a 4–2 victory over Billy Snaddon in a thrilling final at the Ambassador Snooker Club in Kirkcaldy. Henry, the 1988 Scottish Champion, was never behind in the final, although Clackmannan man Snaddon twice levelled the scores at 1–1 and 2–2.

It was a superb climax to a tournament that had attracted a record amateur entry of 3,750 players from all over Scotland.

Scottish success: Drew Henry receives the Benson and Hedges Challenge trophy from B. Faloon of Benson and Hedges.

AMATEUR RESULTS 1988/89

SNOOKER

World Championship (Australia)
James Wattana (Thai) 11
Barry Pinches (Eng) 8

BCE English Championship
Nigel Bond (Matlock) 13
Barry Pinches (Norwich) 11

World Junior Championship (Iceland)
Ken Doherty (Rep Ire) 11
Jason Ferguson (Eng) 5

British Isles Under-19
Paul McPhillips (Glasgow) 3
Kevin Young (Liverpool) 0

British Isles Under-16
Ronnie O'Sullivan (Barking) 3
Andy Hicks (Plymouth) 1

BCE Grand Masters
John Halcrow (Scot) 4
Peter Marshall (Hants) 2

UK Pairs
Jason Weston and Matthew Paffett (Portsmouth) 3
Paul Cavney and Michael Stocks (Leeds) 1

Inter-Counties
Merseyside 5
Surrey 2

Inter-Counties Under-19
Yorkshire 5
Devon 2

Matchroom/IOM Home International
Winners: England

Daily Mirror/Pontin's Junior Home International
Winners: Republic of Ireland

Daily Mirror UK Under-19
Steve Murphy (Rep Ire) 4
Darryn Walker (Wolverhampton) 0

Daily Mirror UK Under-15
Mark King (Romford) 3
Ronnie O'Sullivan (Barking) 2

Rothmans Championship
Peter Ebdon (Islington) 4
Darren Clarke (Dartmouth) 3

Benson and Hedges Challenge
Drew Henry (Rutherglen) 4
Billly Snaddon (Clackmannan) 2

Hainsworth TopTable (Billiards and Snooker Foundation)
Mike Dunn (Redcar) 3
Stephen Taylor (South Yorks) 1

BILLIARDS

English Championship
David Edwards (Abertillery) 2791
Peter Shelley (Stoke-on-Trent) 2345

British Isles Under-19
Glen Cromack (Cleveland) 304
Michael Leach (Doncaster) 202

British Isles Under-16
Lee Cuthbert (Cleveland) 319
David Causier (Cleveland) 235

Inter-Counties
Cleveland 902
Staffs and W. Midlands 645

Billiards and Snooker Foundation Under-18
David Causier (Cleveland) 302
Terry Murphy (NI) 300

THE INTERNATIONAL BILLIARDS AND SNOOKER FEDERATION

The International Billiards and Snooker Federation (IBSF), set up in 1973 to stage and organise the world billiards and snooker championships, officially recognised the rights of its members to play for money in 1988 when it deleted the word 'amateur' from its constitution.

The IBSF, which represents more than forty countries, also announced that it would be arranging its own substantial cash tournaments for the benefit of all its members in the future through the formation of a new company, World Snooker Promotions Limited. This move was made out of IBSF frustration at the restricted entry available to the WPBSA 'professional' ranks.

The current chairman of the IBSF is New Zealand's Brien Bennett.

THE BILLIARDS AND SNOOKER CONTROL COUNCIL

For a century the Billiards and Snooker Control Council (B&SCC) was the world governing body for games played on an English billiards table. In 1985 it handed over this responsibility to the International Billiards and Snooker Federation. However the B&SCC and its administration still retain a vital role within the overall running of both games, and its hard-working team of staff have played a large part in the growth of snooker to its present status as the largest participant sport in the UK.

The duties of the B&SCC include making and revising the rules of snooker and billiards, examining and certificating referees all over the world, listing official break and championship records, and organising the English and British Isles national championships for non-professionals.

Through various types of membership – club or individual – players are entitled to enter these national competitions, while a twice-yearly newsletter keeps members up to date with the latest developments in the sport. For full details of B&SCC membership, write to: Billiards and Snooker Control Council, Coronet House, Queen Street, Leeds LS1 2TN; or telephone 0532 440586.

THE BILLIARDS AND SNOOKER FOUNDATION

Set up in 1968 under the joint sponsorship of the Billiards and Snooker Trade Association and the Billiards and Snooker Control Council, the Billiards and Snooker Foundation exists to train young players under eighteen years of age in the basic skills of billiards and snooker. With this aim in mind, the Foundation ensures that there are sufficient fully trained coaches by means of courses held four times a year at the National Sports Centre at Lilleshall under the leadership of national coach Jack Karnehm. Karnehm, a former world amateur billiards champion, is a professional billiards player, best-selling author and well-known BBC commentator.

Fully aware of the growth of the sport worldwide, the Foundation also takes prospective coaches from overseas on the recommendation of their national associations.

The Foundation provides coaches for Pontin's Holidays during the summer. It also runs the Hainsworth TopTable Snooker event and the B&SF Under-18 Billiards Championship.

Decisions regarding the running of the Foundation are taken by a joint committee consisting of members of the Billiards and Snooker Trade Association, officials of the B&SCC, the national coach and the development officer.

The Coaching Scheme

All prospective coaches must attend a course to be instructed in the basic skills of coaching young people up to the age of eighteen. After gaining a certificate, a coach is expected to arrange courses within his or her own area.

Qualifications Required

A prospective coach should be a reasonably competent player of both billiards and snooker. He or she should be dedicated to the sport and its advancement, be able to talk freely, clearly and without embarrassment, and be able to communicate easily with others, particularly young people.

Coaching Course Syllabus
Aims and objects of the Billiards and Snooker Foundation.
1 Instruction techniques.
2 Basic rules of billiards and snooker.
3 History, characteristics, care and maintenance of equipment.
4 Practical demonstration in instruction.

Examination
A written examination on the basic rules of billiards and snooker. Continuous assessment of candidates takes place during the course.

How to Apply for a Place on the Course
To apply for a place on the course for prospective coaches write to: Development Officer, Billiards and Snooker Control Council, Coronet House, Queen Street, Leeds LS1 2TN. Every candidate is required to obtain a letter of recommendation from the League or Association with which he or she is connected so that it can be established that he or she conforms to the necessary requirements.

RULES OF THE GAME OF SNOOKER *

Authorised by
THE BILLIARDS AND SNOOKER CONTROL COUNCIL

THE BILLIARDS ASSOCIATION
Established 1885

THE BILLIARDS CONTROL CLUB
Established 1908

AMALGAMATED 1919

Chairman: Stan Brooke
Secretary and Chief Executive: David Ford

SECTION 1. EQUIPMENT

SECTION 2. DEFINITIONS

SECTION 3. THE GAME

SECTION 4. THE PLAYERS

SECTION 5. THE OFFICIALS

SECTION 1. EQUIPMENT

1. The Standard Table – Imperial

Dimensions
(a) the playing area within the cushion faces shall measure 11ft 8½ins × 5ft 10ins with a tolerance on both dimensions of ± ½in.

Height
(b) the height of the table from the floor to the top of the cushion rail shall be from 2ft 9½ins to 2ft 10½ins.

Pocket Openings
(c) (i) There shall be pockets at the corners (two at the Spot end known as the top pockets and two at the Baulk end known as the bottom pockets) and at the middle of the longer sides.
(ii) the pocket openings shall conform to the templates authorized by the Billiards and Snooker Control Council.

Baulk-line and Baulk
(d) a straight line drawn 29ins from the face of the bottom cushion and parallel to it is called the Baulk-line and the intervening space termed the Baulk.

The 'D'
(e) the 'D' is a semi-circle described in Baulk with its centre at the middle of the Baulk-line and with a radius of 11½ins.

Spots
(f) four spots marked on the centre longitudinal line of the table.
(i) the Spot: 12¾ins from the point perpendicular below the face of the top cushion.
(ii) the Centre Spot: Midway between the centre pockets and equidistant from the faces of the top and bottom cushions.
(iii) the Pyramid Spot: Midway between the centre spot and the face of the top cushion.
(iv) the Middle of the Baulk-line.

1M. The Standard Table – Metric

Dimensions

(a) the playing area within the cushion faces shall measure 3500 mm × 1750 mm with a tolerance on both dimensions of ± 3 mm.

Height

(b) the height of the table from the floor to the top of the cushion rail shall be from 850 mm to 875 mm.

Pocket Openings

(c) (i) There shall be pockets at the corners (two at the Spot end known as the top pockets and two at the Baulk end known as the bottom pockets) and at the middle of the longer sides.

(ii) the pocket openings shall conform to the templates authorized by the Billiards and Snooker Control Council.

Baulk-line and Baulk

(d) a straight line drawn 700 mm ($1/5$th the length of the playing area) from the face of the bottom cushion and parallel to it is called the Baulk-line and the intervening space termed the Baulk.

The 'D'

(e) the 'D' is a semi-circle described in Baulk with its centre at the middle of the Baulk-line and with a radius of 292 mm ($1/6$th the width of the Playing area).

Spots

(f) four spots marked on the centre longitudinal line of the table.

(i) the Spot: 320 mm ($1/11$th the length of the playing area) from the point perpendicular below the face of the top cushion.

(ii) the Centre Spot: Midway between the centre pockets and equidistant from the faces of the top and bottom cushions.

(iii) the Pyramid Spot: Midway between the centre spot and the face of the top cushion.

(iv) the Middle of the Baulk-line.

2. Balls

(a) the balls shall have a diameter of 52.5 mm ($2^{1}/_{16}$ins) with a tolerance of +0.05 mm –0.08 mm.

(b) they shall be of equal weight within a tolerance of
(i) 3 gms per Snooker set, and
(ii) 0.5 gms per Billiard set.

NOTE: A BALL OR SET OF BALLS MAY BE CHANGED WITH THE CONSENT OF THE PLAYERS OR ON A DECISION OF THE REFEREE.

3. Cue

The cue shall be not less than 910 mm (3ft) in length and shall show no substantial departure from the traditional and generally accepted shape and form.

4. Ancillary

'Rests' may be used to provide a bridge for the cue.

NOTE: IT IS THE PLAYERS RESPONSIBILITY TO BOTH PLACE THE REST ON AND REMOVE IT FROM THE TABLE.

SECTION 2. DEFINITIONS

1. Frame

a frame is completed when
(a) conceded, or
(b) the black is finally potted or fouled.

2. Game

a game is an agreed number of frames.

3. Match

a match is an agreed number of games.

4. Balls

(a) the white ball is the cue-ball.
(b) the 15 reds, and
(c) the 6 colours, are object balls.

5. Striker

The person about to play or in play is the striker and remains so until completion of the stroke or break (Sec. 2 Rules 6 & 12).

6. Stroke

(a) a stroke is made when the striker strikes the cue-ball with the tip of the cue.

(b) for the stroke to be a 'Fair Stroke' the following conditions must be met:

(i) At the moment of striking, all balls must be at rest, and where necessary, colours correctly spotted.

(ii) The cue ball must be struck and not pushed.

(iii) The cue ball must not be struck more than once in the same stroke.

(iv) At the moment of striking, at least one of the strikers feet must be touching the floor.

(v) The striker must not touch any ball other than the cue ball as in section (a) above.

(vi) A ball or balls must not be 'forced off the table'.

(c) a stroke is not completed until all balls have come to rest and the referee has decided the striker has left the table.

7. In-hand

(a) the cue-ball is in-hand when it has entered a pocket or has been forced off the table.

(b) it remains in-hand until played fairly from in-hand or a foul is committed whilst the ball is on the table.

8. Ball in Play

(a) the cue-ball is in play when not in-hand.

(b) object balls are in play when spotted and remain so until pocketed or forced off the table.

NOTE: USING THE CUE TO POSITION THE CUE-BALL
IF THE REFEREE CONSIDERS THE PLAYER IS NOT ATTEMPTING TO PLAY A STROKE, EVEN THOUGH THE TIP OF THE CUE TOUCHES THE CUE-BALL, THE BALL IS NOT IN PLAY.

9. Ball on

Any ball which may be lawfully hit by the first impact of the cue-ball is said to be *on*.

10. Nominated ball

A nominated ball is the object ball which the striker declares, or indicates to the satisfaction of the referee, he undertakes to hit with the first impact of the cue-ball.

NOTE: IF REQUESTED BY THE REFEREE THE STRIKER MUST DECLARE WHICH BALL HE IS ON.

11. Pot

(a) a pot is when an object ball, after contact with another ball, and without any contravention of these rules, enters a pocket.

(b) if a colour, it shall be spotted before the next stroke is made, until finally potted under Sec. 3 Rule 3.

(c) if a stroke is made, with a ball or balls incorrectly spotted, and a foul is not awarded, the ball or balls
   (i) if on the table will be considered to be correctly spotted.
   (ii) if not on the table will be spotted when the foul is awarded.

NOTE:

(I) IT IS THE STRIKERS RESPONSIBILITY TO ENSURE THAT ALL BALLS ARE CORRECTLY SPOTTED BEFORE STRIKING.

(II) SUBJECT TO SEC. 3 RULES 8 & 12, REDS ARE NEVER REPLACED ON THE TABLE DESPITE THE FACT THAT A PLAYER MAY BENEFIT FROM A FOUL.

12. Break

(a) if a ball is potted, the same player plays the next stroke.

(b) a break is a number of pots in succession made in any one turn.

13. Forced off the table

(a) a ball is forced off the table if it comes to rest other than on the bed of the table or in a pocket.

(b) if a colour it shall be spotted as per Sec. 3 Rule 6 before the next stroke is made.

14. Foul

A foul is any act in contravention of these rules.

15. Snookered

(a) the cue-ball is snookered when a direct stroke in a straight line to any part of every ball *on* is obstructed by a ball or balls not *on*.

NOTE: IF THERE IS ANY ONE BALL THAT IS NOT SO OBSTRUCTED, THE CUE-BALL IS NOT SNOOKERED.

(b) if in-hand, the cue-ball is snookered only if obstructed from all positions on or within the lines of the 'D'.

(c) if the cue-ball is obstructed by more than one ball, the one nearest to the cue-ball is the effective snookering ball.

16. Angled

(a) the cue-ball is angled when a direct stroke in a straight line to any part of every ball *on* is obstructed by a corner of the cushion.

NOTE: IF THERE IS ANY ONE BALL THAT IS NOT SO OBSTRUCTED, THE CUE-BALL IS NOT ANGLED.

if angled after a foul,

(b) the referee will state angled ball, and

(c) it may be played from in-hand at the strikers discretion.

17. Occupied

A spot is said to be occupied if a ball cannot be placed on it without it touching another ball.

18. Push Stroke

A push stroke is a foul and is made when the tip of the cue remains in contact with the cue-ball,

(a) when the cue-ball makes contact with the object ball, or

(b) after the cue-ball has commenced its forward motion.
   PROVIDED that where the cue-ball and an object ball are almost touching, it shall be deemed a fair stroke if the cue-ball hits the finest possible edge of the object ball.

19. Jump Shot

A jump shot is when the cue-ball jumps over any ball except when it first strikes the object ball and then jumps over another ball.

NOTE: IF THE CUE-BALL FINISHES ON THE FAR SIDE OF THE OBJECT BALL, EVEN THOUGH TOUCHING IT IN THE PROCESS, IT IS CONSIDERED TO HAVE JUMPED OVER.

NOTE: AFTER STRIKING THE BALL ON FAIRLY IF THE CUE-BALL SHOULD THEN JUMP OVER THE OBJECT BALL AFTER HITTING A CUSHION, IT SHALL BE DEEMED TO BE A FAIR STROKE.

20. Miss

A miss is when the referee considers the striker has not endeavoured to hit the ball *on*.

3. THE GAME

1. Description

The game of Snooker is played on an English Billiard Table and may be played by two or more persons, either as sides or independently.

Points are awarded for scoring strokes and forfeits from an opponents fouls.

The winner is the player or side making the highest score or to whom the game is awarded under Sec. 4 Rule 2.

Each player uses the same WHITE cue-ball and there are twenty-one object balls – fifteen reds each valued 1 and six colours: yellow valued 2, green 3, brown 4, blue 5, pink 6 and black 7.

Scoring strokes are made by potting reds and colours alternately until all reds are off the table and then the colours in the ascending order of their value i.e. – yellow through to black.

2. Position of Balls

At the commencement of each frame the object balls are positioned as follows: BLACK on the SPOT; PINK on the PYRAMID SPOT; BLUE on the CENTRE SPOT; BROWN on the MIDDLE of the BAULK-line; GREEN on the LEFT-HAND and YELLOW on the RIGHT-HAND corner of the 'D'.

The reds in the form of a triangle, the ball at the apex standing as near to the pink ball as possible, without touching it, the base being parallel with and nearest to the top cushion.

NOTE: THE POSITIONS FOR THE OBJECT BALLS ARE COMMONLY REFERRED TO BY THE COLOUR, E.G. BLACK SPOT, PINK SPOT, ETC.

3. Mode of Play

(a) the players shall determine the order of play which (subject to Sec. 3 Rule 10) must remain unaltered throughout the *frame*.

NOTE: THE PLAYER TO STRIKE FIRST AT EACH FRAME SHALL ALTERNATE DURING A GAME.

(b) the first player shall play from *in hand* and the frame starts with the first stroke.

(c) the cue ball
   (i) must first hit a ball *on*, and
   (ii) must not enter a pocket.

(d) a ball not *on* must not enter a pocket.

(e) (i) for the first stroke of each turn, until all are off the table, red is the ball *on*.
   (ii) the value of each red, or ball nominated as red, potted in the same stroke is scored.

(f) if a red is potted, the next ball *on* is a colour, which if potted is scored. The colour is then re-spotted.

(g) (i) until all reds are off the table the break is continued by potting reds and colours alternately.
   (ii) the colours then become *on* in the ascending order of their value (Sec. 3 Rule 1) and when potted remain off the table (except as provided for in paragraph (j)).

(h) if the striker fails to score the next player plays from where the cue-ball comes to rest.

(j) when only the Black is left the first score or foul ends the frame, unless the scores are then equal, in which case:
   (i) the Black is spotted.
   (ii) the players draw lots for choice of playing.
   (iii) the next player plays from *in hand* and
   (iv) the next score or foul ends the game.

NOTE: AGGREGATE SCORES
IN GAMES OR MATCHES WHERE AGGREGATE SCORES ARE RELEVANT IT IS ONLY WHEN THE SCORES ARE EQUAL AS A RESULT OF THE LAST FRAME THAT THE ABOVE APPLIES.

(k) The striker shall to the best of his ability endeavour to hit the ball *on*. If the referee considers the rule infringed he shall call foul and a miss.

NOTE: BALL ON IMPOSSIBLE TO BE HIT
IN THIS SITUATION IT HAS TO BE CONSIDERED THAT THE STRIKER *IS* ATTEMPTING TO HIT THE BALL *ON*.

4. To play from in-hand

To play from in-hand the cue-ball must be struck from a position on or within the lines of the 'D'.

NOTE: THE REFEREE WILL ANSWER IF ASKED IF THE BALL IS PROPERLY PLACED.

5. Hitting two balls simultaneously

Two balls, other than two reds or a *free ball* and the ball *on*, must not be hit simultaneously by the cue-ball.

6. Spotting colours

(a) if a colour has to be spotted, and its own spot is *occupied*, it shall be placed on the highest value spot available.

(b) if there is more than one colour, and their own spots are *occupied*, the highest value ball takes precedence.

(c) if all spots are *occupied*, the colour shall be placed as near as possible to its own spot between that spot and the nearest part of the top cushion.

(d) if, in the case of the Black and the Pink, the space between its own spot and the nearest part of the top cushion is *occupied*, the colour shall be placed as near as possible to its own spot on the centre line of the table below that spot.

7. Touching Ball

(a) if the cue-ball is touching another ball which is, or can be, *on*, the referee shall state TOUCHING BALL.

(b) the striker must play away from it or it is a *push stroke*.

(c) no penalty is incurred for thus playing away if:
   (i) the ball is not *on*.
   (ii) the ball is *on* and the striker *nominates* such ball, or
   (iii) the ball is *on* and the striker *nominates*, and first hits, another ball.

NOTE: MOVEMENT OF TOUCHING BALL
IF THE REFEREE CONSIDERS THAT A TOUCHING BALL HAS MOVED THROUGH AN AGENCY OTHER THAN THE PLAYER, IT IS NOT A FOUL.

8. Ball on edge of pocket

(a) if a ball falls into a pocket without being hit by another ball it shall be replaced.

(b) if it would have been hit by any ball involved in a stroke, all balls will be replaced and the stroke replayed.

(c) if the ball balances momentarily on the edge and falls in, it must not be replaced.

9. Free ball

(a) after a foul, if the cue-ball is *snookered*, the referee shall state FREE BALL.

(b) if the non-offending player takes the next stroke he may nominate any ball as *on*.

(c) for this stroke, such ball shall (subject to para (e) (i)) be regarded as, and acquire the value of, the ball *on*.

(d) it is a foul, should the cue-ball
   (i) fail to first hit, or
   (ii) except when only pink and black remain on the table, be *snookered* by, the *free ball*.

(e) if the *free ball* is potted it
   (i) is spotted, and
   (ii) the value of the ball *on* is scored.

(f) if the ball *on* is potted it is scored.

(g) if both the *free ball* and the ball *on* are potted only the value of the ball *on* is scored (subject to Sec. 3 Rule 3(e)(ii)).

10. Fouls

(a) if a foul is committed:
   (i) the referee shall immediately state FOUL and on completion of the stroke announce the penalty.
   (ii) unless awarded by the referee or claimed by the non-striker, before the next stroke is made, it is condoned.
   (iii) any ball improperly spotted shall remain where positioned, except that if off the table it shall be correctly spotted.
   (iv) all points scored before the foul is awarded or claimed are allowed.
   (v) the next stroke is made from where the cue-ball comes to rest.

(b) should more than one foul be committed in the same stroke the highest value penalty shall be incurred.

(c) the player who committed the foul:

(i) incurs the penalty prescribed (which is added to the opponent's score), and

(ii) has to play again if requested by the next player. Once such a request has been made it cannot be withdrawn.

(iii) If a breach of Section 3.3(k) occurs, the offending player has to play again from the original position, if requested by the next player.

11. Penalties

The following are fouls and incur a penalty of four points or the higher one prescribed.

(a) value of the ball *on*:

by striking

(i) when the balls are not at rest (Sec. 2 Rule 6).

(ii) the cue-ball more than once (2–6).

(iii) with both feet off the floor (2–6).

(iv) out of turn (3–3).

(v) improperly from *in-hand* (3–4).

by causing

(vi) the cue-ball to miss all object balls (3–3).

(vii) the cue-ball to enter a pocket (3–3).

(viii) a *snooker* with *free ball* (3–9).

(ix) a *jump shot* (2–19).

(b) value of the ball *on* or ball concerned:

by causing

(i) a ball not *on* to enter a pocket (3–3).

(ii) the cue-ball to first hit a ball not *on* (3–3).

(iii) a *push stroke* (2–18).

(iv) by striking with a ball incorrectly spotted (2–11).

(v) by touching a ball with other than the tip of the cue (2–6).

(vi) by forcing a ball off the table (2–13).

(c) value of the ball *on* or higher value of the two balls by causing the cue-ball to hit simultaneously two balls other than two reds or a *free ball* and the ball *on* (3–5).

(d) a penalty of seven points is incurred if:

the striker

(i) after potting a red commits a foul before *nominating* a colour,

(ii) uses a ball off the table for any purpose,

(iii) plays at reds in successive strokes, or

(iv) uses as the cue-ball any ball other than white.

12. Ball moved by other than striker

if a ball, stationary or moving, is disturbed other than by the striker it shall be re-positioned by the referee.

NOTE: THIS COVERS THE CASE IN WHICH ANOTHER AGENCY CAUSES THE STRIKER TO TOUCH A BALL. NO PLAYER SHALL BE RESPONSIBLE FOR ANY DISTURBANCE OF THE BALLS BY THE REFEREE.

13. Stalemate

If the referee considers a position of stalemate is being approached, he should warn the players that if the situation is not altered in a short period of time he will declare the frame null and void. The frame shall be re-started with the same order of play.

14. Four-handed snooker

(a) in a four-handed game each side shall open alternate frames, the order of play shall be determined at the commencement of each frame, and must be maintained throughout that frame.

(b) players may change order of play at the beginning of each frame.

(c) if a foul is committed and a request made to play again, the player who committed the foul plays again, and the original order of play is maintained.

(d) when a frame ends in a tie Snooker Rule 3(j) applies. The pair who play the first stroke have the choice of which player plays that stroke. The order of play must then be maintained as in the frame.

(e) Partners may confer during a game but not whilst one is the striker and the striker is at the table or after the first stroke of his break.

SECTION 4. THE PLAYERS

1. Time wasting

If the referee considers that a player is taking an abnormal amount of time over a stroke, he should be warned that he is liable to be disqualified.

2. Unfair conduct

For refusing to continue a frame or for conduct which, in the opinion of the referee is wilfully or persistently unfair a player shall lose the game. He is liable to be disqualified from competitions held under the control of The Billiards and Snooker Council and its Affiliated Associations.

3. Penalty

If a game is awarded to a player under this section the offender shall:

(i) lose the game, and

(ii) forfeit all points scored, and the non-offender shall receive the value of the balls still on the table (each red counting eight points).

NOTE: PROVIDED THAT WHERE AGGREGATE POINTS SCORES APPLY, THE OFFENDER SHALL ALSO FORFEIT 147 POINTS FOR EACH UNPLAYED FRAME, TO THE NUMBER REQUIRED TO COMPLETE THE GAME.

4. Non-striker

The non-striker shall, when the striker is playing, avoid standing or moving in the line of sight; he should sit or stand at a fair distance from the table.

5. Absence

In case of his absence from the room he may appoint a substitute to watch his interests, and claim a foul if necessary.

SECTION 5. THE OFFICIALS

1. The Referee

(a) the referee shall

(i) be the sole judge of fair and unfair play, and responsible for the proper conduct of the game under these Rules.

(ii) intervene if he sees any contravention.

(iii) if a player is colour blind, tell him the colour of a ball if requested.

(iv) clean a ball on a player's request.

(b) he shall not
  (i) answer any question not authorized in the Rules.
  (ii) give any indication that a player is about to make a foul stroke.
  (iii) give any advice or opinion on points affecting play.
(c) if he has failed to notice any incident he may take the evidence of the spectators best placed for observation to assist his decision.

NOTE: THE REFEREE WILL NOT ANSWER A QUESTION REGARDING THE DIFFERENCE IN SCORES.

2. The Marker

The marker shall keep the score on the marking board and assist the referee in carrying out his duties.

NOTE: IF REQUESTED BY THE STRIKER, THE REFEREE OR MARKER MAY MOVE AND HOLD IN POSITION ANY LIGHT SHADE WHICH INTERFERES WITH THE ACTION OF THE STRIKER.

RULES OF THE GAME OF ENGLISH BILLIARDS*

Authorised by
THE BILLIARDS AND SNOOKER CONTROL COUNCIL

THE BILLIARDS ASSOCIATION
Established 1885

THE BILLIARDS CONTROL CLUB
Established 1908

AMALGAMATED 1919

Chairman: Stan Brooke
Secretary and Chief Executive: David Ford

SECTION 1. EQUIPMENT

1.   Table (Imperial)
1M. Table (Metric)
2.   Balls
3.   Cue
4.   Ancillary

SECTION 2. DEFINITIONS

1.   Game
2.   Match
3.   Balls
4.   String
5.   Striker
6.   Stroke
7.   In-hand
8.   Ball in play
9.   Hazard
10. Pot
11. In-Off
12. Cannon
13. Miss
14. Break
15. Forced off
16. Foul
17. Occupied
18. Push Stroke
19. Jump Shot

SECTION 3. THE GAME

1.   Description
2.   Commencement of Game
3.   Order of play
4.   Spotting the red ball
5.   Details of scoring
6.   To play from In-hand
7.   Limitation of hazards
8.   Limitation of cannons
9.   Ball on edge of pocket
10. Ball moved by other than striker
11. Balls touching
12. Miss
13. Fouls

SECTION 4. THE PLAYERS

1.   Time wasting
2.   Unfair conduct
3.   Penalty
4.   Non-striker
5.   Absence

SECTION 5. THE OFFICIALS

1.   Referee
2.   Marker

SECTION 1. EQUIPMENT

1. The Standard Table – Imperial
Dimensions
(a) the playing area within the cushion faces shall measure 11ft 8½ins × 5ft 10ins with a tolerance on both dimensions of ± ½in.

Height
(b) the height of the table from the floor to the top of the cushion rail shall be from 2ft 9½ins to 2ft 10½ins.

Pocket Openings
(c) (i) There shall be pockets at the corners (two at the Spot end known as the top pockets and two at the Baulk end as the bottom pockets) and at the middle of the longer sides.
(ii) the pocket openings shall conform to the templates authorized by the Billiards and Snooker Control Council.

Baulk-line and Baulk
(d) a straight line drawn 29ins from the face of the bottom cushion and parallel to it is called the Baulk-line and the intervening space termed the Baulk.

The 'D'
(e) the 'D' is a semi-circle described in Baulk with its centre at the middle of the Baulk-line and with a radius of 11½ins.

Spots
(f) four spots marked on the centre longitudinal line of the table.
(i) the Spot: 12¾ins from the point perpendicular below the face of the top cushion.
(ii) the Centre Spot: Midway between the centre pockets and equidistant from the faces of the top and bottom cushions.
(iii) the Pyramid Spot: Midway between the centre spot and the face of the top cushion.
(iv) the Middle of the Baulk-line.

1M. The Standard Table – Metric
Dimensions
(a) the playing area within the cushion faces shall measure 3500mm × 1750mm with a tolerance on both dimensions of ± 3mm.

Height
(b) the height of the table from the floor to the top of the cushion rail shall be from 850mm to 875mm.

Pocket Openings
(c) (i) There shall be pockets at the corners (two at the Spot end known as the top pockets and two at the Baulk end as the bottom pockets) and at the middle of the longer sides.
(ii) the pocket openings shall conform to the templates authorized by the Billiards and Snooker Control Council.

Baulk-line and Baulk
(d) a straight line drawn 700mm ($1/5$th the length of the playing area) from the face of the bottom cushion and parallel to it is called the Baulk-line and the intervening space termed the Baulk.

The 'D'
(e) the 'D' is a semi-circle described in Baulk with its centre at the middle of the Baulk-line and with a radius of 292mm ($1/6$th the width of the Playing area).

Spots
(f) four spots marked on the centre longitudinal line of the table.
(i) the Spot: 320mm ($1/11$th the length of the playing area) from the point perpendicular below the face of the top cushion.
(ii) the Centre Spot: Midway between the centre pockets and equidistant from the faces of the top and bottom cushions.
(iii) the Pyramid Spot: Midway between the centre spot and the face of the top cushion.
(iv) the Middle of the Baulk-line.

2. Balls
(a) the balls shall have a diameter of 52.5mm ($2^1/_{16}$ins) with a tolerance of +0.05mm– 0.08mm.
(b) they shall be of equal weight within a tolerance of
(i) 3 gms per Snooker set, and
(ii) 0.05 gms per Billiard set.

NOTE: A BALL OR SET OF BALLS MAY BE CHANGED WITH THE CONSENT OF THE PLAYERS OR ON A DECISION OF THE REFEREE.

3. Cue
The cue shall be not less than 910mm (3ft) in length and shall show no substantial departure from the traditional and generally accepted shape and form.

4. Ancillary
'Rests' may be used to provide a bridge for the cue.

NOTE: IT IS THE PLAYERS RESPONSIBILITY TO BOTH PLACE THE REST ON AND REMOVE IT FROM THE TABLE.

SECTION 2. DEFINITIONS

1. Game
A game is completed
(a) at the expiry of a specified period of play, or
(b) when the number of points agreed on is first scored.

2. Match
A match is an agreed number of games.

3. Balls
(a) the cue-ball is the ball of the striker.
(b) the other balls are object balls.

4. String
To string is to play together from the Baulk-line to the top cushion with the object of leaving the player's ball as near as possible to the bottom cushion.

5. Striker
The person about to play or in play is the striker and remains so until completion of the stroke or break.

6. Stroke
(a) a stroke is made when the striker strikes the cue-ball with the tip of the cue.

(b) for the stroke to be a 'Fair Stroke' the following conditions must be met:

(i) At the moment of striking, all balls must be at rest, and where necessary, object balls correctly spotted.

(ii) The cue-ball must be struck and not pushed.

(iii) The cue-ball must not be struck more than once in the same stroke.

(iv) At the moment of striking, at least one of the strikers feet must be touching the floor.

(v) The striker must not touch any ball other than the cue-ball as in section (a) above.

(vi) A ball or balls must not be 'forced off the table'.

(c) a stroke is not completed until all balls have come to rest and the referee has decided the striker has left the table.

7. In-hand

(a) A player's ball is in-hand when it is off the table, and

(b) It remains in-hand until played fairly from in-hand or a foul is committed whilst the ball is on the table.

(c) When the non-striker's ball is in-hand it remains so until his turn to play or is spotted as in Sec. 3 Rule 7.

8. Ball in Play

(a) A player's ball is in play when not in-hand.

(b) The red is in play when spotted and remains so until potted or forced off the table.

NOTE: USING THE CUE TO POSITION THE CUE-BALL

IF THE REFEREE CONSIDERS THE PLAYER IS NOT ATTEMPTING TO PLAY A STROKE, EVEN THOUGH THE TIP OF THE CUE TOUCHES THE CUE-BALL, THE BALL IS NOT IN PLAY.

9. Hazard

a hazard is

(a) A pot, or

(b) An in-off.

NOTE: A POT IS OFTEN REFERRED TO AS A WINNING HAZARD AND AN IN-OFF AS A LOSING HAZARD.

10. Pot

A pot is when an object ball, after contact with another ball, and without any contravention of these rules, enters a pocket.

11. In-Off

An in-off is when the cue-ball, after contact with an object ball, and without any contravention of these rules, enters a pocket.

12. Cannon

A cannon is when the cue-ball hits both the object balls, without any contravention of these rules.

13. Miss

A miss is when the cue-ball fails to hit any other ball.

14. Break

A break is a succession of scoring strokes made in any one turn.

15. Forced off the table

A ball is forced off the table if it comes to rest other than on the bed of the table or in a pocket.

16. Foul

A foul is any act in contravention of these rules.

17. Occupied

A spot is said to be occupied if a ball cannot be placed on it without it touching another ball.

18. Push Stroke

A push stroke is a foul and is made when the tip of the cue remains in contact with the cue-ball,

(a) when the cue-ball makes contact with the object ball, or

(b) after the cue-ball has commenced its forward motion.

PROVIDED that where the cue-ball and an object ball are almost touching, it shall be deemed a fair stroke if the cue-ball hits the finest possible edge of the object ball.

19. Jump Shot

A jump shot is when the cue-ball jumps over any ball except when it first strikes the object ball and then jumps over another ball.

NOTE: IF THE CUE-BALL FINISHES ON THE FAR SIDE OF THE OBJECT BALL, EVEN THOUGH TOUCHING IT IN THE PROCESS, IT IS CONSIDERED TO HAVE JUMPED OVER.

SECTION 3. THE GAME

1. Description

The game of English Billiards is played by two or more persons, either as sides or independently. Three balls are used, 'plain' white, 'spot' white and red.

It is a game of *pots*, *in-offs*, *cannons* and positional play. Points are awarded for scoring strokes and forfeits from an opponents fouls.

The winner is the player, or side, who has scored most points at the expiry of an agreed period, first scores an agreed number of points or to whom the game is awarded under Sec. 4 Rule 2.

2. Commencement of Game

(a) The choice of ball and order of play, unless mutually agreed upon, shall be decided by *stringing*, the winner having the option, and shall remain unaltered throughout the game.

(b) At the commencement of the game the red is placed on the spot, the first player plays from *in-hand* and the game starts with the first *stroke*.

3. Order of Play

The players play alternately unless a score is made, in which case the *striker* continues the *break* playing from where his ball rests, or, after an *in-off* or as in Sec. 3 Rule 11, from *in-hand*.

4. Spotting the Red Ball

(a) If the red is *potted* or *forced off* the table it is placed on the spot. If the spot is *occupied* it is placed on the pyramid spot. If that spot is also *occupied* it is placed on the centre spot.

(b) If the red is potted from the spot or pyramid spot twice in succession in one break, not in conjunction with another score, it is placed on the centre spot. If this spot is *occupied* it is placed on the pyramid spot or if both these spots are *occupied* on the spot.
If again potted it shall be placed on the spot.

NOTE: IF DURING A STROKE THE RED COMES TO REST ON THE SPOT, IT IS NOT CONSIDERED TO BE SPOTTED.
IT IS THE STRIKER'S RESPONSIBILITY TO ENSURE THAT ALL BALLS ARE CORRECTLY SPOTTED BEFORE STRIKING.

5. Details of Scoring
Points are awarded as follows:
(a) for a *cannon*, *pot* white and *in-off* white, two.
(b) for a *pot* red and *in-off* red, three.
(c) if more than one *hazard* or a combination of *hazards* and a *cannon* are made in the same *stroke* all are scored.
(d) when an *in-off* is combined with a *cannon* it shall score two or three according to whether the white or red was first hit.
(e) should both be hit simultaneously the *in-off* shall count two.

6. To Play from In-hand
The cue-ball must
(a) be struck from a position on or within the lines of the 'D'.

NOTE: THE REFEREE WILL ANSWER, IF ASKED, IF THE BALL IS PROPERLY PLACED.

(b) must hit a ball or cushion out of baulk before hitting a ball in baulk.
(c) may be played against a cushion in baulk to hit a ball out of baulk.

NOTE: IF THE STRIKER IS IN-HAND THE REFEREE WILL ANSWER, IF ASKED, IF A BALL IS IN OR OUT OF BAULK.

7. Limitation of Hazards
Consecutive *hazards*, not in conjunction with a *cannon*, are limited to fifteen.
If more than one *hazard* is made in the same *stroke* it shall count as one for the purpose of this rule but all points shall be scored.
After ten *hazards*, or on request, the referee shall inform the *striker*.
Should the non-striker's ball be off the table as a result of the non-striker's last stroke, it shall be spotted after the fifteenth *hazard* on the middle spot of the 'D', or if *occupied* on the right hand corner of the 'D'.

NOTE: SHOULD THE REFEREE FAIL TO INFORM THE STRIKER AFTER TEN HAZARDS THE STRIKER IS ENTITLED TO PLAY A FURTHER FIVE HAZARDS AFTER HE IS INFORMED.

8. Limitation of Cannons
Consecutive *cannons*, not in conjunction with a *hazard*, are limited to seventy-five.
After seventy *cannons*, or on request, the referee shall inform the *striker*.

NOTE: SHOULD THE REFEREE FAIL TO INFORM THE STRIKER AFTER SEVENTY CANNONS THE STRIKER IS ENTITLED TO PLAY A FURTHER FIVE CANNONS AFTER HE IS INFORMED.

9. Ball on Edge of Pocket
(a) if a ball falls into a pocket without being hit by another ball it shall be replaced.
(b) if it would have been hit by any ball involved in a *stroke*, all balls will be replaced and the *stroke* replayed.
(c) if the ball balances momentarily on the edge and falls in, it must not be replaced.

10. Ball moved by other than striker
If a ball, stationary or moving, is disturbed other than by the *striker* it shall be repositioned by the referee.

NOTE: THIS COVERS THE CASE IN WHICH ANOTHER AGENCY CAUSES THE STRIKER TO TOUCH A BALL. NO PLAYER SHALL BE RESPONSIBLE FOR ANY DISTURBANCE OF THE BALLS BY THE REFEREE.

11. Balls Touching
When the *striker's* ball remains touching another ball, red shall be placed on the spot, the non-striker's ball, if on the table, shall be placed on the centre spot, and the striker shall play from *in hand*.

12. Miss
(a) For a *miss* the striker incurs a penalty of two points.

(b) a *miss* is a foul except when the striker is *in hand* and there is no ball out of baulk.

13. Fouls
(a) if a foul is committed
  (i) the referee shall immediately state foul.
  (ii) unless awarded by the referee or claimed by the non-striker, before the next stroke is made, it is condoned.
  (iii) any ball improperly spotted shall remain where positioned, except that if off the table it shall be correctly spotted.
  (iv) all points scored before the foul is awarded or claimed are allowed.
(b) the player committing the foul incurs a penalty of two points, which are added to his opponent's score.
(c) the next player has the option of playing
  (i) from where the balls are at rest (the red if off the table having been spotted), or
  (ii) from *in-hand*, the red and white being spotted on the spot and centre spot respectively.
(d) the following acts are fouls:
  by striking
  (i) when the balls are not at rest (Sec. 2 Rule 6).
  (ii) the *cue-ball* more than once (2–6).
  (iii) with both feet off the floor (2–6).
  (iv) out of turn (3–3).
  (v) improperly from *in-hand* (3–6).
  (vi) with a ball incorrectly spotted (2–6).
  (vii) a ball other than the *cue-ball* (2–6).
  by making
  (viii) a *jump shot* (2–19).
  (ix) a *push stroke* (2–18).

(x) more than fifteen *hazards* (3–7).
(xi) more than seventy-five *cannons* (3–8).
(xii) by touching a ball with other than the tip of the cue (2–6).
(xiii) by forcing a ball off the table (2–6).
(xiv) by using a ball off the table for any purpose.

SECTION 4. THE PLAYERS

1. Time wasting
If the referee considers that a player is taking an abnormal amount of time over a stroke, he should be warned that he is liable to be disqualified.

2. Unfair conduct
For refusing to continue a frame or for conduct which, in the opinion of the referee, is wilfully or persistently unfair a player shall lose the game. He is liable to be disqualified from competitions held under the control of The Billiards and Snooker Council and its Affiliated Associations.

3. Penalty
If a game is awarded to a player under this section the offender shall:
(i) lose the game, and
(ii) if the game was to be decided on a number of agreed points he shall forfeit all points scored and the non-offender shall receive the agreed number of points, or
(iii) if the game be decided at the expiry of a specified period of play and forms part of a team match the whole match shall be forfeited.

4. Non-striker
The non-striker shall, when the striker is playing, avoid standing or moving in the line of sight; he should sit or stand at a fair distance from the table.

5. Absence
In case of his absence from the room he may appoint a substitute to watch his interests, and claim a foul if necessary.

SECTION 5. THE OFFICIALS

1. The Referee
(a) the referee shall
(i) be the sole judge of fair and unfair play, and responsible for the proper conduct of the game under these Rules.
(ii) intervene if he sees any contravention.
(iii) if a player is colour blind, tell him the colour of a ball if requested.
(iv) clean a ball on a player's request.
(b) he shall not
(i) answer any question not authorized in the Rules.
(ii) give any indication that a player is about to make a foul stroke.
(iii) give any advice or opinion on points affecting play.
(c) if he has failed to notice any incident he may take the evidence of the spectators best placed for observation to assist his decision.

NOTE: THE REFEREE WILL NOT ANSWER A QUESTION REGARDING THE DIFFERENCE IN SCORES.

2. The Marker
The marker shall keep the score on the marking board and assist the referee in carrying out his duties.

NOTE: IF REQUESTED BY THE STRIKER, THE REFEREE OR MARKER MAY MOVE AND HOLD IN POSITION ANY LIGHT SHADE WHICH INTERFERES WITH THE ACTION OF THE STRIKER.